1 MONTH OF FREE READING

at
www.ForgottenBooks.com

By purchasing this book you are eligible for one month membership to ForgottenBooks.com, giving you unlimited access to our entire collection of over 1,000,000 titles via our web site and mobile apps.

To claim your free month visit:
www.forgottenbooks.com/free181729

* Offer is valid for 45 days from date of purchase. Terms and conditions apply.

ISBN 978-0-267-47046-4
PIBN 10181729

This book is a reproduction of an important historical work. Forgotten Books uses state-of-the-art technology to digitally reconstruct the work, preserving the original format whilst repairing imperfections present in the aged copy. In rare cases, an imperfection in the original, such as a blemish or missing page, may be replicated in our edition. We do, however, repair the vast majority of imperfections successfully; any imperfections that remain are intentionally left to preserve the state of such historical works.

Forgotten Books is a registered trademark of FB &c Ltd.
Copyright © 2018 FB &c Ltd.
FB &c Ltd, Dalton House, 60 Windsor Avenue, London, SW19 2RR.
Company number 08720141. Registered in England and Wales.

For support please visit www.forgottenbooks.com

THE FATHERS OF THE DESERT

TRANSLATED FROM THE GERMAN OF
THE COUNTESS HAHN-HAHN

By

EMILY F. BOWDEN

*With a Chapter on The Spiritual Life of
the first Six Centuries*

By

JOHN BERNARD DALGAIRNS
(Priest of the Oratory)

In Two Volumes: Volume I

BURNS AND OATES
28 ORCHARD STREET
LONDON W

First Edition 1867
Second Edition 1907

CONTENTS

Essay on the Spiritual life of the last six centuries. By John Bernard Dalgairns. Priest of the Oratory . i-lxiv

CHRISTIANITY IN FREEDOM.

How it took possession of the world; by the doctrine of its being the only way of salvation; by the connection between the ancient prophecies and their fulfilment; by learning; by its civilization of mankind: by works of love 1

CHRISTIAN WORSHIP.

Why Christians rejoiced over each new Church—Description by Eusebius of the Church at Tyre—Basilicas—Their decoration—The cross, images and votive offerings—The Liturgy of the Church—Oblation—Eulogia—The Holy Sacrifice of the Mass—Low Masses—Votive Masses—Masses for the Dead—The Canonical Hours 13

FEASTS AND FASTS.

Sunday—Easter—Ascension Day—The Rogation days—Pentecost—Christmas—Epiphany—The feasts of the Blessed Virgin Mary and the Saints—The spirit of penance—Secret and public confession—The four degrees of public penance—Relaxation of the spirit of penance 28

THE BOSPHORUS AND THE NILE.

Byzantium; its situation, environs, greatness, riches, beauty, palaces, churches and treasures of art—The Nile and its banks 39

THE ANCHORITES.

How the anchorites strove to live according to the three evangelical counsels given by Christ—The evangelical counsel founded the state of perfection by means of

CONTENTS

PAGE

Christian asceticism—Its fruit, mysticism, is the union of the soul with God—Penance or suffering for the love of God must precede the kingdom of God in the soul . 52

THE DESERT.

The Deserts of the East—The Great Syrian Desert from Anti-Lebanon to the Euphrates—Damascus at its entrance—The Lesser Arabian Desert between Gaza and Cairo—The Egyptian Desert between Cairo and the Great Cataract of the Nile—The Thebaid between the Nile and the Red Sea—The caves and the ancient Egyptian rock-sepulchres 68

PAUL OF THEBES.

Born 229—Died 342.
Patriarch of solitaries—He flies from the world and finds God—He is discovered by Antony—His death . . 7

ST. ANTONY.

Born 251—Died 356.
His parentage and education—The Gospel leads him to the state of perfection—He practises holy asceticism—The tempter torments him—He goes to Thebais and shuts himself up in a ruined tower for twenty years—His influence upon his own and future ages—His miracles—His rewards—His prophecies—He goes to the mountains of Colzim—The end of his life . . . 91

ST. HILARION.

Born 291—Died 371.
At the age of fourteen he seeks the guidance of St Antony—He withdraws to the morasses on the shore of the Mediterranean near Gaza—The severity of his mortification—His prayers work miracles—His hermitage becomes a place of pilgrimage—Disciples collect around him, and lauras with anchorites and monasteries with monks arise and flourish in Palestine, Syria and Mesopotamia—He flies from worldly honours to Egypt, Sicily, Dalmatia and Cyprus—His death 139

PAUL THE SIMPLE.

Died at the end of the 4th century.

At the age of sixty he became a disciple of St Antony, and attains to perfection through childlike obedience . . 158

AMMON, ABBOT OF NITRIA.

Died about the middle of the 4th century.

He marries and, together with his bride, lives in a state of virginity—After eighteen years they separate, and he settles in the desert of Nitria—A numerous community assembles there by degrees—Their mode of life, occupation and hospitality—The still more remote seclusion of some in the Desert of Cellia—Antony in spirit sees Ammon's death 165

ST. PACHOMIUS, ABBOT OF TABENNA.

Born 292—Died 348.

The impression made by Christians upon the heathen youth—His campaign, his baptism and resolution—He goes to the aged Palemon to be exercised in asceticism— A presumptuous solitary—Pachomius founds monasteries and the Order of Tabenna, and prescribes their rule —The life of the monks—The life of the nuns—Brother Zaccheus—Pachomius obeys a child—Brother Sylvanus — Macarius of Alexandria and the Egyptian Macarius— Brother Titheos—Pachomius tames crocodiles and is calumniated—He dies of the plague 174

SERAPION THE SINDONITE.

Died in the 4th century.

At Corinth he becomes slave of an actor, whom he converts At Lacedæmon he sells himself to a Manichee and converts him—He sells himself twice more in Rome—He returns to the Egyptian Desert and dies 210

CONTENTS

ST. ARSENIUS.

Born 355—Died 450.

He goes from Rome to Constantinople, and from thence to the Desert of Scete—He is tried by Brother John the Dwarf—He considers himself as one dead—His humility and silence—Brother Alexander—An aged solitary—A noble Roman lady—Arsenius flies from one desert to another—His peaceful death 216

THE BLESSED MOSES.

Died in the 5th century.

He is a slave in Ethiopia and then a robber—He flies to the Desert of Scete, where he undergoes terrible struggles—He is consoled by St Isidore—The teaching of Moses—Brother Zacharias—The reception Moses gives to visitors—He is ordained priest—His end . . . 231

BROTHER VALENS, BROTHER ERO AND BROTHER PTOLEMY.

Died in the 5th century.

Brother Valens falls a prey to presumption and goes out of his mind—Brother Ero begins piously, but lets himself be beguiled by vanity and falls into misery—Brother Ptolemy becomes a victim to self-will 243

ST. EPHREM THE SYRIAN.

Born 306—Died 378.

His origin—His spirit of penance—His ascetic life with St James of Nisibis—His friendship with the monk Julian—St. James and King Sapor—Ephrem becomes deacon, preacher of penance, doctor of the Church, poet and missionary—His praises of the Holy Mother of God—He undertakes the charge of the plague-stricken in Edessa and dies 253

ST. MACRINA.

Born 328—Died 379.

Her grandmother, Macrina the elder—Her parents, St. Basil and St. Emmelia—Her childhood, education, betrothal

CONTENTS

and consecration to God—Her virtues—Her monastery—Her sufferings—Her death. 274

THE BLESSED MARANA AND THE BLESSED CYRA

Died in the 5th century.

These two rich and noble virgins lead, at Berea in Syria, a life of severe penance for love of Christ in bonds. . 283

ST. THAIS.

Died in the 4th century.

She leads a sinful life in Alexandria—The Abbot Paphnutius goes to her—She is converted and does penance for three years immurred in a solitary cell. 288

ST. PELAGIA.

Died in the 5th century.

Mount Olivet near Jerusalem—Brother Pelagius does penance in one of its caverns—James, deacon of Edessa visits him—He is found dead—How Bishop Nonnus of Edessa had converted the actress Pelagia, at Antioch. 292

ST. SIMEON STYLITES.

Born 388—Died 459.

His birth in the village of Sisan in Syria—His childhood as a shepherd—His love of God—His joy in sacrifice—His entrance at the age of fourteen into the Monastery of Teleda—His austere penance—His trials—He leaves Teleda. He goes to the deserted monastery of Telnesche—At the age of twenty-four he enters the mandra—At thirty-five he mounts first low and then higher columns—His mode of life on the same—His clothing, devotion, sermons, and sufferings—His miracles—The concourse of people to him—How he receives his mother—The Emporor Theodosius II. Pulchoria Eudocia Nestorius and his heresy condemned by the Council of Ephesus, 431—Eutyches and his heresy condemned by the Council of Chalcedon, 451—The Empress Eudocia espouses the latter heresy, but listens to Simeon and is converted—Earthquakes at Antioch—Simeon's death—Other Sty-

CONTENTS

lites:—Daniel at Constantinople, who died in 489, and Simeon the younger, who died 596, on the marvellous mountain near Antioch, after he had stood upon columns from his sixth year upwards. 306

ST. NILUS.
Died in the 5th century.

Born in Ancyra, studied in Antioch, lived at Constantinople, in a happy marriage, and loaded with honours—About the year 390, he goes with his son Theodulus to the Desert of Mount Sinai—He receives a gift of illumination and becomes by means of his writings a teacher in the Church—The holy virgin Magna—The onslaught of the Saracens—Theodulus is taken captive—He is restored to Nilus—Both father and son are ordained priests and return to Sinai. 371

ST. JOHN CLIMACUS.
Born 525—Died 605.

Palestine his native country—He is well educated—At the age of sixteen he enters the Desert of Sinai, where he becomes the disciple of the anchorite Martyrius—He takes the religious vows, and attains to the highest virtue—At the request of the Abbot of Raithu, he writes "the Ladder to Paradise"—On obedience—Brothers Abbacyrus, Laurence, Menas, and Isidore—On penance—On meekness and humility—On prayer and the peace of the soul—John is made Abbot of Sinai—After four years he retires again into the desert at Thola—He dies peacefully. 382

THE DAUGHTERS OF THE GRACCHI.

The great number of religious of both sexes in the East, and especially in Egypt—St. Athanasius takes to Rome an intimate and deep knowledge of the religious life—The life of the noble ladies of heathen Rome—Their female slaves—Their luxury in dress, ornaments, and furniture—Their cruelty and pride. 402

CONTENTS

ST. MARCELLA.
Died 410.
PAGE

Her family—The influence of St. Athanasius upon her and upon her sister Asella—Her marriage—Her widowhood—Her occupations—Her salutary influence over women—Her holy zeal—Her friendship with St. Jerome—Her adopted daughter Principia—The sack of Rome, by Alaric king of the Goths—Marcella's death. . . 418

THE BLESSED FABIOLA.
Died 400.

She leaves her first husband and marries another—She does public penance—Her glorious conversion to God—She founds the first hospital in Rome, and serves in it as nurse—She makes a pilgrimage to Jerusalem, where she acquires the friendship of St. Jerome—Her return to Rome, and her death. 428

THE BLESSED PAULA.
Born 347—Died 405.

Bethlehem and the Holy Cave—Paula's ancestry—Her husband Toxotius—Her happy marriage—Her five noble children—Her grief at the death of her husband—Her conversion to God—Her ascetic life—Her spiritual direction by St. Jerome—Her studies of the Holy Scriptures with her daughters—Eustochium dedicates herself to a life of virginity—Blesilla marries, and dies young—Paulina marries Pammachius and Rufina Aletius—Paula goes with Eustochium to Palestine—She travels all over it, and visits Egypt—In Bethlehem she builds a monastery for monks, with a refuge for pilgrims, and a monastery of nuns which she governs—She invites Marcella to come to Bethlehem—Death of Rufina and Paulina, 398—Pammachius builds a hospital at Ostia, and dies in 410—Paula's son Toxotius marries Læta, and dies young—His little daughter, Paula the younger, is sent to her grandmother, at Bethlehem—Death of St. Paula—Eustochium becomes Superioress of the monastery—She is honoured by St. Jerome. 436

THE TWO MELANIAS.

Died 410 and 439.

The Roman widow Melania arranges her household and travels to Egypt, in 372, to visit the solitaries—St. Isidore, master of the hospital at Alexandria—The blind Didymus—The blessed Alexandra—An avaricious virgin—Hor, abbot of Nitria—St. Pambo and the silver vessels—The exhortation of Pinuphius—Sayings of the ancient fathers—Why the abbot Sylvanus loved Brother Mark—Brother John captures a lioness, and waters a stick—Two peaceful ascetics—Persecution of the solitaries—Melania protects them—She founds a monastery at Jerusalem, and lives there in the practice of good works Evagrius Ponticus—Rufinus—Melania inclines towards heresy—Her son Publicola, and Albina his wife—Her granddaughter Melania and her husband Pinian, strive after evangelical perfection—Melania goes to Italy, and with her family visits St. Paulinus at Nola. In Rome she converts Apronianus—In 408 she goes with her family to Tagaste, to the holy Bishop Alypius.—Their mode of life there—Melania the elder returns alone to Jerusalem, and dies there in 410—In the year 417, Pinian, Melania the younger, and Albina journey to the East—Their ascetic life—Volusian summons his niece Melania to Constantinople—She converts him to Christianity—Her friendship with the Empress Eudocia—Finian's death in 435—Eudocia makes a pilgrimage to Jerusalem—Melania's holy death in the year 439 471

INTRODUCTION.

ESSAY ON THE SPIRITUAL LIFE OF THE FIRST SIX CENTURIES.

The lives of the Saints of the Desert have ever exercised a wonderful influence over the minds, not only of Catholics, but of all who call themselves Christians; nor is it difficult to comprehend why it should be so now, more than ever. The age in which we live distinguishes itself above all others by a restless longing to realize the past. Men are searching bog and marsh, moor and river, the wide expanse of downs, the tops of mountains and the bottom of lakes to find out how our ancestors lived, and to reproduce the men of the age of stone, bronze, or iron. The same sort of yearning curiosity exercises itself on the early Christians. If we had only Eusebius and Sozomen, it would be utterly impossible to picture to ourselves what were our ancestors in Christ. The Catacombs tell us much, but they are comparatively dumb. In the lives of the Desert-saints, we have a most strangely authentic insight into the very hearts and thoughts as well as the way of life of men and women who lived hundreds of years ago. They are extraordinarily authentic, for the marvellous facts which they contain are vouched for by writers such as St. Athanasius, who probably knew St. Antony and by St. Jerome. In most cases we have the account, almost the journals of men, who, like Cassian, Palladins and Moschus, travelled conscientiously to visit the marvellous population of Nitria and the Thebaid. Palgrave and Livingston tell us far less of the tents of the Bedouins and the huts of the negroes, than these writers tell us of the daily life, and the very gossip of the monastery. There is a freshness and a bloom, a cheerfulness and a frankness about these monks and hermits, which has an inexpressible charm. It seems as if the men who had been trained to silence and contemplation, when they did speak, spoke like children, with their heart on their lips, so good humouredly did they answer the somewhat tiresome questions of inquisitive travellers. Such men as these are too real to bo accounted for on any theory of myths, and, wonderful as are the tales told of them, they can hardly be consigned to he class of legendary literature, when vouched for by such men as St. Athanasius. These monks look out upon us from the darkness of the past with a vividness and simplicity, which shew that they considered that their existence in this busy world needed neither apology nor proof. The strangely beautiful virtues which they practised serve as their defence even with the most unascetic. Even writers of a school, most opposed to mysticism, have forgotten its principles and been caught in the net of the charity and sweetness of these solitaries. Their usefulness has found favour for them in the eyes of the most hostile. It is impossible to find fault with a man who, like St. Antony, presents himself after years of silence, prayer and fasting, at the door of his cave with a bloom on his cheek, and a smile on his lip, and who condescends to use something like gentlemanly chaff with the philosopher who came to see him. There is at once a gulf between him and a fakir. He fully vindicates his usefulness, who is the consoler and the confidante and spiritual guide of half Egypt. Even St. Simeon Stylites can hardly be said to be lost to the world when he converted Arabs and Barbarians of various races. There is evidence enough in the following pages, that the cell of the hermit in the fourth, fifth and sixth centuries was the refuge of the poor and the suffering and the outcast. The monk of the desert was a Carthusian, a Sister of St. Vincent of Paul and a nun of the Good Shepherd, all in one. Never were men less rigorous to others than these who were so rigid to themselves. No man of the world was ever less narrow-minded than those solitaries of the desert. At the time when the Church was most severe in her discipline, they are ever preaching that a repentance of one day* is enough, if it be profound, ever singing hymns of joy over sinners, who instantly receive the Holy Communion, ever dwelling on stories like that of St. Pelagia who bears down all the canons which would delay her reception into the Church, by the fervour of her conversion.

Qualities, such as these, constitute the chief charm of the lives of the Fathers of the Desert; yet after all they by no means furnish the key to their marvellous mode of living. All this does not in the least explain their love of solitude. When St. Antony hid himself in the desert, he never anticipated that the mountain of Colzim would become one great monastery and resound day and night with the chanting of the Psalms. When Ammon left his virgin bride, he little thought that the wild solitude of the dark pools of Nitria would be peopled with five thousand monks, of whom he was to be the spiritual father. It was in spite of himself, that St. Hilarion was the founder of the monastic state in Palestine. When Abbot Paphnutius retired from the world, he certainly never anticipated that he would go to Alexandria to bring back Thais with him. All these actions were afterthoughts, but their greatest attraction, their original vocation was to the desert, where was their real home. This is the point which demands explanation and on which we will

* Rosweide, p. 676, 600.

dwell. Their great work, that by which they have an influence upon us at this day, was the foundation of mystical theology.

Christianity appeared upon earth as an essentially social religion. It was planted in the world, says one of its earliest writers, as the soul is in the body, and if it vivified the dead mass, that body in its turn seemed a condition of its operation. "Christians are neither different from other men in country, nor in language, nor in manners. They have no cities to themselves, nor use a peculiar tongue, nor lead a singular life. They are scattered among Greek and barbarian cities alike, just as each has had his lot assigned him; in their dress, food and customs they are like the rest of the world, they marry and have children."* Their devotions seemed essentially social. It could not be otherwise with a worship the chief rite of which was Holy Communion. The Catacombs prove that the assembling together was a necessity to them; in after times the Apostolical † Constitutions make it one of the ten commandments of the new law, that daily the morning dawn should find the faithful in church, and that after their work, in the evening they should repair thither, as even now French villagers say their evening prayers together in the parish church. We know from St. Athanasius that

* Ep. ad Diog. 5.
† Lib. ii. 36.

they passed long nights together in their vast basilicas singing psalms and hymns. Their duties lay in the world; and as members of the Catholic Church they seemed planted inevitably in the very heart of the world. The proximity of priests seems a necessity to a catholic. Yet lo! a strange phenomenon. There is a rush towards the desert as now to the gold fields of California. Men and women go out from civilized life into the wilds. They are not misanthropes; they have met with no disappointments; no physical force drives them, for the time of persecution is over; they are not weary of life, for many are too young. Their apparent duty and their taste alike bid them stay in the city; yet some strong counter-attraction draws them into the solitude. Here is evidently some enthusiasm, which is not for their fellow-creatures. The love of man is not the ruling passion of Christendom. The secret of this mighty exodus is a passionate yearning for union with God.

Mystical theology is an essential part of the Christian religion, for it is nothing else but the science which regulates the intercourse of man with God. The moment that we know that God has come down from heaven and unites closely to Himself all who choose to receive Him, at once numberless questions rise within us, and crave for a science to answer them. Is this union sensible or not? Can we be conscious of it? By what faculty can we embrace our God? Is it intellect, or will, or both? or some unknown undiscovered power, not yet catalogued by psychology? Does He communicate Himself through some secret unknown channel, and set up His throne in some hidden depth? Does He manifest Himself to our feelings, and if so, which are real and which are false? Is His love equally distributed to all, or are there some who are called and attain to a closer union than others? All this evidently calls for a science, and what is more, its possibility is plainly its justification. If it be possible for the soul to be united to God, then evidently it is right for the soul to put itself into the requisite condition for that union, since it could not be possible unless God willed it. Unless God steeps to the human soul, it can never reach Him. He must make the first advances or it could not be united to Him; and as soon as He moves towards it, it becomes lawful for it to leave all to seek Him. If Christ calls Follow Me, on the seashore, then it is right to leave all to obey His call. The moment that intercourse with God is real, (which I am here supposing,) then at once it is lawful. If God is the bridegroom of the soul, then His bride may and must leave father, mother, brethren and sisters, and all to follow Him.

It is plain that this science must be an experimental one. It would be impossible to tell beforehand, how and how far God would please to manifest Himself to the soul. Accordingly, all definitions of the science refer in some way explicitly or implicitly to the experience of the individual. Take for instance the following descriptions from the course of Mystical Theology by Joseph of the Holy Ghost. "First, John Gerson thus defines it: It is an experimental knowledge of God through the embrace of unitive love: again, Mystical Theology is an experimental and gratuitous union of the mind with God. Denys the Carthusian defines it to be 'a most secret speaking with God.' Lastly, Valgornera frames this definition out of St. Thomas: It is a most perfect and high contemplation of God, and a love full of joy and sweetness resulting from the intimate possession of Him." All these point to feelings and states of mind which it would be impossible to describe in words till they were experienced, and about the frequency or rareness of which no one could pronounce, till time had told. There, if nowhere else, development was necessary. There also, as in all other developments of a revelation given once for all, is implied a very real idea apprehended from the first. The exclamation of St. Ignatius: "My Love, my Eros is crucified!" contains a whole Mystical Theology in itself. That thought, with which the mind of the early Church was perfectly possessed, that the steps of man's return to God correspond to the steps of his outgoing from Him, produced two fruits closely connected with each other, devotion to Mary and Mysticism, sometimes found together, sometimes apart. In St. Irenæus we find the marvellous retrospective effect on Eve of the faith of Mary, the necessary channel of grace to her.* On the other hand, in the epistle to Diognetus, quoted above, the author, a disciple of the apostles, holds out to his heathen correspondent the promise of a mystical state in which man returns to, nay becomes himself, the old paradise of God, for in his heart are planted the tree of knowledge without its poison, and the tree of life, a blessed place where "Eve escapes corruption, and a virgin shews her faith."† The foundations of all future mysticism were based by the author of the books of St. Denys the Areopagite on the same idea of man's return to the unity of God by reversing the multiplicity which was his path of departure from Him. Whenever the author lived, and whoever he was, he certainly gathered together the Mysticism floating about the ancient Church, and can be adduced as a proof of its existence. But I find the best proof of the influence and the vagueness of early mysti-

---

* Eam quæ est a Maria in Evam recirculationem significans: *quia non aliter, quod alligatum est solveretur, nisi* ipsæ com pagines alligationis reflectantur retrorsus.—St. Ir. 3, 22.

† Ep. ad Diog. in fin. The passage is obscure and probably corrupt; but the comparison of the Church to Paradise and the allusion to Mary are plain. For an analogous use of the passive of πίπτω v S. Justin, Apology 2. 10.

cal ideas in the three treatises on prayer by
Origen, Tertullian and St. Cyprian. All show
how thoroughly the necessity of prayer had
seized upon the Christian mind, and how new
was the notion to converts from heathenism.
Their language proves that the conception of
intercourse with God in the Christian sense
was as new to the ordinary Roman, as it was
to the Red Indian, who when the Jesuit mis-
sionaries appeared in his forests, called Christianity "the prayer." All three show the
same anxiety to make all Christians "pray
always," and the same elementary difficulty as
to how this is to be made compatible with life
in the world. All three are inferior in every
respect to the commonest modern writer on
Prayer, such as Rigoleuc or Segneri, whose
books are in the hands of every one. St.
Cyprian, it is true, abounds in beautiful
thoughts and pregnant principles. "Let heavenly reading be ever in your hands," he says,
"and the thought of the Lord in your inmost
feelings." Nevertheless, his direction has a
regimental character about it, which belongs to
the African church. If it could be carried
out, we can only say that Christians at Carthage had very little to do.* Origen however
especially has left the impress of his mind on
mystical as on every other theology. It is
strange how few have noticed in that great

* V. De Dom. Or. 11. and De Zelo et livore 4.

man the same yearning after some state of perfection, as we have noticed in other writers; stranger still that controversy should hardly have noticed, how this is connected in his mind with that Mary, of whom elsewhere he had spoken so hastily. The same application of the words of Jesus on the cross to St. John, which is so common in modern writers, and which to many may have appeared strained, is to be found in Origen. From these words he argues that every Christian, in proportion as he is perfect, is given to Mary as a son. He takes it for granted that every " perfect Christian no longer lives, but Christ lives in him; and since Christ lives in him, it is said of him to Mary, Behold thy son, the Christ."* In other words the life of Christ in us implies that Mary is our mother. So close is her union with Christ that no one can be identified with Him without being her son. The absolute union of Mary with Him is a necessary premiss to Origen's argument, the very same as that on which Grignon de Montfort bases his devotion. "O my loving Jesus, I turn for a moment towards Thee, to complain lovingly to Thy divine Majesty, that so few Christians perceive the necessary union between Thee and Thy holy Mother. Thou art, O Lord, ever with Mary and Mary ever with Thee, and she cannot be without Thee, otherwise she would

---

* Com. in Joan. tom. i. 6.

cease to be. She is so transformed by grace that she no longer lives her own life. Thou, O Jesus, alone dost live and reign in her."* In Origen's book on Prayer we find no longer indeed the same principles with respect to Mary, but remarkable anticipations of what we should have been inclined to call modern methods if we had not seen them in him. His division of prayer is nearly the same as that in the Brief way of mental prayer† in Thomas of Jesus, and in that of Father Quental of the Lisbon‡ Oratory. There are descriptions of states of prayer in him which are not unworthy of St. John of the Cross.§ Yet in this, as in everything else in this great man, notwithstanding his mighty gifts of intellect, and the magnanimity of his character, there is something disappointing, a promise which is not fulfilled. It is hopeless to expect any progress in prayer in one who uses language implying that prayer in the sense of petition (ἔντευξις) can only be offered to God the Father, not to Christ. His hold on doctrine was too slippery, his grasp of dogma too feeble, his theological insight too vague and undefined to enable him to pray, like a man, who has a clear view of the Sacred Humanity as an object. There could hardly be a distinct image of

* Traité de la Vraie devotion, p. 44.
† Via brevis, c. 3.
‡ Idea. degl. Esercizi del' Oratorio. Appendix.
§ De Or. c. 9. 30.

Christ even on his imagination, since he seems to have held that the face of Jesus appeared to vary according to the mind and disposition of the beholder.* Speculative and scientific theology was certainly not in his case favourable to contemplation. Perhaps his Absolute God was too much of an abstraction, and at times his Supreme Being too metaphysical, and too destitute of attributes, to serve as an object for prayer. His stormy life of struggle and of controversy was not favourable to the peace of the Holy Spirit, especially when his strong passions are taken into account. Nor were the streets of Alexandria a help to prayer; the many-coloured stream of life which poured down them, their motley groups and hubbub of dialects furnished his impressionable mind with pictures and sounds, which but too readily turned into those images ($\varphi\alpha\nu\tau\alpha\zeta\iota\alpha\iota$) of which, in common with all men of mystic tendencies, he complains with sadness. But I doubt whether the catechetical school was not even worse than the noisy thoroughfare. I would speak most gently of one to whom the Church owes so much. Never was man, more raised above the bitterness and littleness of controversy than Origen, and there was a tender piety in him, which is not unusual in high-minded men, and which has placed his name by St. Bernard's side in the pages of medieval mystics.† It seems to me that the

---

* Contr. Cels. lib. 6, 689, &c.
† S. Bonaventure de 7, Itin. disp. 4. art. 4.

Saint of Clairvaux must have read the Commentary on the Canticles, where Origen celebrates the marriage of the Word with the soul His bride. In one place he even anticipates the devotion to the Sacred Heart, and says that St. John sought in the depths of that princely Heart for the treasures of wisdom and science hidden in Christ Jesus.* There is no doubt that he had a true personal devotion to the Eternal Word; and his very errors are owing to his attempts to give a scientific basis to the separate personality of Him, whom he knew to be true God. Yet there is no true mysticism without the sharp, clear outlines of the Manhood of Jesus, and the soul must ever have, living and moving before it, the scenes of His life and Passion. The movement of dialectics is but a poor substitute for the Stations of the Cross. St. Thomas and Suarez might be mystics, but I doubt whether the method of the De Principiis, its headlong plunges into bottomless depths of thought and bold looking with unwinking eyes into the furnace of burning questions, could ever have been compatible with even what we should call daily meditation. We can discern in Origen passionate cries of the soul to its God and Saviour, exclamations probably in the language of Holy Writ, for strength in the fiery trial of martyrdom, approaching terribly near, and for help in the hotter fire of temptation.

* In Cant. i. 33

Yet if we have read aright the life-battle of that noble soul, we should be surprised to find much prayer of quiet. The intellectual gymnastics, which form his excuse with St. Athanasius, were no help to contemplation. Three times a day we know from himself that he prayed, and he avows his predilection for a quiet corner of the house, set apart for prayer; yet he draws without disapproval an uncomfortable picture[*] of Christians standing to pray in the open air ovei the impluvium of a Roman house or in the peristyle of a Greek one, with eyes fixed and arms stretched towards heaven; a position which, like the cruciform attitude of Tertullian, does not look as if the prayer could last very long.

From all this it follows that the mystical life existed from the very first, and, on the other hand, that few distinct rules had been given for it. It is held out to Diognetus by his Christian correspondent. It is the "most sweet rest" offered to Tryphon the Jew by St. Justin.[†] Even the restless mind of Tertullian longs after "the school of quiet";[‡] in that franticly savage pamphlet in which he bids a final farewell to the bar, and assumed the pallium for a cassock. Yet if we listen to the terms of boastful contempt in which he speaks, we augur ill for his vocation. "I owe nothing to the forum, nothing to the field, nothing to the senate house. I pay my respects to no one in

---

[*] De Or. 270.　　[†] Dial. 8.　　[‡] Magisterium quietis, de Pallio.

the morning, I take not to the stump, I hang about no law court, I snuff up no stink of gutters in the forum, I fawn at no bar, I thump no benches, I throw no law into confusion, I roar out no pleading, I am neither judge, nor soldier, nor king; I have given up the world. My one thing needful is with myself. A man has more enjoyment in solitude than in public life." If Ravignan or Lacordaire had left the French bar in this spirit, St. Sulpice would have suspected their vocation. It was not to Tertullian, nor to Origen, nor even to St. Athanasius, that God entrusted the task of being the Rodriguez of the ancient Church. There is hardly a page of the "Christian Perfection" which does not cite some story or some saying of a hermit of the desert.

It shewed a tremendous consciousness of strength in the Church, and a confidence in the loyalty of her children, to allow them to go out into the wilds and lead a solitary life. The enormous majority of the monks were laymen, nor generally speaking were even the abbots priests; yet so secure was the Church that the necessity of belonging to her and obeying the one visible body was a first principle with them, that she allowed them to stray into the desert, and to plunge into all the dangerous depths of contemplation. It was not till long afterwards that the yells of the wild Egyptian monks, dis- 'urbing the propriety of councils, showed the necessity, which afterwards produced St. Columban and St. Benedict. Meanwhile the solitaries were left to win their own spiritual experience. The first pioneers in the wilderness, the pilgrim fathers of the wilds, communicated their spiritual feelings to each other, and instructed their successors. We ourselves in our daily life, our temptations, our struggles, our examination of conscience, our mental prayer, are following the lights held up to us by the saints of the desert. Not only St. Benedict and St. Teresa, but even ordinary Christians are living at this day on the record and experience of many a fight with the devil and many a lonely midnight prayer in the wilderness. Christian mysticism is quite different from any other, though mysticism exists everywhere in all races, however cold and matter-of-fact, in all religions, however false; and these peculiarities of Catholic mystical life are to be seen in all their essential outlines in the men and women whose lives are here presented to the reader. A short account of their peculiarities will both show the amount of gratitude, which we owe to our forefathers in Christ, and how their lives bear practically upon ours.

As in Germany, while philosophy was running its course of speculation and mysticism from Kant to Schelling, the hands and feet of Catherine Emmerich, the Addolorata and Maria Mörl were dropping blood, so while St. Paul, St. Antony, St. Macarius and Arsenius were leading their wonderful lives in the desert, in the same country and at the same time Plotinus and Hierocles were lecturing, and Hypatia was bewitching Alexandria with her eloquence and her beauty. There is, however, a much more direct connection between the schools of Alexandria and of Nitria, than between the mysticism of Jacobi and Schelling, and the ecstatics of Munster and the Tyrol. Neoplatonism was a doctrine of which the end and object was union with God; and though their God was impersonal, yet their system was a real mysticism, the climax of which was extasy. Porphyry declares that Plotinus often and especially four times when they were together was raised to a state of ecstatic intuition of the Sovereign Good. "As for myself," he adds, "I have only been united to God once in my forty-eighth year." "Eunapius writes," says Cardinal Bona,* "of Jamblichus, that he was sometimes raised ten cubits from the ground. Porphyry, in his life of Plotinus, tells us marvellous things of his contemplation; Proclus also, in his books on the Theology of Plato, and Plotinus himself in many places, speak much of extasy and of abstraction from the things of sense, in a way not contrary to the maxims of Christian wisdom. Again, the autnor of the Heavenly Wisdom according to the Egyptians, thus writes of himself: I often, when engaged in mental contemplation,

* Via. Comp 8, 4.

seem to leave my body and to enjoy the possession of the Highest Good with marvellous delight." Where did this system of union with God differ from that of St. Antony?

1. Heathen mysticism at its best, when cleared of magic, witchcraft, Canidian drugs and general devilries, was an intellectual system addressing itself to the choice spirits of the human race and leaving vulgar uninteresting souls in the mire. I do not mean to say that Platonic ethics were not lofty, nor that in practice Hypatia's life was not spotless, nor that prayer and love were not taught to be necessary instruments, in order to fulfil this great aspiration of the human spirit to its God. Science and intellect, however, were absolutely necessary conditions for the attainment of this object. A man must have gone through the whole field of dialectics, have mastered the ens unum in multis, have proved that multiplicity is essential to reason and all its products, have seen the last duality of thinker and thought, of subject and object, expire with the extinction of personality, before the great act of union, extasy, can ensue. But no Platonic logic is necessary for the Christian life. The christian mystic is not made of finer clay than his neighbour: the common red earth of Adam with the common human soul is quite enough with the grace of God. The spirit bloweth at its own sweet will and urges on pure hearts and simple minds. The Saints of the desert are made out of such

men as the illiterate St. Antony, Paul the Simple, Moses, the negro robber, and Mary the sinner of Alexandria. This has been its characteristic in every age. Brother Egidius could boast that by God's grace he could see as deep into the abyss of love as Father Bonaventure. The highest phenomena of Christian mysticism appear to this day in the soul of a poor village girl in the Tyrol, who has learned no science but that which can be gained at the foot of the crucifix. But this fact by no means gives us the measure of the essential difference between the two systems. I have been speaking here of that part of the mystical life which is not essential to it. Instead of being the aim of christian life, extasies and raptures are not even a necessary portion of it; nay, if they are aimed at or desired, in the smallest degree, ever so indirectly, the whole life is vitiated, and if outward symptoms of them occur, they are necessarily false. So little are they necessary, that in some races, they hardly ever occur For instance Ireland with all its virtues has not produced a mystic, for very many centuries; and even its earlier Saints differ to an extraordinary degree, from those of Italy or France. The Celtic race has in this sense very little mysticism. But the gulf between the Museum and Thebaid is not to be measured by the fact that in the one case, extasies were the rare reward of painful intellectual endeavour, in the other they came unbidden and unsought to the unlettered christian girl or mechanic. It would be more true to say that all christians without exception are in one sense called to union with God. The following passage deserves to be well pondered by all of us. "Because there are very many of us who wishing neither to learn, nor to observe the rules of christian perfection handed down to us by Christ, excuse themselves from the appearance of despising them, by asserting that those rules concern those who are shut up in cloisters, and are free from the cares of the world, I will now shew clearly how vain and false is their persuasion, that this error may be destroyed, and the truth made clear. It is most true that Christian life may be divided into two states, the secular and religions. Both, however, though by a different route, tend to the same end, and as far as the practice of virtue, contempt of the world, poverty of spirit, and love of the cross, the condition of each is identical, with this only difference, that religious being bound by the ties of solemn vows and rules, are obliged more strictly to perfection than those who live in the world. In other respects, one and the same way of life is required of both, one and the same Gospel has been preached to both. Since God commands nothing but charity, forbids nothing but self-love, there is no difference as far as that is concerned, no exception of persons. Our Saviour has commanded that no one should speak an idle word, or he will have to render an account of it at the day of judgment. No one is to be angry, no one to give way to wrong desires; here is no distinction between the monk and the married Christian. In the same way, when He says, Blessed are they who mourn; woe to those who laugh now; when He taught us to pray always, to renounce all things, to hate our life, to deny ourselves, to bear injuries patiently, to enter the narrow gate, He makes no exception in favour of any member of the human race. When Paul the Apostle writes to all Christians, even those who are married and have children, does he not exact from them all the discipline of the monastic life? 'Having food and raiment,' he says, 'let us be content.' What could he require more of an anchorite? Were not Peter and James writing to all Christians when they exhort them to be holy, perfect, wanting in nothing? When Christ said, Be ye perfect, as My Heavenly Father is perfect; He spoke to all the faithful, to whom He appointed the highest aim of sanctity, that all we who are called and are sons of God, should strive after the perfection of our Father. There is, therefore, a great necessity of sanctity laid upon all Christians, lest they should be excluded as degenerate children from their Father's inheritance."* This is a very important passage; the modern type of a worldly Catholic would not have been considered safe

---

* Bonæ. Principia Vitæ. Christ. c. 6.

when that was written. He existed, doubtless; but he would not have considered himself safe. This perfect self-satisfaction is our characteristic. We enjoy this world not viciously, but without reference to God, and think ourselves quite sure of heaven though we make no attempt at the perfection of our state, and hardly any prayer, though we give but scanty alms, and aim at no interior life of intercourse with God. Such a man or woman would have been thought half a heathen by St. Antony, and would have been pitied as in a dangerous state, for the call to some kind of perfection would have been considered as involved in Christianity itself.

2. Not only does it appear that some sort of intercourse with God is held out to all Christians in general, and that perfection belongs to no state in particular, but it is also true that the first steps in the spiritual life are the same in all. Any one who has read the life of St. Antony, must have been struck with wonder, and perhaps feel some kind of disappointment, on reading the apparently commonplace and matter-of-fact instructions, given by him to his monks. After years spent in the desert, his first discourse to his disciples is in a great manner made up of such sentences as these: " Of what profit is it to seek things which we cannot take away with us ? Why should we not rather acquire those things which we are able to take away with us, such as prudence, justice, temperance, fortitude, intelligence, (σύνεσις)

charity, love of the poor, faith in Christ, meekness, hospitality." A strange list this of virtues for a monk of the desert, but a stranger result for days and nights spent in prayer, fasting, and vigils, in utter solitude in the depths of the desert. Very unromantic platitudes those, when we remember the speaker and his audience with the scene around them, St. Antony and his monks, with his cavern for a background. Unromantic, perhaps, but most necessary for monks and all Christians whatsoever. It was the announcement, that before man can attain to the unitive life, he must pass through the purgative and illuminative. Christian virtue is the beginning, middle, and end of the cloister, and of perfection in general. Many a soul dreaming about perfection, might profit by St. Antony's speech. To many such, we would say, Madam, keep your temper, and give alms. St. Antony knew human nature well when he bade his monks disbelieve the devil, if the evil spirit promised to reveal to them the moment of the rising of the Nile. Human nature aims at the supernatural, and despises the commonplace, forgetting that the supernatural is often very commonplace in its outward aspect. Moreover, however sublime may be the prayer of the saints, however wonderful their intercourse with God, the first steps in prayer are identical for the saints and the most ordinary amongst us. All begin with meditation, and go on through affective prayer. With patience and perseverance, all souls can go a certain way, a considerable way in prayer, without trenching on the really supernatural. Ordinary grace will carry you through many stages of prayer without landing you in those heights of passive contemplation which require extraordinary help. The fact is, that there is no gulf between the ordinary and the supernatural in prayer. The soul of a saint passes on through unconscious and undistinguishable steps, just as the old year melts tranquilly into the new, without any sound breaking the silence of midnight. Theologians even differ as to where the precise point begins, when the ordinary ceases and the supernatural prayer begins. For instance, Cardinal de Laurea looks upon acquired contemplation as within the compass of ordinary grace : "I seriously warn novices and the faithful, who are inexperienced in spiritual thoughts and prayers, not to be frightened when they hear of contemplation, as though it were a hard and difficult thing, yea, morally impossible, and only conceded to anchorites by a most singular favour of God. This is not the case, if we speak of common, or acquired, or as it is commonly called, natural contemplation, for, with respect to the subjects who are capable of contemplation, St. Gregory says, that persons of every sort, of both sexes and of all conditions, are capable of contemplation, if they are instructed. And St. Bernard and St. Bonaventure say, that unlearned simple persons are most apt for contemplation. Of infused or supernatural contemplation, of course it is true that it does not belong to all of every state, and of a common order, but only to very few who are perfect, or on the way to be perfect. As, however, all the faithful, if they are instructed, are capable of meditation on the objects of revelation, so, if they are instructed, they are capable of common or acquired contemplation, because the transition from meditation to contemplation is in the regular order of things. It is enough for my purpose at present to touch upon the easiness of common or acquired contemplation."[*] It is plain, then, that the prayer of the saints of the desert, in its ordinary state, was not so far removed as to be useless to us. We may parody the words of the poet, and say, "One touch of grace makes the whole world kin." It is therefore with no antiquarian curiosity that we gaze down into the hearts of those old hermits. Their fragmentary sayings, their simple, pious, almost humorous utterances are indeed remarkable, if only as waifs and strays from that great ocean of the past, flung up on the shore out of the depths where so much has sunk for ever. Even as men we listen with interest to those voices of the dead, and love to think of those uncouth hermits, and of Mary of Egypt wandering about the solitude of Moab covered with her long, black, rusty hair. She, too, was

[*] Laurea. de Or. Christ: Op. 3. c. L.

a veritable child of Eve, with her heart full of the memory of life's sorrows and sins, and her eyes no longer lit up with the wild light of the delirium of vice and of Alexandrian orgies, but glowing softly with the blessed peace of conscious forgiveness. They were no stargazers, no idle dreamers, these hermits of the wilderness, but the first teachers of the spiritual life. They went out into the desert, conscious of no grand aim, led by the spontaneous impulse of their simple hearts, with no reflection on self, but wishing to obey literally the words of Christ. They had no views, no high ideal before them of what they themselves would become. They anticipated no contemplation, they sought for no particular prayer. The desert was their purgative life, their novitiate. They committed themselves quietly to God's guidance, and let His Spirit carry them whithersoever He would, living day by day on whatever of temptation, of desolation, or spiritual sweetness it pleased God to send them. They chatted simply together of their experiences, and thus they planted for us the landmarks of the Christian life. They examined their consciences, they had their directors, and to this day their prayer is held out to us as a model. At times it took the shape of what we should now call meditation, as in the case of the monk who records his thinking on the crucifixion,[*]

[*] Rosweide, lib. vi. 659.

and of Abbot Pæmen who meditated on the sorrows of Mary, but in general it appears to have been principally the prayer of aspiration or of ejaculation. Their prayers were far less regular and methodical, more impulsive and less self-restrained, more instinctive and less dependent on reflection than those recommended in ordinary books of devotion. They would have agreed with St. Philip, who taught an old woman mental prayer by bidding her dwell on the words of the Pater Noster, and with St. Teresa, who gave the same advice to her Carmelite Sisters. In general, the prayers of saints and even of medieval writers are more antique than those now in common use. Listen to another Cardinal and monk. "Verily Christ the Saviour taught us this mode of prayer by His example; for in the garden He repeated over and over again, 'My Father, if it be possible, let this cup pass from me, nevertheless not My will but Thine be done.' Thais, once a sinner, was taught by Abbot Paphnutius to pray continually, 'My Creator, have mercy on me.' Cassian in his collations recommends the frequent use of this little verse: God, hasten to my help. Many such things are found in the lives of the Fathers. Abbot Isaac saw the prayer of a certain monk rise while he was eating, like fire in the sight of God. Another monk, while he was conversing with others, made a hundred and three ejaculations. Abbot Macarius, when some one asked him about his prayer, answered: 'It is not necessary to speak much in prayer, but to spread out your hands frequently, and say, 'Lord, as Thou willest, and knowest, have mercy on me.'" Moses, the Ethiopian, once a robber chief, made fifty prayers a day; Paul, the monk, three hundred; a certain virgin seven hundred. Theodoret relates that Simeon Stylites made numberless acts of adoration a day, so that a bystander counted sometimes one thousand two hundred and forty-five."* Here Cardinal Bona evidently holds up the prayers of the desert Saints as a model to the modern Christian. St. Simeon on his pillar was not so very unlike either in his work or his interior, the Curé d' Ars in his parish church. And if you descend into the ranks of ordinary, commonplace Christians, it will not be hard to find out that there is much in their spiritual life which connects them with the old desert Saints. Their temptations were the same. The noon-day devil walks about the streets of London, and the drawing-rooms of Mayfair, as he made his rounds in the desert. The cell of the modern nun is not more free from his visits, than the cavern of the wilderness. It is for this reason, that the records of the temptations and struggles of the ancient monks are so valuable to us. They are precious for the tempted, and precious for all who have to deal with souls. It would be well if we priests

* Bona. Via. Comp. 6.

knew more of the mystical theology to be learned in the pages of Rosweide; and if superiors of religious houses studied the gentleness and sweetness of the abbots of the deserts, and remembered that they are fathers and mothers of individual souls. If it be true that there are dangers of illusion in the study of mysticism, it is also true that there is greater danger in the ignorance of it. God's dealings with souls are very marvellous, and it needs not to be a saint to feel the crucifixion of His operations. The tediousness and the weariness and disgust of the monotony of the spiritual life which makes up what is called *acedia*, and appears so often in the pages of Cassian and Moschus, are not confined to the banks of the Nile. It is even true that, in some of the earlier stages of that life, there are anticipations of the pains which, in an infinitely greater degree, saints have suffered. After narrating some of the most terrible trials of the life of the Ursuline Mary of the Incarnation, suffered while she was teaching the savages in Canada, Father Charlevoix adds: "All this account is very instructive, and if those who are tempted were to behave as she did, they would spare much trouble to themselves and their directors also. It is not rare to find even in persons but little advanced in the spiritual life, states of mind such as we have described. It is not always God who acts immediately on the soul; He has only to let the tempter have his way. Even natural disposition has much to do with it. The design of God in allowing it, is to humble the soul. What the soul has to do is to practise patience, to keep silence, and to be humble and submissive."* It would be well also if the director was patient as well as the penitent; and he would be patient, if he knew more of the ways of God even from books, and respected the work of God in souls. We should do well to remember the advice of Abbot Apollo to the monk, who was himself tempted because he had been harsh to his brother : " This has happened to thee because you drove into despair the youth who was attacked by the evil one, and whom you ought to have anointed for his fight with the devil by words of consolation. You never thought of our Lord's words, break not the bruised reed."† Alas! poor reeds! terrible sufferings are often inflicted on souls because we are too much hurried away by the tumult of life to pray, or to think, or to study anything whatsoever, far less the science which the old monks taught us in the solitude and silence of the desert.

3. A third characteristic of Christian spirituality is what is called the interior life, and I dwell upon it principally because it gives me an opportunity of noticing the influence of the desert on Christian doctrine. It is sometimes said

* Vie de la Mere M. de l'Inc. book 5 p. 25.
† Roswcide lib. 5. p. 572.

that all doctrines which are subjective, and have to do with the analysis of man, his states of mind, and his relations to grace, are modern, and were little considered in the ancient Church.* It seems to me that those ancient Christians were far more like ourselves than is commonly thought, and this part of the subject will enable me to point out both the likeness and the difference between them and the modern Catholic.

Let us begin by quoting a description of the interior life from a well-known writer. "The interior life consists in two sorts of acts, viz., in thoughts and affections. It is in this only that perfect souls differ from imperfect, and the blessed from those who are still living on earth. Our thoughts, says St. Bernard, ought to be 'ever following after truth, and our affections ever abiding in the fervour of charity.' In this

---

* Of all theories about the early Church, none is so offensive as that which affects to point out the precise moment when certain doctrines were supposed to be taught for the first time, because the errors which denied them first brought them into prominence. Mr. Ffoulkes, for instance, tells us that "Pelagianism was a heresy born out of due time," (Christendom's Divisions, p. 69,) which means a heresy inconvenient for Mr. Ffoulke's theory according to which heresies and truths ought to arise at certain times and in certain places. There are a good many heresies which labour under the same misfortune as the Pelagian. We can scarcely believe our eyes when the same author actually writes as though the individual christian first arrived at the consciousness of the possession of a conscience in the 16th century under the auspices of Luther. (Ibid, pp. 96, 182. (Let us trust that the estimable and industrious author really attached no meaning whatsoever to his words.

manner, our mind and heart being closely applied to God, being fully possessed by God, in the very midst of exterior occupations we never lose sight of Him, and are always engaged in the exercise of His love. The essence of the spiritual and interior life consists in two things: on the one hand in the operations of God in the soul, in the lights that illumine the understanding and the inspirations which affect the will; on the other in the co-operation of the soul with the lights and movements of grace. One of the occupations of the interior life is the examining and ascertaining particularly three sorts of things in our souls. First, what comes from our own nature, our sins, our evil habits, our passions, our inclinations, our affections, our desires, our thoughts, our judgments, our sentiments: secondly, what comes from the devil, his temptations, his suggestions, his artifices, the illusions by which he tries to seduce us unless we are on our guard: thirdly, what comes from God, His lights, His inspirations, the movements of His grace, His designs in our regard, and the ways along which He desires to guide us."* It is plain, then, from this passage that what is called the interior life consists in the substitution of heavenly thoughts for evil or natural thoughts. It means that it is reasonable and right for a christian to aim not only at keeping God's commandments and doing

---

* Lallemant, Spiritual Doctrine—English translation. p. 209.

good works, but also at a continual thought of God's presence, and a constant obedience to the movements of grace, as the supernatural spring of our actions instead of following merely natural and simply human feeling. That this can never be perfectly realised in this life is certain: but that it should be aimed at as partially possible, that without fanaticism, without singularity, without crushing nature it should be possible so to penetrate and imbue it with the life of God that it should seldom move alone, this is an idea, to speak humanly, as peculiar to christianity, as novel and original as Transubstantiation. That it was a totally new notion to a converted heathen is perfectly manifest. Immersed in the outer world, which poured itself into him through his five senses, and ever fed his imagination with the many-coloured images of a life without restraint, and the thinly-disguised outlines of dangerous forms, he never progressed even as far as the notion of an indoor existence or a home. The idea of a heavenly life within himself would be utterly unintelligible. I doubt, whether, even now, outside the Church, it has progressed as far as to be even a dream. The use, for instance, of the word recollection, is as thoroughly Catholic as confession or absolution, nay, it is even more exclusively Catholic, for it has nothing to do with either ritual or vestment. Within the Church it is the great distinction between the worldly and unworldly christian. In proportion as our faith thoroughly seizes hold of us, we are recollected and filled with the thought of God. I suspect that the worst times of ecclesiastical history, such as those which immediately preceded the great modern heresy, were those in which the proportion of worldly christians was greatest, that is, of christians on whom their faith sat, like an external thing.

This idea of the interior life was principally brought out by the hermits of the desert. The real doctor of the wilderness, who reduced their religious practice to theory was St. Macarius, and his homilies preached by him probably in the church of the monastery of Scete, after he was ordained priest, in the year 340, furnish us with as good a notion of the inward life of the members of that Libyan solitude as the sermons of St. Bernard give us of that of the Cistercians of Clairvaux. There we find the doctrine of original sin brought out with a clearness which rivals St. Augustine, while his descriptions of states of the soul remind us of St. Teresa, or Henry Suso.* The greater part, however, of the teaching of the saint relates to the establishment of the interior life as described

* For instance, for original sin v. Hom. xi. with the beautiful description of Jesus entering into the utmost depth of the heart (βάθυς κόλπος) and xii. For supernatural states Hom. viii. Some expressions, e. g. Hom. xv. 22, have been accused of semi-Pelagianism, a heresy quite foreign to the saint's whole spirit. It is true, however, that a curious tract on Baptism in Gallandius, Tom. 8, ascribed, I know not with what reason, to Mark, a later hermit, has a very Pelagian look.

by Lallemant:* "In this do true Christians" he says, "differ from the whole race of men, and the great difference between the two, as we have said, consists in that the intellect and reasoning power are ever occupied with heavenly thoughts, and contemplate the noble things of eternity through the participation and communication of the Holy Spirit. They are supernaturally born of God, and are reckoned to be sons of God in reality and power. They have attained to a state of unshaken tranquillity, of quiet and of rest, through many struggles and troubles and much length of time, and are not tossed wildly as in a sieve, or flung about by the waves of restless and empty thoughts. They are greater and stronger than the world in that their mind, and the thought of their souls are in the peace of Christ and in the love of the Holy Ghost. For not in outward shapes and types does the speciality of Christians consist, though many think so, and in consequence men are like the world in their intellect and reasoning. There is an earthquake and a tossing, a faithlessness and confusion, an unquietness and a trembling in the thoughts, just as though they were not Christians, but simply men like others. On the surface and in certain outward practices they are not heathen. But in heart and mind they are bound by the chains of earth, for they have not the rest of God and the fear of the

---

* Hom. v.

Spirit in their interior life. They have never sought it by prayer from God, and have never believed it to be possible."

A homily this which might have been delivered with effect elsewhere, to the courtiers of Constantinople, or the ladies of Antioch; indeed it would not be out of place if addressed to worldly Catholics of all generations.

While, however, it is plain that the interior life of a Christian of the fourth century does not differ from the Christian life of the nineteenth, it is certain that there are differences in the modes recommended at different times for the practice of the interior life. It is certain that in our time there is a far more frequent reference to the details of the Life of our Lord, especially to His Passion, a far more minute analysis of His feelings as Man, and a deeper entrance into the joys and sufferings of His Sacred Heart than in the first ages of the Church. That these were never wanting in any age is proved by a few instances which have already been given from the saints of the desert, and could be proved by passages from early writers. Nothing can exceed the tenderness with which St. Clement* appeals to all that Jesus had suffered for Christians, and how His words were received into their bosoms and inmost beings, and His Passion ever before their eyes. St. Justin has written words quite

* 1 ad Cor. 2, and Ep. 2, 1.

modern in his appreciation of the interior sufferings of the Heart of Jesus in His agony, as if he had made his meditation upon them in the morning.[*] "For in the records which I say were composed by His apostles and those who followed them, it is written that His blood flowed like great drops of blood, while He was praying: Let this cup pass from Me, if it be possible. It is plain then that His Heart was trembling, and His bones likewise and His Heart felt like wax melting within Him, that we might know that His Father willed that His own Son should in very deed go through such passions for us, and that we should not say that being the Son of God He did not feel the things which happened to Him." Again, Origen[†] speaks of the image of the wounds of Jesus impressed on the minds of Christians. It would be absurd to suppose that the Passion had no influence over the feelings and perseverance of the saints of the desert, when St. Macarius exhorts them to bear their hard life by the thought that they must be crucified with the Crucified One, and that the human soul which is the bride of Christ must suffer with her Bridegroom. In the same place he bids them remember Him "who as a mark of insult bore the crown of thorns on His Head and endured spittings,

---

[*] Dial. cum Tryph. 103.
[†] Cont. Cels. lib. vi. 636.

buffets, and the cross."* Nevertheless it is generally the glorious rather than the suffering Christ who appears in the early Church. In the visions of martyrs, Christ appears splendid and radiant, and their dreams were peaceful and full of beautiful poetry. St. Stephen saw Jesus standing in glory at the right hand of God. "In the midst of my cruel torments," says St. Victor, "I invoked the merciful Saviour; and lo! all at once I saw Him carrying in His hand the heavenly sign of our redemption. And He said to me: Peace be with thee, Victor. Fear not, I am Jesus, and it is I who send suffering and pain to My saints." Saint Marianus sees lovely meadows, planted with dark cypresses and pines, and drinks a cup of delicious water from a cool stream. Children come crowned with roses, and present a palm to the martyrs, bidding them welcome to the heavenly banquet. It seems as though amidst their terrific sufferings God sent them visions of glory to sustain the fainting flesh. In exhortations to martyrdom, the sufferings of Christ are not so prominently put forward as the joys of paradise. How unsatisfactory is Origen, in his address to martyrs, when he accounts for the Agony of Jesus! how eloquent when he speaks of throwing off "this mortal coil," and of the sight of the Eternal Word! Tertullian, in his *Ad Martyras*, does not mention the Passion once.

* Hom. xii. 5.

St. Cyprian speaks of the Passion in his exhortation, but far more of the Maccabees.* In early writings the Passion appears almost always as an element of triumph. Never are the most ancient Fathers so explicit and peremptory in their assertion of the Godhead of Jesus as when they speak of His cross. The Patripassian heresy would have been impossible, if the Church had not constantly and unequivocally declared the sufferer on the cross, to be absolutely and in the strictest sense the God who created all things. St. Clement and St Ignatius speak of the Passion of God. Tertullian† forgets his usual ferocity in the beautiful treatise on the flesh of Christ, to speak eloquently and lovingly of his "crucified God." The taunts of the heathen about the dead malefactor under Pontius Pilate by a sort of natural reaction forced Christians to be proud of His ignominy, and to forget the agony of shame in the intensely human soul of their suffering God. The awful pains of the flesh were hidden, in the blaze of the grand achievement of redemption. It seemed to them a glorious thing, worthy of a God, to come down from heaven to reunite them to God, to save them by an act of self-sacrificing love, from the

* He uses a truly African topic of consolation when he thus represents the feelings of the Maccabees: "How great a relief was it in their martyrdom, how vast, how immense a consolation, during their tortures, not to think on their own sufferings, but to prophesy the torments of their torturer."
† De Carne Christi, c. 5

empire of Satan, from sin and passion, and to work a moral renovation on the earth; and the splendour of this victory of the Godhead served to throw a veil of glory over the poor suffering Manhood. They knew that He was Man, and we know that He was God, even when we enter most deeply into His human pains; but in their case the earthly shame was swallowed up in the grandeur of success. "The Son of God was crucified," continues Tertullian, "I feel no shame precisely because it was shameful." Some even pushed the feeling to an excess, and shock us by maintaining that the Sacred Humanity was the reverse of beautiful. The Virgin and Child were an object of devotion in Christianity long before the cross. Our Lady is often seen in the catacombs, the cross never.[*] Nearly the earliest form of the symbol of salvation appears in triumph on the Roman eagles or in the jewelled cross of the old mosaics. Something of the same feeling appears in the hermits of the wilderness. It was perhaps also owing to a reaction against the Arian heresy that the homilies of St. Macarius are full of the Godhead of Christ. The union of our souls with the Godhead through the instrumentality of the Sacred Humanity forms the essence of his interior life. The Manhood is

[*] Wherever it appears, De Rossi says that it is the work of comparatively recent hands. Martigny, Dictionnaire. Art Croix. The Tau, I believe, is sometimes found at a somewhat earlier period.

rather according to the beautiful expression of Clement of Alexandria, "The breast of the Father," to which we poor fallen mortals attach our lips and receive the stream of God's life within us. Jesus appears at times on His cross in St. Macarius, as we have seen, but most frequently it is the sweet image of Him at whose feet Mary Magdalene sat, and the thought of whom draws delicious tears from the eyes of those who contemplate Him.* The object of their love, their desire, their burning affection,† was the same as that which we have before our eyes, Jesus yesterday, and today, and the same for ever; but the point of view from which they regarded Him was somewhat different. They rather considered the victory of the Man-God than the battle and the suffering. It was reserved for a later age to enter more deeply and minutely into the details of the Passion, and to make it the basis of their interior life. The pale face of the Man-God, and His arms outstretched in agonized love upon the cross, and His hands and feet dripping blood, have sunk more and more deeply into the heart of suffering humanity. The figure of our crucified God has long been the central point around which have moved all the profoundest feelings of our souls.

The stigmatized saints, the wayside crucifix

---

* Hom. xxv.

† Καῦσις πρὸς τὸν κύριον—Hom. xv. 1

and the mystery-plays of the Tyrol are all in their way proofs of what I mean. The visions of modern mystics are far different from the joyful scenes which cheered the Martyrs. Jesus sweating blood, or scourged at the pillar, or staggering under His cross has replaced the same Lord, appearing in His glory to the Saints of the early Church. For this many subjective reasons may be given. I cannot help thinking that our hearts are more tender than those of the converts from that old Greek and Roman world. Classical poetry sings of the straightforward joys and pains of the old Adam, but it has far less minute analysis of feeling, of sorrow and sadness than ours. Domestic affections, the product of Christianity, have refined and deepened our emotions, and given them a greater capacity at once of tranquil joy and of sensitive sorrow. This may be one reason why we enter more deeply into the sufferings of Christ. Again, there was in that young Church, with the world all before it, a certainty of prompt success which now we cannot realize. Was not the day of judgment coming soon? Was not the reign of justice to begin and Christ's kingdom to appear? Why waste time in mourning over a world which must so soon come to an end? It may be that the nearly expected approach of the end of the world and the consequent triumph of the Church contributed to render the hearts of those first Christians of the Roman world less sensible to suffering. As the Church grew older, Christians entered more minutely into the feelings of their Lord. There is a far more modern aspect, for instance, in St. Gregory Nazianzen. In one of his most beautiful orations, he tells his people that he had been in retreat by the seashore, and how he had enjoyed the sight of the waves, and even the pebbles and shells and seaweed on the beach. He then turns to the Passion of our Lord, and after going through its details, he enters more deeply into His mental sufferings, and reminds his hearers that 'God must have the preeminence in suffering, because dishonour was worse for Him to bear.'[*] And now, that the Church has struggled on through fifteen fresh centuries of sin and sorrow since Constantine, we have learned to sympathize more with the agony of His soul, and with all that the anticipation must have cost Him. Certain of final success, we are certain also that successes on a grand scale are few and far between. His kingdom is not yet come. In the meanwhile, individual sufferings and public miseries are rife, and we feel the want of the Cross and the crucified One more intimately than did the first Christians. We rush to the Heart of Jesus for sympathy in desolation and sorrow. The real reason however of the difference probably comes from Christ Himself. Not only do we seek His sympathy

[*] Or. 26.

but He seeks ours. To Him martyrdom is a triumph, while the sins of Christians are a shame. For this reason He comes to ask us to feel for and with Him. He appears to modern Saints under all the indignities of the Passion. He would have us realize the fact that His Godhead spared Him no pang, but added poignancy to all His sufferings. It only made flesh and heart more keenly alive to physical and mental pain. The consciousness of infinite greatness only gave Him a profounder sense of shame under indignity, and unbounded lovingness only made the disappointment of unrequited love more unmitigatedly bitter. Because His Person was divine, all the sinless feelings of our nature were in Him intensified, and possessed a strength even beyond those of us ordinary men, with all our egotism; and this served to enhance the pain of His unreserved self-sacrifice by raising to an unlimited degree the sensitiveness of His suffering Heart. There is something awful in the shame of God, and modern visions are meant to teach us that the accumulated shames of centuries were felt beforehand by Jesus, in His Agony and on His Cross. And not only shame, but the pain of all other human feelings formed a part by anticipation of His bitter cup. Hence, all woes have ever run to hide themselves in His Sacred wounds. Hence, time has only enabled us to realize better how much it cost Jesus to redeem us. Hence, though St. Teresa like St. Macarins, bids us look for the presence of God in our own hearts, yet she also warns us never to lose sight of the Sacred Humanity. Hence, though the object on which our interior life is fixed is the same Jesus, God and Man, who occupied the minds and hearts of the hermits of the desert, yet there is no dead monotony in the life of the Church. The heavenly figure which appeared to Martyrs and Saints in the primitive ages has gained in clearness and in beauty, in tenderness and pathos through the lapse of time. It may be that the spiritual state of the Saints of the desert coincides with those more advanced stages of mystical theology, when the union with God is greater and images fewer. The spiritual state of St. Macarius, of course, is more like that of St. John of the Cross than like those earlier stages of prayer, which we find in ordinary spiritual books. Nevertheless, even in the highest modern Saints, we hear more of the Sacred Humanity than in lives of the Saints of old. Even in the advice, given to the common run of Christians, the same difference is observable. The following passage, from one who has been supposed to exaggerate the possibility of union with the Godhead, will fitly close this part of the subject, and illustrate the contrast between the ancient and the modern Church. In Tauler's Imitation of the life of Jesus, the following rules are given for keeping up the sense of the presence of God. "A man must contemplate the sufferings of Our Lord. He must imprint them upon his heart. Through them he will learn how he must avoid all which is not God, how he must exercise himself in every virtue in order to arrive at God. Through the contemplation of our Lord's Passion, God pours a strength into him, by which He draws him to Himself with power; and this is the effect of the force which lies in the sufferings of Jesus. And when a man earnestly turns himself towards the thought of the Passion and dwells in it, God reveals to him the fruit of His suffering, which is so great that it flows out upon and around the man, and he is thus forcibly drawn through the rushing of grace towards God. The mighty stream seizes on all things and hurries them along in its strength, and in like manner it happens to a man, who diligently contemplates the Passion. The flow of grace bears him along out of himself, back to his first origin, the God from whom he came. On the contrary, he who gives himself to good works without any such application of his interior to the thought of the Passion of our Lord, has his face indeed towards God, but often stands stock still or even retrogrades instead of advancing; while they who occupy themselves with the sufferings of Jesus, do not walk but run as fast as men who have enemies behind them. They never stand still, they never go backwards, but ever without intermission advance forwards. This however comes not from their own strength, but it is heavenly power lent them through the contemplation of the Passion of our Lord."*

4. There is another characteristic of the mystical life of which little appears in the following pages. I mean the devotion to the Blessed Virgin. We can hardly conceive an identity between ourselves and the monks of old, unless we find in them some traces of what is now considered to be essential to the very notion of the spiritual life. Let me say something upon this subject before I conclude.

We hear a great deal about the practical system of devotion to our Lady, which is supposed to be perfectly modern, and which is over and above the dogmatic decrees of the council of Trent. That there is such a system we readily admit; it is not explicitly contained in formal documents, but it is preached by parish priests in their sermons, taught by nuns to girls who are about to make their first communion, pervades the whole life of the Church, is sucked in by Catholics with their mother's milk, surrounds us all like an atmosphere and is breathed in with every breath we draw. To this we must submit or we are bad catholics, and keep ourselves aloof from the mystical life of the Church. In point of fact a practical system of some kind over and above authorized formulas there always must be, because our faith is too vast and magnificent to be expressed in words. Now it is

---

Nachfolge, 1. 123.

precisely to this fact, that I wish to draw attention; if there must have been such a system in the Church from the first, what was it? how far especially did it appear in the mystical life of the Saints of the wilderness? has it utterly perished? did it contain anything about Mary? If it can be made out that in the early Church there existed a system, in its leading features like that which shocks the sensibilities of men who eliminate Mary from the Christian life, it renders their position more untenable and illogical than ever. I am willing to allow at once that the practical system of the Church has developed; but by development I mean nothing vague or indefinite. Some writers speak of development as though they believed in a theological transmutation of species; as if one doctrine could come out of another utterly different in kind. Others write as though the process of development was a contest, the result of which has been that, by a sort of natural selection, the strong doctrines outlived the weak, as though the truths thus developed were only connected together by historical sequence, without any internal cohesion. On the contrary, doctrines were delivered whole, and their growth is a process of evolution by which the hidden harmony of the parts is rendered visible, though all those parts were previously taught or implicitly held. The development consists in bringing to light by reflection, what was spontaneously believed before. It is the unfolding of an idea, which was given whole.

Christian truths were thus planted whole like the trees in Paradise; they grew, they unfolded blossoms and they developed into fruit, but they never sprang from seed. If the principle is to be of any scientific use, we must not be content with indistinct germs, any more than we could hope to satisfy a man who asked for an oak, by showing him an acorn. Can we then by any fair use of recorded facts shew the existence of any practical system of devotion to our Lady, floating about the ancient Church, and especially about the cells of the desert? It would not be surprising if we could not discover a vestige of it. There is no difficulty whatsoever in showing that on state occasions, four hundred years before the division of the East from the Catholic Church, sermons were preached by St. Proclus or by St. Cyril of Alexandria, which prove that the doctrine of Christendom was then what it is now. The practical system however of an age gone by is precisely what is most perishable, because it is not contained in documents. Fifteen hundred years hence, it is very unlikely, that one Garden of the Soul will remain, while the canons of the council of Oscott have a chance of being preserved in some future Hardouin. Grand dogmatic treatises remain to reveal the great truths, which occupied the then religious world, but history is silent about the prayers, and the aspirations, and the special devotions, and the spiritual reading of the layman, and about the sermons of the obscure priest, at the time when the Nicene council met. Is there however anything which will render it perfectly conceivable that a Hail Mary or something like it might have been said in the desert? Let us begin with what is certain.

At the end of the sixth century, there is no doubt whatever that the devotion of a monk of Palestine to the Blessed Virgin was precisely what it would be now. John Moschus, accompanied by Sophronius, afterwards patriarch of Jerusalem, set out on a voyage in which he visited the principal monasteries of the East, about the year 578. He tells us stories which read like pages from the Glories of Mary, and which prove that the cells of hermits had images of the Blessed Virgin with the Infant in her arms, that they prayed to her, and burned candles before them. In one case Abbot John the Anchorite, who lived in a cavern, twenty miles from Jerusalem, when about to go on a pilgrimage to the Holy Cross, or the relics of the Saints, used to pray thus to the Blessed Virgin: " Holy Lady, Mother of God, since I am about to travel a long way, take care of thy lamp and do not let it be extinguished, for I am going away trusting to have thy help for a companion of my way." The story goes on to say that the lamp continued to burn miraculously in his absence. Another story* is told of a hermit on the Mount of Olives, whom the devil tempted to put out of his cell an image of our Lady with the Holy Child, and to whom Abbot Theodore said that he had better commit any sin than cease to adore Jesus Christ, God and Lord, with His holy Mother. In another place, our Lady appears in a vision to a monk who had a volume of Nestorius in his cell. I am not defending the truth of these miracles, though I see no reason to doubt them; I bring them forward to prove that in the sixth century the devotion of the monks needs no application of the principle of development to prove its identity with that of the nineteenth. We have not advanced much since then. And these facts throw light on others of the same period.† In the year 555, on the 4th of June, St. Simeon Stylites the younger, solemnly erected his pillar in the presence of the monks of his monastery and called on our Lord, His mother, and the holy angels to witness the truth of the words which he then spoke. The same saint wrote to the Emperor to complain

---

* This story is in Rosweide, p. 368. It is not found in the Greek, published by Cotelerius. That MS. however, omits many other stories, and the passage is quoted in the second council of Nicæa, with the observation that heretics had mutilated the codex. The controversy about images had already begun during the Monophysite controversy, Xenaias and Severus having declared against them in the beginning of the sixth century. Several stories in connection with that controversy appear in Moschus.

† Assemani, quoted by Marin, lib 9, 22.

of the destruction of an image of our Blessed Lady. The thought and the name of Mary must evidently have been in his mind, and have cheered him throughout his marvellous mystical life.

I, however, go much further than this. It is quite plain that so great a devotion could not be of recent growth. It springs up before us all at once as a grand river. Even if its course was unknown to us, so wide and so full a stream must have passed through many lands, and its fountains must be sought for in a distant country. Let us trace it upwards as far as we can. About the year 480, some monk in Palestine wrote a narrative of an event, which took place on the Feast of the Exaltation of the Cross, probably in the year 383, the conversion of Mary of Egypt.[*] In the time of her sinfulness she endeavoured to enter the church of the Holy Sepulchre and found herself repelled by an invisible force. She lifts up her eyes and sees an image of our Lady over the porch, and she bursts out into the following prayer: "O Lady and Virgin, who didst bear the Word of God according to the flesh, I know that it is neither reasonable nor decorous that I, so foul with sin, should look on thine image, who wert ever a stainless virgin; nevertheless, since thy Son became man to save sinners, help me in my desolation, order the door to be opened even to me that I may adore the holy

---

[*] *V.* the proofs in Bollandists, April 2

Cross." It is no wild conjecture, then, that the cry, "Lady, lady, forsake me not," which she afterwards used, must have been ever on Mary's lips during her long wanderings, in the desert. Again, in October, of the year 367, St. Gregory of Nazianzen narrated in one of his first sermons in his new church at Constantinople, that St. Justina invoked our Lady and was heard. Evidently, St. Gregory, himself a monk, was no stranger to devotion to Mary, though his great works may contain no further invocation of her. The next example carries us back to the first ages of monachism. About the year 355 a young Egyptian of fifteen, conversed with St. Antony, and afterwards became well known as Abbot Pœmen. One day, we cannot now tell at what period of his long life, he fell into a state of extasy; and when he was coming to himself, Abbot Isaac bent over him and said to him: "where wert thou?" He answered: "my mind was where the Holy Mary, the Mother of God, stood weeping at the cross of the Saviour, and I was all the while wishing evermore to weep like that."* These words are the first chords of the Stabat Mater stealing over the Church in the desert, like the music from the fabled statue at the dawn of day. It was a nearer approach to modern devotion than the words of St. Ambrose: I have heard

* Cotel. p. 621.

of Mary standing at the foot of the cross, but not of her weeping.*

Now let me connect the monastic devotion to Mary with the common spiritual life of the Church before I have done. We have seen in the passages quoted from St. Irenæus and Origen the two ideas on which the modern devotion to Mary rests; in the former we have found what may be called its hypothetical necessity, that is, its necessity on the supposition that God willed to make the redemption of mankind correspond to its fall. In Origen we have seen how that devotion is personal, that is to Mary as to a person, who stands to our individual soul in the place of a mother Did these ideas develop, that is bear fruit, become living parts of the spiritual life of Christians, and spread into the practical system of the Church in the fourth and fifth centuries, at the time when St. Athanasius, St. Gregory, St. Basil, and St. Chrysostom were alive? I believe that, necessarily few and scanty as are the relics of such a system, the deeper we dig into the buried remains of antiquity, the more we shall be convinced of its existence. There are several instances of what I mean, which have been too lately discovered to be generally known. Let me begin with two, about which I can only speak second-hand.

* De Ob. Val

because I am ignorant of the languages in which they are written.

Nothing can be a better index of the mind of Christians than their popular hymns. The vernacular hymns sung, for instance, all over England may be considered as a very practical test of the trains of devotional thought, and the imagery peculiar to our people. Now it so happens that a Protestant missionary has lately brought to Europe the hymnal of Jared, a hymn-book of the Abyssinian Church. Some of the hymns are very ancient, and are anterior to the time of the Eutychian heresy. Here we have the words which burst from the lips and hearts of the children of the Abyssinian Church before the work of St. Frumentius was corrupted by the Monophysite heresy. In one of the hymns* we find the Archangel Gabriel clothed in the purple gar-

* It is curious that in Monophysite art angels were always painted white, and purple was especially excluded, v. 2, Council of Nicæa. The hymnal seems thus to contain hymns written before Abyssinia became Monophysite. From the close connection between Alexandria and Abyssinia I should think that that heresy must have been making its way in the latter country from the time of Timothy the Cat, that is from the fifth on through the first half of the sixth century. Severus came to Alexandria in 518. When it is said that Abyssinia was converted in the sixth century, Nubia is meant. In Dilman's Catalogue the accounts about Jared are very confused, but pp 32, 50, he is assigned to the reign of Elesbaan and his son, in the beginning of the sixth century. The hymn, however, may be earlier than Jared, who was a compiler. Dilman assigns the hymns to later dates, but says that the book contains fragmenta perantiqua I judge of the date of this hymn chiefly by internal evidence. The translation is by the Rev. J. M. Rodwell, a learned orientalist

ments of which Severus the Monophysite had stripped the angels; while the hymn to our Lady, to which we refer, could never have sprung from a heart which disbelieved in the two natures of her Son. Men and women in Axoum in the sixth century did not essentially differ from what they are in London, and as our English hymns are sung by many a labourer and workwoman in courts and garrets, so we may be sure that the Abyssinian poor carried home from church the hymns of Jared to cheer them in their labours in the fields or at the loom. No hymn, however, sung at the Oratory could surpass in glowing expressions that sung in Abyssinia. It reads like a portion of the Litany of Loretto, of which it anticipates many invocations. "Our Mother," it says, "and the Mother of our Lord, Angels with pen of gold shall write thy praises; thou art the bush, which was truly called Holy of Holies; thou art the light, the treasure-house of the Word; Mary, pray for us." She is called the mother of martyrs, the ark which contained the law, the gate of salvation. There is evidently a personal devotion to Mary at work in the hearts of the faithful.

I now go back to an earlier time and to a different country. It is strange that, as if to reward the faith of the Church in the declaration of the Immaculate Conception, testimonies previously unknown are springing up which prove the fact asserted in the Bull that it formed part of the original revelation of Christianity. Voices are reaching us from various parts of the ancient Church, which bear witness to the identity of the spiritual life of their people with our own. A schism, of which all record had perished, desolates the church of Edessa, and St. Ephrem could appeal in a popular hymn or rhythmical discourse to the Immaculate Conception, as a doctrine to which all hearts would respond. He pleads for indulgence to our Lord on behalf of the afflicted Church in these words: "Truly Thou and Thy Mother are the only beings who are beautiful altogether and in every respect; for there is no spot in Thee, Lord, nor in Thy Mother any stain."[*] When we remember St. Ephrem's clear views of original sin, and his reverence for the souls of baptized infants who died without actual sin, these words are perhaps the

---

[*] V. Carmina Nisibena, published last year at Leipsig by Dr. Bickell, from a MS. in the British Museum. The editor's observations, p. 28, are as follows: Probatione vix eget Ephraemum hoc loco S. Virgini immunitatem non solum ab actuali, sed etiam ab originali peccato tribuere. Adscribit enim ei talem sanctitatem, quam cum solo Christo participat, quaque omnes reliqui homines carent. Alias autem Ephraem semper primum locum concedit infantibus qui post baptismum sine peccato actuali e vita decesserunt, eosque omnes sanctos honore et dignitate superare contendit. (Cf. iii. ed. Rom. 300, c. 582, hymn. Nis. 63, 23) Si ergo de actuali tantum peccato ageretur, Maria Virgo non sola præter Christum hoc immunitate gauderet, sed in eundem cum infantibus post baptismum mortuis ordinem releganda esset. Cœterum notandum est hanc doctrinam apud Ephraemum, eo majus astimandum esse, quo clarius et accuratius idem peccatum originale docet.

clearest testimony, which has reached us from antiquity, of its belief in the perfect immaculateness of Mary's conception. Unless she were in the grace of God from the first instant of her existence, her stainlessness could not be paralleled with our Lord's, nor could she stand alone with Him in solitary purity, unshared by a single human being. The nineteenth century has not improved upon the fourth. Who dictated the words, which had lain hid for more than a thousand years in an Eastern monastery, and which have just come to light from the British Museum? He was a monk, at once of the desert and the city. We have in one breath the witness of the wilderness and of the schools. Strange combination of the hermit and the modern Benedictine, St. Ephrem issued from the wilds, and became the master of a wide-spread theological school. Like everything else supposed to be of late growth in the Church, scientific theology began far earlier than is thought. Even Rome, which the shallow imagination of historians had supposed to be, from the earliest times, the very home of mental stagnation, has been lately discovered to have possessed a school in the second century.* Alexandria and Antioch each formed a separate scientific centre, more or less Greek in its origin; but the university of the far east was Edessa. There

* V. Hageman. Romische Kirche 108.

was the chief seat of the genuine oriental Church, with the least admixture of the Greek. ✢ There was the point where Christianity came in contact with all the philosophies and religions of the East, Buddhism, the worship of fire, the doctrine of the good and evil principle, and the tradition of the Brahmins. It was one of the earliest centres of Christianity, and its fame for science was almost equal with its faith. In the second century the Bible was translated there, and its version was used by all Christians who spoke the Syrian tongue. The capital of the ancient kingdom of Osroene, it was a light to countries where Christianity is now unknown or disguised under the tenets of miserable sects. It was over its school that St. Ephrem presided, and his influence extended to Armenia, Parthia, and even through Syro-Persian merchants to the coast of Malabar. Though the Persian school at Edessa was probably distinct from his own, yet Persia also knew his name and felt his power. He represented the doctrine of St. James of Nisibis, whose favourite disciple he was, who was one of the fathers of the Council of Nicæa, and whom he is said to have accompanied thither. On his deathbed he could appeal to Jesus by all the moving details of His Passion to bear him witness that he had only taught the doctrines of the apostles. But he was far more than a monk and a doctor. He was a popular preacher, and his hymns were sung all over the east. He was within the walls of Nisibis when it was besieged by Sapor, and his songs cheered the hearts of its defenders and celebrated their victory, when the broken troops of the heathen turned away baffled from its walls. Never was hermit more popular. Gentle, courteous, loving, he entered into conversation with all, even the most degraded women. A man of the people, he shared their danger in war, wept over all their sorrows, and suffered with their sufferings. He fearlessly attacked the selfishness of the Roman government in devastating the country for fear of the Persians. By his hymns, however, above all, he leavened the minds of the people. He wrote them and set them to popular tunes, in order to counteract the heretical songs of Bardesanes and Harmodius. He formed a choir of young girls to sing them, and thus they penetrated into the homes and domestic life of his countrymen. He exhausts all the imagery of an oriental imagination to express his own tender feelings towards the Mother of God, and make the love of her sink deep into the minds of the people. He taught them the power of her prayers with God: "But most of all," he prays to God, "again and again I entreat and adjure Thee, that Thou wouldst put down the monstrous enemy of the human race by the prayers and merits of Thy Mother." "To Thee, Lord," he says, "together with the sweet smell of sacrifice, we offer the merits of the most blessed Virgin Mary." "O Jerusalem the blessed, may thy gates be open to all and shut out none; may our prayers and supplications be admitted before the throne of the Lamb by the intercession of the Virgin Mother of God and of all the blessed, and may they obtain mercy and pity."* His teaching was not lost upon the Syrian Church. In the beginning of the fifth century, St. James of Sarug † taught the Immaculate Conception. Even the Nestorian heresy, which overwhelmed the East like a deluge, could not obliterate it. In the 13th century, a Nestorian hymn declares Mary to have been sanctified in the first moment of her conception. It is perfectly plain from all this, that in the early Church the doctrine of Mary's greatness was not a sterile idea, but was reduced to practice. "Parthians and Medes and Elamites, and inhabitants of Mesopotamia," were

* Ed. Rom. III. 481, 487, 532.

† Quoted in Bickell's preface to St. Ephrem's Carmina Nisibena, p. 30. The passage quoted from the Carmina Nisibena throws light on many others which previously seemed obscure. Let any one read Rhythm 8. 41., in my old friend Mr. Morris's beautiful and learned translation; I am sure that "bride by nature" will be interpreted by any unprejudiced person of the Immaculate Conception. It expresses a privilege which she alone possessed. Other holy women were brides, she alone bride by nature. Again, the antithesis is to our Lord's miraculous conception "not by nature;" surely the corresponding "nature" must mean a natural conception. The reference to φύσει υἱός is quite irrelevant. St. Cyril there means by participation of the divine nature; while the Syriac (according to the translator) means "by the established course of things."

taught the value of her prayers. If we invoke the principle of development, it is not on account of any deficiency of proof. That development is not a progress from doctrine to practice, but from a less to a more extensive practice. Devotion to Mary is now more widely spread and more universal: it is not more intense or more practical. That St. Athanasius says comparatively so little about the subject, proves that our Lady was not so prominently put forward at Alexandria in his time; but it does not prove that in his day the Immaculate Conception was unknown, nor that in other parts of the Church devotion to her was not as great and as practical as in the nineteenth century, since his contemporary, St. Ephrem, is as clear as St. Alphonso Liguori. The only legitimate conclusion to be drawn from the facts is, that the practice of Alexandria was, as far as our present knowledge extends, less like our own than that of Edessa. At the same time I see nothing incredible in the notion that the faithful who crowded around the pulpit of S. Athanasius invoked our Lady, when they heard their great pastor call her the All-holy and the Godlike Mary.*

---

* παναγία and Θεοειδής. In an author whose every word is theological, like St. Athanasius, the word is peculiarly remarkable Compare F. Newman's translation, p. 422. It occurs in a fragment of a commentary on St. Luke, published since Montfaucon by Gallandius, tom. 5. p. 187.

Again, there is a class of literature of which sufficient use has not as yet been made; I mean spurious and apocryphal writings. It is considered enough to banish a work from controversy, if the Benedictines have declared that it does not proceed from the pen of the author, whose name it bears. *If however its age can be ascertained,* a book may be an unexceptionable witness, without being an authority. We have been too apt to look upon individual fathers as authorities in doctrine, which they are only to a limited extent: even St. Athanasius is more valuable as bearing testimony to what was taught by the Church in his day, than as a teacher. It is no paradox to say that a nameless writer may be a better witness of the popular system of the Church. It would be absurd to suppose that works like those of that great saint in general, his treatise De Synodis, for instance, represent the common spiritual reading of the faithful at Alexandria. Just as the Golden Legend in the middle ages was certainly in the hands of the faithful to an incalculable extent more frequently than the Summa of St. Thomas, so we may be sure that an apocryphal Gospel was popular in the early Church, in a sense in which St. Augustine was not. Many of these writings were perfectly orthodox, and represent legends which were current among Christians.* Though the Church always pro-

* V. instances of the use made by various Fathers of the apocryphal writings in Nicolas, Etudes sur les Evangiles Apocryphes.

tested against their being Scripture, yet they were often tolerated till the decree of Gelasius; and the number of manuscripts which are preserved, and the traces of their contents which remain even in medieval legends, are proofs that they were widely spread. We may therefore safely assume, that in some of them we possess books, which represent a popular system in the early Church. One of them has just come to light, which is pronounced by Tischendorf to have been written not later than the fourth century, though it may have been composed even earlier.* It is an account of the death of the Blessed Virgin, written in the form of a narrative put into the mouth of St. John. Its doctrine is perfectly orthodox, and it contains throughout a singularly straightforward assertion of the absolute Godhead of Christ, yet without any of the theological terms which were peculiar to a later period.† In this book we find

p. 293. See again the remarkable reference to the Gospel according to the Egyptians in S. Clement Ep. 2. St. Jerome says of St. Barnabas, "Unam ad ædificationem Ecclesiæ pertinentem epistolum composuit, quæ inter apocrypha legitur."

* V. Tubingen Quartalschrift for 1866, 3rd part. "As for the date of the whole work, there is no imperative ground to put it with Wright and Ewald as late as the latter half of the fourth century, for Wright's arguments respect only the Syriac, not the original Greek. Even Tischendorf supposes that the writing may very well be older than the 4th century." Thus the passages cited from these documents are probably older than St. Ephrem.

† Compare for instance the unequivocal ὁ τῶν ὅλων Θεός, ἀληθινὸ Θεός, applied to Christ, with the most suspicious passage either of Origen or attributed to him in the commentary on

the whole doctrine of the intercession of our Lady. She prays on her deathbed that Jesus should grant help to all who invoke her name. The answer of our Lord is: "Rejoice, and let thine heart be glad, for every grace and gift has been given to thee by My Father who is in heaven, by Me, and by the Holy Ghost. Every soul calling upon thy name shall not be ashamed, but shall find mercy and consolation, help and confidence both in this world and the world to come, before My Father who is in heaven." Accordingly, after her death, a sick man, by the command of St. Peter, cries out, "Holy Mary, Mother of Christ our God, have mercy on me," and is cured. In a document belonging to the same cycle, the very manuscript of which is of the 6th century, it is said that "the blessed one was holy and chosen by God from the moment that she was conceived in her mother's womb."* I do not think that there is any extravagance in the assertion that Mary entered into the spiritual life of the men who wrote and read these books; nor should I be at all surprised to hear the Ave Maria coming from their lips, nor even to find in their souls a devotion to her name and her heart.

St. John 2, 50-51. On the other hand, our Lord is not even called the Λογος much less ὑπερτιος. This appears to me to prove the antiquity of the document, and perhaps its Roman origin.— v. Hageman, Römische Kirche, 102.

* I quote from the German translation in the Tubingen Quartalschrift for 1866. v. also Journal of Sacred Literature for 1865.

One more instance before I have done. There is no stranger collection in all literature than the motley one, called the Sibylline Oracles. No one, of course, imagines that they are what their name indicates that they claim to be. They are the productions of men of the most various creeds at very different times, sheltering under the Sibyl's name descriptions of contemporary events. Jew, heretic, and Christian, have contributed to the motley assemblage of heterogeneous poetry. It looks like a vast tesselated pavement made up of fragments of various mosaics, all thrown together, where arabesque patterns, the most grotesque, are cemented together with tragic masks and fragments of graceful forms. It reminds us of a discordant concert, where the organ's solemn tones mingle with the wild roll of the barbaric gong and the crash of oriental cymbals. The strangest heretics stand side by side with faithful Catholics. But whoever is the writer, or whatever his creed, we have at least the passionate outburst of genuine feelings, which agitated human breasts in the 2nd and 3rd centuries of our faith. We have the savage exultation of the Jew that the day of vengeance is at hand; and we have the hopes and the fears, the joy and the despondency of Christians. The wounds of Jesus, and the crown of thorns, with the details of the Passion, appear sometimes to console Christians under persecution. Much more frequently, however, the poems dwell on the ap proaching judgment and the consequent triumph of the Church. As we have heard the prelude of the Stabat Mater in the desert, so we find the germs of the Dies Iræ in the famous Sibylline acrostich of the name of Christ. But, amidst all the terrible images of the day of doom, and the scarcely disguised triumphant expectation of God's vengeance on the heathen, there is one image of peace and compassion which breathes a pitying charm over the awful picture. It is that of the pure Virgin, who, at the Archangel's bidding, received her God in her bosom, and to whose outstretched hands, pleading for mercy, Christ granted a space for repentance, even to the Pagan. Evidently, in the age of martyrdom, Christians would have found nothing strange in the intercession of Mary.*

I trust that I have said enough to show the bearing of such books as that here presented to the public on the history of the Church, and the use which we can draw from them for our own spiritual good. The more we study that ancient Church, the more we shall be convinced of what our faith has already told us, that we are abso-

* In the Sibylline oracles, the words παρθένος ἁγνή and equivalent expressions are constantly recurring. The prominence of our Lady is easily explained if we remember that those poems were written with Esaias and the Jam redit et Virgo of Virgil's Eclogue before the eyes of the authors. Evidently this personage is our Lady, for she is the Virgin who conceived and bore a Son. Her virginity was absolutely necessary to distinguish our Lord's birth from others so common in mythology, for the birth of a god was no new idea to heathens. The lines referred to in the text are assigned by M. Alexandre in his excellent edition of the Sibyl-

lutely one with it. This is true, not only in great dogmas, but also in our life and practice. I hope that I have already elsewhere shown that, if we take into consideration the actual practice of the ancient Church, its conduct in the confessional was by no means so different from ours, as the mere study of the canons might lead us to suppose. Something has been done in these few pages to point out the same fact as to our interior life, though volumes might be written upon the subject. The lives of the desert saints may thus be useful in regulating our own life. The insight, which is here given into these peaceful solitudes, may help us to correct the tendency to over-activity, which penetrates even into our very religion. The railroad pace of the world hurries even good Christians along with it, and they fling themselves into schemes of active benevolence, in a way which is often injurious to their interior life. It produces a combined restlessness and languor, a physical exhaustion of nerve and brain, which is very perilous. Never did Christians want more prayer than now, for the world is all in confusion, and the time is out of joint, and before we attempt to set it right, we had better begin with our.

---

line oracles to the year 187, the sixth of the reign of Commodus. They also appear in the second book, which however was written probably in the reign of Decius. The words are:—

Καὶ τότ' ἀταρτίψει φανερῶς τὸ πρόσωπον ἐπ' αὐτῶν
Ἑπτὰ γὰρ αἰώνων μετανοίας ἥματ' ἔδωκεν
Ἀνδράσι πλαζομένοις διὰ χειρῶν παρθένου ἀγνῆς.—viii. 355.

selves. All is floating and uncertain. Landmarks, intellectual and political, are torn up and men are drifting they know not whither Nothing will save us from danger but an intellect, a heart, and a mode of life, entirely one exteriorly and interiorly with the ever-living Church of Christ. There is no possible Christian life but in the old path of mortification and prayer. Along this path the saints, in every age, have borne their cross. Throughout all its various forms, sanctity is still identical, nor do I see very much difference between St. Simeon Stylites on his pillar, and the Curé d'Ars in his cramped confessional. May they obtain grace for us to follow them, if not in their heroic penance, yet at least in their interior life, in boundless charity for our sinful and suffering brethren, and their burning love for Jesus and Mary.

Nor can I finish my task, without turning to you, who are attempting to renew outside the Church the monastic system, which except within her pale can only be stagnant or awfully perilous. Not in a spirit of ridicule, but of the profoundest pity do I think of you. While my whole soul revolts with indignation at the presumption of those who without mission, without jurisdiction, without the requisite gifts, presume to take upon themselves the guidance of souls, I feel the deepest compassion for those, who are their victims and who are on their way with them to the inevitable ditch. To us who are looking on, it seems nothing less than a judicial fatuity to put oneself under the guidance of men, who never speak of a sacrament, without betraying a confusion of thought, which shews them to be incapable of seeing clear into any theological question whatsoever. How dare they touch the keys without a semblance of jurisdiction? With what face can they urge any one to make a confession when they inform the penitent that after all the misery and the agony of the avowal of guilt, forgiveness might have been cheaply purchased without it? How can they pronounce an absolution which they themselves loudly assert to be unnecessary?* But, above all things, I am struck with wonder at their presumption in pronouncing on vocations. It is just such tricks as these played before high heaven, which make the angels weep, when they see rash men rushing in where they would fear to tread. A Catholic priest, with the tradition of eighteen centuries at his back, with the living Church to guide and to check him, trembles when he has to pronounce on a vocation, and when he meddles with the spiritual life of a soul, redeemed by the blood of Christ. He knows well that

---

* It is evident from Dr. Pusey's correspondence with the Times that he does not consider absolution, even where it could be had, as necessary to forgiveness. He has thus incurred by implication the anathema of the Council of Trent, Sess. xiv. Can. 6.

nature can take the semblance of grace, and that not all who desire the most perfect life are called by God's Holy Spirit. Alas, poor souls! when at the bidding of some Anglican clergyman you have given up all the dearest ties of life, and entered into a mock convent, or taken unauthorized obligations, what guarantee have you that one day you will not discover, when it is too late, that you have made an irremediable blunder? When, under the monotony and the labour of wearing work, a Catholic nun at times feels fainting and overpowered, what will become of you, poor sheep without a shepherd, or, what is worse, with sham sacraments and false guides? May God, in reward for your goodwill, bring you into the true fold, before you fall into the hardened sobriety of hopeless pride, or the terrible delusion of false mysticism.

It only remains for me to say a few words on the work now translated. Its author is the Countess Hahn-Hahn, long a well-known German writer. She was not originally a Catholic, and was only converted at an advanced age. Married very young, it is commonly known that her marriage was not a happy one, and she spent a great portion of her life in travelling about Europe, as well as in countries which at that time were but little visited, especially by ladies. She first became famous by her "Letters from the East," a book which attracted great attention by the boldness and originality of her views, the vividness of her descriptions of scenery, and the beauty of the style. She has also written many novels, said to be distinguished by striking sketches of character, life-like dialogues, and a total absence of plot. She was converted to the Catholic Church by the excellent Bishop of Mayence, Monsignor von Ketteler. Since her conversion she has lived a devout and solitary life in a convent at Mayence. Notwithstanding her advanced age, her mind is active as ever, and she has been employed in writing works which are very deservedly popular. Her novels, one of which has been translated in the Month, are beautifully written and well conceived, though the dialogue is at times rather garrulous, and the artistic faults as well as the excellencies of her old writings are not absent. Besides works of fiction she has written a series of books on the History of the Church, one of which is now presented to the reader in an English dress. She has embodied in it many of the beautiful descriptions of scenes visited by herself and published in her earlier works, as well as a great deal of information on heathen as well as ecclesiastical subjects. Though it is not free at times from the fault of prolixity, and though her expressions are not of course always as accurate as if she were a theologian, yet it is by far the fullest and best picture of the primitive monks which has appeared in

English. To take but one instance, the life of St. Simeon Stylites contains circumstances which, as far as I know, will hardly be found elsewhere in the language.

We are indebted for the excellent and careful translation to a lady whose accurate knowledge of languages is a guarantee for its fidelity.

 The Oratory,
Feast of St. Agatha. 1867.

SOLI DEO GLORIA.

CHRISTIANITY IN FREEDOM.

THE Emperor Constantine, as the instrument of God, delivered from outward oppression, and defended from heathen persecution, the faith which the Son of God brought down from heaven for the redemption and salvation of mankind, which He sealed with the miracles of His life and death, and which He ordained for the safe keeping and propagation of an institute whose holy constitution He had Himself in His divine wisdom arranged and established. But this faith did not take its place amongst other religions as merely of equal birth with them; it laid claim to the spiritual government of the whole world, as being the only one revealed by the Eternal Wisdom itself, and therefore possessed of the sole right to it. Other religious systems—those of the Egyptians and of the Greeks, of the Indians and of the Persians, as well as of the Romans, and even that of the Israelites—belonged always to their own country, and their own people; they were separated from one another by mountains and rivers, bounded by diversity of language, and confined by the various modes of thinking of the nations that adhered to them. The deity which was worshipped on the southern coast of the sea was unknown on its northern coast; and there stood on the western slopes of a mountain temples and altars whose rites were strange or despised on the eastern ones. Nations took a kind of pride in this very thing, that their gods were the gods of their own land. The likeness of God in which they were created was defaced in them, because they had fallen away from eternal truth, and the impress of grace had given place to that of nature. As all their powers of mind, of will, and of feeling, took root in this natural soil, they sank into a state the opposite to that of grace; they created their own gods, and created them such as in all times egotism without faith creates them, for self, for its own ends, for its own wants and inclinations. These idols were images of the godless interior of man, and man served them under the delusion that they served him in return—that they granted him their power and their protection, and that they defended his own home, while to foreign peoples and lands they were hostile and threatening. Had he been obliged to share the gods of his own country with another people, he would have considered it prejudicial to his possessions, and destructive of his rights. These trivial, narrow-minded divisions had developed into the extreme confusion of polytheism, and had reached their greatest excess when the Son of God became man in order to transform this pitiable dismemberment into blissful unity, and to make all peoples and nations of the earth now and for ever the children of one Father, and the worshippers of one God. The religion of Jesus lay claim to one attribute which for four thousand years had never yet been claimed; it was divinely infallible, it alone bestowed salvation, and therefore it was not to be restricted to any one time or nation. For to all men, and in every time, Christ spake, " I am the way, the truth, and the life;" the way that you must follow, the truth that you must receive, the life that you are to enjoy to all eternity. The first centuries showed what an echo these words found in the hearts of men; for during them was fulfilled the prophecy of Christ, "If I be lifted up from the earth, I will draw all things to myself." This attraction was so powerful and so universal, that instead of being extinguished and repressed by the lives and deaths of the martyrs of those three first centuries, it was enkindled and animated by them. At the end of those three centuries, Christianity had triumphed over heathenism.

But it did not follow that each individual Christian had, in union with his divine Saviour, "overcome the world." The preference openly shown by Constantine for Christians, the outward privileges with which he favoured them, the great respect which he expressed on every occasion for bishops and priests, his care for the worthy celebration of the divine mysteries, the extraordinary generosity with which he raised the houses of God to the highest pitch of magnificence—all this contributed to induce many to join a religion which so powerful and so wise an emperor valued thus highly. For he always considered himself, and announced himself to be a Christian although he was not baptized,[1] because the opinion was then prevalent, that baptism should only be administered on the deathbed for fear of the misfortune of losing the grace of baptism by sin. Constantine spoke and acted as a Christian, though not always as a perfect one, and this was sufficient to cause many to follow his example. They had formerly worshipped the heathen emperors as gods, they had cursed and persecuted according to their every caprice and humour, and had acknowledged

---

[1] There are, however, some grounds for the supposition that Constantine was baptized long before the end of his life by Pope Sylvester.

no higher rule of faith than their will. The immense revolution of ideas which now changed the inmost hearts of many, affected others only outwardly, and led them merely in form along the path trodden by Constantine. The example of those in power works in wide circles, but it is impressive and attractive only in proportion to the holiness of him who gives it. Therefore streams of men now poured into the Church of Christ, who remained ignorant of her nature, who moved only on the surface of life, and never reached the treasury of graces nor attained the object for which graces enable us to strive.

But the elder Christians who had become confessors through the hardships of the days that were past, and who had come out of the great tribulation, rejoiced and praised the wonderful works of God which He had done for them in the world, till lately so heathen and so hostile. Many thousands of them came forth from the mines of Numidia, from the quarries of Upper Egypt, from the mountains and forests of Asia Minor, from the deserts of Arabia, where they had lived in banishment or voluntary exile, to return to their homes and families, to their own hearths and the beloved sanctuaries of their religion. After a separation of years, the father once more beheld his children, the husband his wife, the friend the companion of his youth, and the priest and bishop were reunited to their beloved flocks. Many of the confessors bore upon their bodies the marks of the sufferings which they had undergone on account of their constancy in the faith; they were one-eyed, or they had been lamed in the knee-joint with heated iron to make flight impossible for them, and so sent to work in the mines. Others had become gray and infirm through sickness, ill-usage, and unheard-of privations. But this caused them to take part all the more joyfully in the exultation of their brethren in the faith; for they could say with the Apostle St. Paul, "I am not ashamed; for I know whom I have believed."[1] They had experienced with him that "though our outward man is corrupted; yet the inward man is renewed day by day."[2] They knew that the genuine Christian life is always outwardly Passion-week, and inwardly Easter, a daily death and resurrection; and that "the present tribulation, which is light and momentary, worketh for us above measure exceedingly, an eternal weight of glory."[3] An earthly reflection of this glory was now shining upon the world: the truth had triumphed, the truth was worshipped, and men considered it a happiness and an honour to be counted amongst its worshippers. And because their joy was directed to heavenly things, it was pure, and free from rancour against their former persecutors, and from over-estimation of self in the present triumph. For it was not they who had wrought the triumph, but it was the fulfilment of the prophecy of the holy Psalmist, King David. "The kings of the earth stood up, and the princes met together, against the Lord and against His Christ. Let us break their bonds asunder, and let us cast away their yoke from us. He that dwelleth in heaven shall laugh at them: and the Lord shall deride them. Then shall He speak to them in His anger, and trouble them in His rage. And now, O ye kings, understand; receive instruction, you that judge the earth. Serve ye the Lord with fear, and rejoice unto Him with trembling. Embrace discipline, lest at any time the Lord be angry, and you perish from the just way."[4] These few words contain a brief prophetic sketch of the fate of the Church in the first centuries. Then the Emperor Constantine began to "understand," and the war

[1] 2 Tim. i. 12.
[2] 2 Cor. iv. 16.
[3] 2 Cor. iv. 17.
[4] Ps. ii.

came to an end, which his predecessors had carried on against the everlasting God, to their own prejudice and infamy.

The historian Eusebius, Bishop of Cesarea, an eye-witness of those times, relates that the Christians sang with delight the hymns of David, in which, fourteen centuries before, he had prophesied the conversion of the world. "Sing to the Lord a new canticle: sing to the Lord all the earth. Declare His glory among the Gentiles: His wonders among all people."[1] "The Lord hath reigned, let the earth rejoice."[2] "The Lord hath made known His salvation: He hath revealed His justice in the sight of the Gentiles. He hath remembered His mercy and His truth toward the house of Israel. All the ends of the earth have seen the salvation of our God."[3] For Christianity did not now enter the world as a stranger, unauthenticated and unannounced. A solemn succession of heralds had preceded her, and her first promulgation sounded in paradise when the Lord God himself awakened a distant hope in the hearts of the two most miserable of the human race as He spoke to the serpent, "I will put enmities between thee and the woman, and thy seed and her seed: she shall crush thy head, and thou shalt lie in wait for her heel."[4] Thenceforth the hope of this Messias, this Deliverer, who was to tread the serpent under foot, spread through the whole race of the people of Israel like a vein of pure and shining gold in the hard and dark rock. Thenceforth the inspired prophets, whose clear sight penetrated beyond this world and rested on the divine promise, revived by their predictions the sparks of hope often too feebly glowing in a people who preferred sensual idolatry to faith in a Redeemer, and consoled the better part of the nation by the thought of the brighter times that were to come.

[1] Ps. xcv.   [2] Ps. xcvi   [3] Ps. xcvii.   [4] Gen. iii. 15.

"For they strengthened Jacob, and redeemed themselves by strong faith."[1] Then Isaias spoke, pointing out the coming of the Messias. "The Lord himself shall give you a sign; behold a virgin shall conceive, and bear a son, and His name shall be called Emmanuel, God with us."[2] "Send forth, O Lord, the Lamb, the ruler of the earth."[3] He said to the faint-hearted, "Take courage and fear not; behold, God himself will come and will save you."[4] And he exultingly sang, "For a Child is born to us, and a Son is given to us, and the government is upon His shoulder, and His name shall be called Wonderful."[5] Then he mourned over the "Despised, a man of sorrows, who hath borne our infirmities and carried our sorrows; He was wounded for our iniquities, He was bruised for our sins, He was offered because it was His own will."[6] Again, He broke forth in triumph, "Arise, be enlightened, O Jerusalem for behold darkness shall cover the earth, and a mist the people; but the Lord shall arise upon thee, and His glory shall be seen upon thee."[7] The prophets all spoke in this manner, invariably pointing out the coming of the Messias, and even its minutest circumstances. More than five hundred years before Isaias, David had said, "They have dug my hands and feet, they have numbered all my bones, they parted my garments amongst them, and upon my vesture they cast lots."[8] And the nearer the fulfilment approached, the more precise was the prediction. Daniel, "the man of desires," calculates the coming of the Lord accurately, under the form of weeks. Aggeus cries, "Thus saith the Lord of hosts: Yet one little while and I will move the heaven and the earth, and the sea and the dry land. And I will move

---

[1] Ecclus. xlix. 12. [2] Isa. vii. 14. [3] Isa. xvi. 1.
[4] Isa. xxxv. 4. [5] Isa. ix. 6. [6] Isa. lii. 1-5.
[7] Isa. lx. 1, 2. [8] Ps. xxi. 17-19.

all nations: and the desired of all nations shall come... and I will give peace."[1] And Zacharias asks, "What are these wounds in the midst of thy hands?"[2] But Malachias, the last of these holy seers, exclaims, "Behold He cometh,"[3] and the voice of the prophets ceased with him. The heathen heard with amazement of these things, of this marvellous connexion of the present with the past, of the destinies of man with the designs of God, of these prophecies, all of similar nature, which fell from so many different lips, in the course of thousands of years, and, unconfused by the storms which disturbed and ravaged nations and kingdoms, and undeviating in the midst of the deep immorality in which mankind was wearing itself away, announced a powerful Saviour, a Redeemer for the whole world. And many of the heathen embraced the faith in this Redeemer from deep conviction. What grace began, science carried on, in order to win souls in all ways for the spiritual kingdom. Lactantius the African, the tutor of the Emperor Crispus, wrote several works in Ciceronian Latin, in which he enlightens the ignorance of the heathen, clears away misunderstandings, points out the road to the truth, and strengthens and encourages those who are already following it. He explains thus the final end of man, and the object of his existence. " The world was created that we might be born. We were born that we might know the Creator of the world and ourselves. We know Him that we may worship Him. We worship Him that we may receive immortality in reward for our sacrifice, because the worship of God requires from us the offering up of all our powers. We are endowed with immortality that we may, like the angels, serve for ever our sovereign Lord and Father, and form for God an everlasting kingdom." The Christian

[1] Hag. ii. 7-10.   [2] Zech. xiii. 6.   [3] Mal. iii. 1.

Cicero, as he was accustomed to be called, on account of his refined and winning eloquence, died about the year 330. At the same time Eusebius, Bishop of Cesarea, one of the most learned men of his time, or indeed of antiquity, wrote two works in the Greek language upon the "Preparation for the Gospel," and the "Proofs of the Gospel," which form together one whole, wherein are contained more full and convincing proofs of the divinity of the Christian religion than are to be found in any other book of Christian antiquity that has come down to us. The dark sides of it are the errors against orthodoxy of the learned bishop. He was prevented from penetrating beyond the surface of things by a certain dryness of understanding which often accompanies learning, with its compilations and its comparisons, but which is opposed to the flight of the soul and the abstraction of the mind in an invisible world and its divine mysteries, of which the kingdom of grace and of redemption is the most sublime. This was the excuse of the assent given by this renowned writer to the erroneous and degrading idea of the Son of God which is branded with the name of Arius. The fundamental doctrine of Christianity, the mystery of the three Persons in God, was sealed to him. The man of knowledge should be in an especial manner a man of faith and of prayer, lest he should be deprived of the choicest fruits of his intellect.

Whichever way the spirit of paganism turned, it encountered adversaries instead of support. On the throne, the Emperor Constantine and his family; in the world, the most eminent, the most respected; in science, the most learned. The idols had fallen in spite of emperors, they would fall still more readily when no imperial hand was stretched out for their support. Christian ideas and opinions pervaded daily life: marriage was raised to the dignity of a sacrament, to a figure of the union between Christ and His Church, therefore sanctified and indissoluble. What a civilising influence would this alone exercise over all the relations of life! For by this woman was placed by the side of man, on the same footing, and with equal privileges. She ceased to be a thing which could be bought, which could be forsaken and resumed. The benediction of the priest blessed the covenant which two redeemed souls made in order to form themselves and their children, the children of God, for the kingdom of heaven. The whole education of the children was transplanted into another soil and a different atmosphere when the mother ceased to be considered as a thing or as a slave. The child inherited its share of advantages in the reinstatement of woman in her lost rights. The child that had also been looked upon hitherto as a thing or a slave, the possession of its father, which he was at liberty to repudiate and to slay, was considered and treated as a creature of God, and became a member of an institution which Christianity alone has produced, namely, the family; and as such it had its rights, its claims, and its duties.

Slavery was too deeply interwoven into all the habits of ordinary life to be suddenly and universally uprooted. The slaves formed the majority of the population, and being without property or possessions, had neither the means, nor in many cases the power or the capability of procuring an independent livelihood. It often happened that when rich people were converted to Christianity they gave their slaves their liberty, and the necessary means of subsistence. But others either could not or would not do this. This gave occasion to the great bishops, the renowned teachers in the Church, to insist with fiery zeal upon a purely Christian relation between masters and slaves, upon the education and training of the latter, and even upon their emancipation. This zeal was so successful that a series of laws was enacted in favour of the slaves, those very slaves who, two years before, were trodden under foot by their heathen masters like very worms. The sunshine of the new era also brought forth into sight the holy blossoms of brotherly love. Works of mercy had been at all times the favourite occupation of the Christians, but hitherto, on account of persecution, they had been hidden in the darkness of the dungeons and the catacombs, or confined to the privacy of their own houses. Christ, the Judge of the world, will one day reward or condemn souls, will lead them into the kingdom of heaven, or banish them into everlasting fire, according to the works of mercy they have accomplished or neglected, and by no other rule.[1] How zealous therefore would the Christians be to prepare for the day of judgment now that the field for this holy activity was open to them, bearing in mind the promise, " Blessed are the merciful for they shall obtain mercy."[2] Refuges for pilgrims, and hospitals for the sick and plague-stricken, were established; orphans and foundlings, of which there were so many amongst the heathen, were cared for; and institutions for tending the infirm, the crippled, and the aged, took their rise. The bishops suggested these things, and the faithful carried them out. Immense sums, and even whole estates were given in this way to Christ in His poor. Holy people, both men and women, did not content themselves with sacrificing their goods and possessions, but they gave themselves up to the service of our Blessed Lord in His suffering members, and laboured humbly and devotedly in the hospitals. In smaller places where the laity did not possess the means, pious bishops turned

---

[1] Matt. xxv. [2] Matt. v. 7.

their own houses into hospitals and refuges, or tenderly took the needy to live with them in order to perform services of love towards them, and thereby to participate in the blessing which God has pronounced upon such deeds. St. Augustine, Bishop of Hippo, ate at the same table with the sick. The holy Pope Gregory the Great waited daily at table upon twelve poor men. The legend relates that a thirteenth was once found amongst them, and that St. Gregory recognised in him with surprised humility our Blessed Lord Himself. At that time the doctrine of the meritoriousness of good works had not been called in question by the assertion that good works should be done without any regard to merit, which is equal to saying without any love of God. For as the Son of God has expressly said that He will give "life everlasting" to the "blessed of His Father" who have fed Him in the hungry and covered Him in the naked, it follows that those who perform good works with a different intention from the hope of a reward in everlasting life, with which He wills they should be performed, do not believe in the Son of God, do not love Him, and consequently do not love God. And in what does this reward consist? This He also answers with the promise, "I myself will be your exceeding great reward." And "He who has promised is faithful." No Christian doubted that these precepts and promises proceeded directly from the Heart of God, and therefore that they would conduct those who faithfully followed them back to the Heart of God. Hospitality was also lovingly exercised in honour of the Divine Stranger upon earth. To guard against its abuse, it was the custom that each wayfarer should exhibit a certificate from his bishop, so as to be able everywhere to prove himself to be a member of the Catholic Church. The richer churches showed sympathy to the poorer ones, and sent them assistance, a liberality which the Roman Church exercised to the greatest extent of all. In one word, wherever suffering, infirmity, or want showed itself, there was the hand of love ready with its helpful deeds; and this was the first use which Christianity made of its youthful freedom, beginning thus its dominion over the world.

CHRISTIAN WORSHIP.

DURING the last and terrible persecution, which is called the persecution of Diocletian, because it was begun by that emperor, although it continued to rage many years after his abdication, innumerable churches were destroyed or laid waste. Their restoration and solemn public dedication was the cause of much holy rejoicing on the part of the Christians. For not only did the population of each place, with their bishop and clergy, thankfully and joyfully celebrate this great festival, but crowds of the sympathising faithful poured in from all sides, and bishops from the neighbouring dioceses, and sometimes even from great distances, hastened thither to take part in it. Now, what was the real cause of all this interest? What was the joy which united all these hearts? Is a magnificent building, are marble pillars and golden chalices, even though they be destined to noble uses, are they worthy of such rejoicings? Oh, no; the real reason is widely different.

In the portion of the Apocalypse, which is annually read at Mass on the feast of the consecration of the church, it is said, "Behold the tabernacle of God with men, and He will dwell with them."[1] And in the gospel for the same day,

[1] Apoc. xxi. 3.

"He was gone to be a guest with a man that was a sinner."[1] It was this, it was the faith in the mystery of the Real Presence of God in the Holy Eucharist in the midst of sinners, the faith in the hidden and gracious life and tarrying of God with the children of men. Hence the churches were holy and solemn places, and men looked upon them as truly the houses of God, because He Himself descended upon the altar in order to be near to help His redeemed, but yet so feeble children. The hearts of Christians full of this faith overflowed with joy that "the hidden God,"[2] under the mystical veil of the sacred Host, took possession of the earth, and raised His Calvary and His throne on each altar. A church would be a meaningless building without the mystery of the Real Eucharistic Presence. For the fields and the woods, or the peaceful chamber, would be more fitting places in which merely to think of God or to speak of Him than a confined and empty space. But "the ing of Glory entered in," and "the princes lifted up their gates,"[3] and His visible Church stepped joyfully forth from the catacombs into the adoring world. In the Real Presence and the visible Church, man found the complete satisfaction of his twofold wants as a spiritual and a corporeal being; and faith, the most sublime faculty of his soul, found its Object, and could accomplish its desire of offering to this Object the most perfect expressions of adoration. Catholic worship so immeasurably rich to the mind, so ineffabl sweet to the heart, unfolded itself around the holy sacrifice of the Mass like a glorious flower out of the bud which had waited three hundred years in the catacombs for its development. Interior religion could now venture to show itself outwardly. It is soul-stirring and exciting as no other is, and must possess a thousand means of animating to the observance of the

[1] Luke xix. 7. [2] Isa. xlv. 15. [3] Ps. xxiii. 7.

commandments in order to work upon all; for it must, in a deeper sense than that in which the great Apostle speaks of his own ministry, "become all things to all men," and draw down the powers of a higher world upon the earth in the celebration of its mysteries. Hence this indescribable exultation in the consecration of the houses of God which were now raised again from their ruins or newly built, larger and more sumptuous than before. Eusebius gives a description of the festival held on the occasion of the consecration of the new church at Tyre, which caused a commotion in the whole of Palestine.

Tyre lies on the coast of Syria to the north of Mount Carmel, and Cesarea, the bishopric of Eusebius, to the south of it. Two or three days' journey divided the two cities, which were both full of the magnificence and luxuries collected by oriental riches and Roman love of pleasure, although Tyre had long ago lost the power she possessed in former days as the capital of the Phœnicians. Cesarea is now a gigantic heap of ruins, and in Tyre the prophecy of Isaias is fulfilled, "Thou, O Tyre, shalt be forgotten, that wast formerly crowned,"[1] for she has lost her very name, being called Sur. She has also a more silent and forsaken appearance than any other city on that coast, because entirely destitute of the gardens which luxuriantly and smilingly surround almost every other oriental town, causing each one to assume more or less the aspect of a bright and friendly oasis in the desert, green and shining amid the yellow sand and rocks like an emerald in a setting of gold. Such are Beyrout and Sidon on this side of Lebanon, and such beyond it is "the heavenly-scented Scham," as Damascus is named by her poets. But Tyre lies all bare and desolate on a promontory of the coast.

[1] Isa. xxiii. 15.

The riches and good taste with which the Christians built the houses of God is evident from Eusebius's description of that church. A lofty portico, which was visible from a great distance, and seemed to invite all to enter in, led into the eastern side of an open and spacious court, surrounded on all sides by covered colonnades. In the middle of the court were fountains, which served partly for ornament and the cooling of the air, and partly for ablutions. Opposite the outward portico there were three doors, the middle one very high and majestic, being the entrance into the church. The doors themselves were of bronze, beautifully and artistically ornamented. The interior of the church was divided by two rows of lofty columns into three naves, so called because they typified the bark of Peter. The middle nave, which was higher and broader than the side ones, corresponded with the largest doorway. At the other end of it, raised by a few steps, and shut off by an extremely beautiful screen, was the choir, with the altar in the centre. The wall behind it was built in a semicircle, and called the apse. The bishop's throne stood there, and the raised seats for the clergy were ranged on each side of it, all tastefully carved. The canopy was of cedar, also richly carved, and the floor was composed of slabs of marble of various colours and designs. The walls were inlaid with mosaics. Light and air penetrated within by means of windows pierced above the columns of the nave, and closed with fine lattice-work instead of glass. Lesser doors in the side aisles led into the sacristy, where the holy vessels and the priestly vestments were kept, into rooms where the catechumens were instructed, and into the baptistery where the font stood, which in those days, owing to the custom of complete immersion, was no mere vase, but a large bath sunk in the ground. The church with the buildings appertaining to it, and the court, were moreover enclosed with a wall to keep off as much as possible all worldly disturbance. With the exception of this wall, the church of St. Clement's at Rome is to this day a faithful model on a smaller scale of that church at Tyre, of which there is not a vestige left; and indeed the present form and arrangement of our churches has remained on the whole such as Eusebius described it fifteen hundred years ago.

Heathen temples, which were generally small, because not destined to contain many people at a time, were sometimes changed into Christian churches; but the large roomy buildings called Basilicas, used for the administration of justice, were more frequently taken for the purpose. Hence the name of Basilica was conferred upon all the larger churches. The usual form was the long triple nave, but the cruciform plan came gradually into vogue, that is to say, the fabric was enlarged on each side between the choir and the nave so as to form transepts. Sometimes, although very rarely, the octagonal form was used for churches, but more commonly for baptisteries, which were also built quite round, and being separated from the church, formed small and richly decorated independent edifices.

Outside the entrance doors, which were called the great" or "royal" doors, were the vestibules, supported on pillars, where the catechumens, the penitents, and the unbelievers remained during the celebration of the Divine Mysteries. The faithful were in the nave, the two sexes being separated from each other, and amongst the women, in a still further division, were the consecrated virgins and widows. At the side of the choir, or sometimes in the nave itself, was the Ambo, a raised platform, from whence spiritual lectures were read. The choir, sometimes called also the presbytery, was raised more or less above the nave, but always divided from it by a barrier, and it was entered by none but the clergy.

Besides the throne at the back of the choir, the bishop had another especial place, a raised platform by the altar, from whence be addressed his instructions to the faithful. In the larger churches there hung over the detached altar sometimes a canopy, and sometimes a representation of the Holy Ghost in the form of a dove. Lamps perpetually burned as a symbol of the everlasting glory and worship due to the unchanging God.

On account of the heathen idolatry of images, the early Christians had none in their churches lest they should be dangerous to recent converts, or awaken misconceptions in unbelievers. The faith had been so much concealed during the long persecution, that its symbols were more eloquent to the Christian mind than actual images. There were, however, a few in the catacombs. After the overthrow of Paganism the fear of the profanation and misunderstanding of images also disappeared, and the first place amongst them was taken by the Cross, which from being the token of malediction and of extremest punishment had become the emblem of salvation and of love. It not only shone over the altars and upon the walls of churches—it not only adorned private dwelling-places—but it towered over the roofs of houses and the masts of ships; it was planted on the summits of lofty hills; it surmounted weapons, and everywhere reminded Christians upon earth of their vocation—to suffer for the things of God, and, by suffering, to enter with Christ into everlasting glory. Every possible honour and veneration was shown to this symbol of redemption, and hence the heathen reproached the Christians with being worshippers of the Cross, which only proved that they could charge them with no greater crime. Soon arose also images out of Bible history, images of Christ, of the blessed Virgin Mary, of the Apostles Peter and Paul, images of the martyrs in the churches dedicated to their memory; and holy Fathers of the Church and pious bishops urgently recommended this custom, because images were an excellent means of instruction, especially for those who could not learn from books. Amongst these holy men were Gregory of Nyssa Paulinus of Nola, and Pope Gregory the Great. The latter mentions as one of the customs of his time, (he died in the year 604,) that of prostrating themselves before the Cross,—so completely had the fear of idolatry disappeared. Votive images, that is, gold or silver models of healed limbs, or other representations of the redress of suffering, were accustomed to be hung, as early as the fifth century, in the churches of the martyrs to whose intercession the cure was attributed.

In the fourth century Rome already possessed forty basilicas. Seven of these were built and adorned by Constantine himself. The principal and the most ancient of them is St. John Lateran. The Lateran palace had formerly belonged to the Roman family of that name, and latterly to the Empress Fausta, Constantine's second wife. A basilica was now built next to it; it was for several centuries the residence of the Popes, in which many councils were held. In our days there reigns a marvellous stillness around this basilica. The whole of ancient and modern Rome lies behind it; nothing worldly approaches it; and from its gigantic vestibule the eye gazes uninterruptedly over the melancholy campagna towards the blue outline of the Alban and Latin hills on the eastern horizon. Attached to this basilica was a separate baptistery, dedicated like all others to St. John the Baptist, and from him the church received its name. To honour the grave of the Prince of the Apostles in the catacombs of the Vatican hill, Constantine built the basilica of St. Peter on the ruins of a temple of Apollo. He also built that of St. Paul on the spot of his martyrdom, on the road to Ostia; that of St. Agnes, together with a baptistery, at the request of his daughter and his sister Constantia, both of whom had been baptized by Pope Sylvester. Then that of SS. Peter and Marcellinus, in which his mother the Empress Helena was buried; that of St. Lawrence, on the road to Tibur; and lastly, that of Santa Croce in Gerusalemme, which received its name from a portion of the Holy Cross preserved there. This basilica is also in a very retired situation, not far from the Lateran. Constantine bestowed upon these churches, estates situated in Italy, Sicily, Africa, Egypt, and Asia Minor, which brought them a yearly income of about £25,000. The church of SS. Peter and Marcellinus possessed the whole island of Sardinia, that of St. Peter houses in Tyre and in Alexandria, and lands at Tarsus in Cilicia, and on the Euphrates. Besides this, the East was bound to provide them annually with 20,000 pounds' weight of the most valuable spikenard, balsam, storax, cinnamon, and other aromatic substances for their censers and their lamps. Costly oils and frankincense burned in golden lamps and thuribles, and golden chalices were used at the Holy Sacrifice. Massive silver candlesticks with wax lights surrounded the altar, and even the chandeliers suspended from the roof were of silver. Nothing was too beautiful, too rich, or too precious, to be employed in honour of the mystical celebration in which the Blood of Christ was ever being newly offered to the Father as an atonement, and flowing over the souls of men for expiation and sanctification.

It is evident from ancient documents that there was at this early period a certain order of prayers and solemn ceremonies,—a liturgy, of which the Holy Sacrifice of the Mass is the origin and centre, and that its nature was the same in all the churches of the various countries and nations. This is shown, for instance, in the First Apology of Justin the Martyr, (A.D. 167,) where he gives a succinct account of the Holy Sacrifice, which in essentials was exactly the same as it is in our time. Longer or shorter prayers, some invocations, single acts, or a different order of them, made certain exterior varieties in the several liturgies which were used by individual cathedrals, and which received the name of the founder of the Church, or of its most renowned bishop. Thus at Jerusalem and in Syria the liturgy of St. James was used; in Alexandria, that of St. Mark; in Constantinople, St. Chrysostom's; in Milan, the Ambrosian; and in the East, various others. In Spain the Mozarabic was used. The Roman one was derived from apostolical tradition. It is certain that the most important and most sacred portion of the Mass, the Canon, has remained unaltered in its present form, even down to its very words, ever since the fifth century, and that there has not been the smallest change in it since the time of Pope Gregory the Great. This holy doctor put the "Our Father" in another place, and inserted the prayer, "Give peace in our days." This Canon has been inseparable from the Holy Sacrifice of the Mass, the living Sun of this world, for more than twelve hundred years, in all the length and breadth of the Roman Catholic Church.

The public Mass, which was intended for the whole congregation, was offered by the bishop assisted by the priests and deacons, and the people took an actual part in it at the oblation and the communion. The oblation was the offering of the bread and wine required for the Holy Sacrifice, the consecrated portion of which was consumed at the communion; that not consecrated was laid aside for the clergy and the poor, or in some places blessed, and distributed to the laity as a token of Christian love and fellowship when they no longer received daily communion. The bread thus blessed was called bread of eulogy. This custom of carrying round blessed bread cut into small pieces, and distributing it in the church on Sundays at the end of the service, has been retained in some places ever since. The oblation included also certain first-fruits, which were brought by the faithful during the Mass, and blessed by the bishop, but only those which had some connexion with the altar and the sacrifice, such as fresh grapes, corn, oil, and incense. Those who brought them gave their names in writing to the deacon, and the priest remembered them in the secret prayers. In the sixth century the custom of these oblations became confined to Sundays only, and in the seventh it was altogether discontinued in the West, because the priests had then begun to prepare the unleavened bread for themselves. Offerings of money then took the place formerly occupied by these gifts in kind.

Private Masses were also said by a single priest, without any communion of the laity, in small chapels dedicated to the martyrs, in country places, in private houses, and, in times of persecution, in the prisons. When Bishop Paulinus of Nola was lying on his deathbed, he caused an altar to be erected, and Mass to be said by his bedside. Votive Masses for particular intentions, for the salvation of souls, for the cessation of rain, for averting unfruitful seasons, or to thank God for some particular benefit, were frequently said. So likewise were Masses for the faithful departed, which were always repeated on the anniversary of their death, and with an especial office. The whole life of a Christian stood in such close and intimate connexion with the faith, that he sought the sanction of the Church for each act of his existence. Masses in honour of the memory of the martyrs on the days of their triumph, at which selections from the acts of their martyrdom were read, and sermons preached in praise of them, came very early into use, and, soon after, similar Masses in honour of other saints. If the Object of the worship of the Catholic Church were not in Itself worthy of the adoration of angels and men, her most ancient liturgy would be entitled to veneration as a sacred thing, which has passed unchanged through the vicissitudes of so many centuries and races.

Before the invention of bells in the seventh century, the stroke of a hammer upon metal called the faithful together, both to the Holy Sacrifice of the Mass, and to the prayers in common in the morning and evening. Every one obeyed the call, and quietly took his appointed place. The Mass was divided into two principal parts, the Mass of the catechumens, and that of the faithful. Pagans, Jews, penitents, and even heretics, might be present at the first. It began with psalms sung by the people, either altogether, or divided into two choirs, with antiphons and responsories. The bishop or priest prepared himself to approach the altar by a general confession of sins, and the psalm that was sung as he ascended the steps was the Introit of our present Mass. Then followed the supplication for mercy, the Kyrie eleison, which so well befits the children of the earth, especially before they venture to sing in the Gloria the praises of the All-holy. Next the bishop greeted the people with the *Pax vobis*, " Peace be with you ; " and, as their spiritual father, gathered together in one short prayer, the Collect, the wishes and prayers of all, and offered them up to the Heavenly Father, concluding with the invocation of the Son of God. The bishop then proceeded to his throne, and the lector ascended the ambo and read the lection out of the Epistles or the Old Testament, and sometimes also out of the writings of very holy men; but this last was discontinued after the fourth century. At the end of the lection, a psalm was sung called the Gradual, and the deacon read a portion of the Gospels. The people rose to listen to it with great reverence, and the bishop, either from his throne, or standing at the altar, interspersed explanations and practical remarks, or preached a separate sermon.

This brought the Mass of the catechumens to a close. At a summons from the deacon the unbelievers and penitents withdrew from the nave of the church into the vestibule, the doors were shut, and the profession of faith recited; for the sublime mystery which God was about to accomplish by means of His priest could be comprehended only in the light of this faith. Those who were present, being inflamed with the love of Him who became incarnate in order to make all men brothers, greeted each other with the kiss of peace in this way. The bishop embraced the deacon, and the deacon his neighbour, and so on, each one embracing whoever was next to him, which was rendered practicable by the division of the sexes, and the great humility which prevailed amongst Christians possessing rank or position. Here took place the oblations on the part of the faithful, which have been before alluded to, out of which the deacon and the subdeacon selected what was necessary for the communion, and the bishop recited the offering of the propitiatory sacrifice, which was to be consummated by the consecration. After the offertory, the deacon presented water for the washing of hands to the bishop, who then recited the Secret, usually a supplication to God that He would mercifully accept the offerings, and that He would Himself render the faithful worthy to offer to Him an acceptable sacrifice. In the beautiful Preface he exhorted the faithful to raise their hearts to God, (*Sursum corda*,) and to worship and praise with all the heavenly hosts His infinite majesty, omnipotence, and glory which He causes to shine forth to our salvation in the inscrutable mystery of His love. This most sublime hymn, changing with the feasts and seasons of the ecclesiastical year, ended with the seraphic song Sanctus! Sanctus! Sanctus! in which all the people joined. After the invocation of the angels, who are present in adoration at the most Holy Sacrifice, the Canon, the most important part of the Mass, began with prayers for the whole of the Church militant, in which the name of the Pope was mentioned first. Then followed the invocation of the Church triumphant, of the blessed Virgin, the Mother of God, of the Apostles and Martyrs, that their love and intercession might procure help and protection in the conflict. After this the bishop pronounced the consecration of the bread and wine, with the words spoken by Christ himself, in which dwells the power of the "Word that was with God and was God,"[1] and the transubstantiation is accomplished. At the elevation the bishop raises on high the Sacred Host and the holy chalice in turn, bends his knee, and adores the living Victim present on the altar, while the people throw themselves upon their knees, and worship. In this sublime moment the Church, impelled by the love which dwells in a mother's heart alone, remembers her dead, who have departed in the grace of God, and who are waiting for heaven in the sufferings of purgatory. The first supplication of the priest is for them—he bestows upon them the first drop of the Blood of the Lamb. Surely never did love for the dead find a stronger or more touching expression. And now that all the children of the Eternal Father—who are indeed divided in their separate abodes of heaven, earth, and purgatory, but most intimately

[1] John i.

united by sanctifying grace — are, as it were, assembled together by the priest, that each may receive their share in the sacrifice, **he recites the Pater noster**, implores mercy from **the Lamb of God**, (*Agnus Dei*,) makes a humble preparation, and receives the communion. The ejaculation, "Behold the holy of holies," to which the people answered "Amen," preceded the general giving of communion. After the bishop or priest the clergy were the first to receive communion, and always at the altar, then the ascetics, monks, and nuns, and after them the remainder of the faithful received it at the rails of the sanctuary.

The priest who distributed the communion said to each person, either "May the Body of Christ," or "the Blood of Christ," or "the Body of the Lord keep thy soul." Psalms were sung during the communion. Then followed a thanksgiving, the blessing of the people by the bishop, and the dismissal, spoken by the deacon, (*missa, dismissio*, hence, Mass.) At the public celebration of the Eucharist communion was generally given under two kinds, but it was always believed that the whole substance of the sacrament was perfectly contained in one alone, as the Apostle has already said, "Whosoever shall eat this bread *or* drink,"[1] &c. It was permitted in times of persecution, or on long journeys, especially by sea, or to hermits in the desert, and to monks in their retired cells, to take with them the Eucharistic Bread, for there was then no fear that the Body of the Lord would be less reverently handled or consumed out of Mass than it would have been during it. This custom unmistakably expresses faith in the Real Presence under one kind only. The pious awe and reverence of the faithful caused them voluntarily to receive communion fasting; but this custom was soon made an ecclesiastical pre-

[1] 1 Cor. xi. 27.

cept, in order to obviate all possible occasions of dishonour. Besides this, prayer six times a day, if possible in church, was required of the faithful, by the ancient Apostolical Constitutions.[1]

At cock-crowing, on account of the returning day; at sunrise, to praise God for the new day; at the third hour, because our Blessed Lord was then condemned to death; at the sixth, the hour of His crucifixion; the ninth, that of His death, in the evening, in remembrance of His rest in the grave, coupled with the thought of each one's eternal rest after his life is happily ended. When the first love of the great mass of the people for their Redeemer grew cold, their fervour in prayer gradually diminished also. But the Church did not, therefore, by any means relinquish this demand, she only confined it to those who had dedicated themselves by preference to a life of prayer, the cloistered of both sexes, who have to say certain prayers together in the choir of their church at the canonical hours, to canons and prebendaries, and finally to all the clergy, beginning with subdeacons, who are bound to the recital of the Breviary, not in common, but each one separately. Thus was the incense of prayer to rise uninterruptedly through the ages of the redeemed world before the heavenly throne of God, simultaneously with the offence of sin, and to surround the mystical throne of God in the tabernacle. Faith in the mystery of the Real Presence brings with it continual prayer, for love speaks to its Beloved.

[1] In the very early times the Church was governed not by written laws, but by the tradition of the apostles and of their first and most noted disciples. The six first books of the "Apostolical Constitutions" are the oldest work in which are described the laws, regulations, and customs of the Church, the duties of clergy and laity, religious ceremonies, the service of God, and the feasts and doctrines of the faith. The author was probably a Syrian bishop or priest, who lived towards the end of the third century. The form is the same as that of the Apostolical Epistles.

FEASTS AND FASTS.

The ancient doctors of the Church, such as Origen and Clement of Alexandria, look upon the Christian life as one continual festival, not indeed as one of those which are kept by feasting and worldly indulgence, but as a day of holy joy, because the night of sin has been overcome by redemption, because reconciliation with God has brought peace and true joy to the soul, and because from this joy no one is excluded who does not voluntarily separate himself from God. For this the angels sang on the holy night of Christmas their song of jubilee, "Glory to God in the highest, and on earth peace to men of good will."[1] The Prince of Peace, as Isaias had named Him, had come into the world, and brought down with Him from heaven peace and joy, which are enumerated by St. Paul among "the fruits of the Spirit."[2] But in order that the Christian might the more surely be the figure of Christ, and the more perfectly bear the image of the heavenly man, as Christ had borne the image of the earthly,[3] it was necessary that he should suffer himself to be continually penetrated and sanctified by the saving mysteries of Christianity, and that he should imitate the Saviour, contemplating His life step by step, and dwelling in this contemplation. For this reason particular times were set apart as festivals, which, like faithful messengers of religion, returned every year, unceasingly announcing the work of redemption, and by their attractive festivity enkindling and animating the sensual nature of man, and preparing his soul for the everlasting feast of heaven. The festival which returned the oftenest, because it could never be sufficiently celebrated, was Sunday, or, as it was more commonly called, the

[1] Luke ii. 14. [2] Gal. v. 22. [3] 1 Cor. xv. 49.

Lord's-day, (*Dominica*,) which was dedicated even in apostolic times to the remembrance of the Resurrection of Christ. On that day work was not permitted, and all the infirmities and miseries of this earthly life were banished from the mind, for it commemorated the triumph of the eternal life. The case was very different on Wednesday and Friday. The day on which Judas betrayed the Lord, and the day on which the Lord died on the Cross, were observed by fasting till three o'clock and fervent public prayer. They were called Days of the Stations, days on which the warriors of Christ kept watch at their posts. In Rome the remembrance of these days of the stations is still kept up. There is daily in Lent, and frequently during the rest of the year, a station, that is, a devout assembly of the faithful in certain churches, as arranged by Pope Gregory the Great. The prayers recited in each church on that day are enriched with an indulgence.

The most ancient festivals were those of Easter and Pentecost. The groundwork of Christianity was Christ crucified and Christ glorified. From that foundation arose the practice of the imitation of Him, which entered in a thousand ways into the life of the faithful. A period of penance, of long and uncertain duration, now restricted to the forty days' fast of Lent, (*Quadragesima*,) preceded the celebration and contemplation of the sufferings and death of our Lord in the "great week," as it was called. The universal characteristics of the ecclesiastical fast were the late hour of the one meal, which was not taken till sunset, and the abstinence from meat and wine; and during its continuance neither marriage nor christening festivities were allowed. But the fervour of the faithful led them to practise still greater mortifications, especially in the East, where it was the custom to restrict themselves on all fast-days to bread and water, with at the utmost a few vegetables or dried fruits; while in the West this was only the case on Good Friday. They were anxious, on the other hand, to strengthen and fortify their souls, and for this purpose there were continual sermons all through Lent, as, for example, those preached daily by St. Chrysostom at Constantinople. A specimen of these is given us by Origen:—"Abstain from all sin, take to thyself no food of sin, enjoy not the indulgence of thy passions, drink not the wine of thy desires. Refrain from evil deeds and words, and from still more evil thoughts. Seek not the bread of false doctrine, and thirst not after a deceitful philosophy which is far from the truth." It was not sufficient that the body should be denied all sensual delights, the soul was also to be exercised in self-mastery; and the chief advantage of the mortification of the senses lay in this, that it facilitated the victory in spiritual things by keeping men constantly in the habit of fighting against the coarser passions.

Thursday in Holy Week was dedicated to the institution of the Eucharist, and was therefore in the morning a day of joy. After the fifth century the bishops took this day for the consecration of the Holy Oils for Baptism, Confirmation, and the Sick. In the evening began the anticipation of the solemnity of the day of the Holy Passion, the day of the Cross. All the people assembled in the church, and the history of the Passion was read. The day was passed in prayer, labour, mortification, and fasting, never in repose from work or in amusement. The prayers for infidels, Jews, heretics, and schismatics, on that day, together with the adoration of the Cross, which follows them, have been in use ever since the fifth century, and are in perfect accordance with the mind of Him who died upon the Cross for all men, and who prayed for His enemies and tormentors, saying, "Father, forgive them, for they know not what they do." The great vigil of the festival of Easter began on Saturday evening, and lasted till daybreak on Sunday, so that the faithful remained in church uninterruptedly for ten or twelve hours. Then came the Benediction of the Paschal Candle, and the Blessing of the Font, with most beautiful prayers and lessons out of the Old Testament. This was also the time for the Baptism of the Catechumens, and last of all, on Easter Day itself, came the Mass of the Resurrection. This was truly a day of rejoicing. The faithful embraced each other with the greeting, "The Lord is risen. He is risen indeed." The neophytes celebrated their own resurrection from the death of sin, their being born again " of water and the Holy Ghost," simultaneously with the Resurrection of their Redeemer. This rejoicing lasted not only during Easter week, but the whole time till Pentecost, so that Tertullian undertook to show that the Christians had even more feasts than the pagans.

The jubilee of the Alleluias rises up afresh on the day of the Ascension of our Blessed Lord. He had spent the forty mysterious and gracious days since His Resurrection with His disciples, and promised to send them the Holy Ghost from on high, who was to comfort them when they no longer saw His form or heard His voice amongst them. He had then so spiritualised them that they did not look upon the separation from Him with feelings of earthly sorrow, but in holier dispositions received it as an additional grace. There lies a veil over the forty days in the desert which preceded His appearance in the world as the Messias, and on the forty days which precede His departure from the world there rests a veil also. The two mysteries of the combat in which He overcame the world, and of His supernatural glory, must **alike be contemplated** and adored in silence and in faith.

After the fifth century, three days of prayer before the Ascension were likewise occupied in calling down the blessing of God on the germinating fields and meadows. The whole of nature was involved in the consequences of sin by the fall of the first man, so that she could not bring forth her blossoms and her fruits without the sunshine and the dew of grace. As man had dragged her down with him in his fall, he must seek to free her from the curse by prayer. Mamertus, Bishop of Vienne in France, was the first who ordained these days of prayer to be observed with processions through the fields, in the year 469, after his city had suffered severely from earthquakes and scarcity. From thence they spread over the whole of Catholic Christendom.

Ten days after the Ascension there came the sweet feast of Whitsuntide, which brings the fulness of the grace of the Redeemer, the Holy Ghost, the Fruit of His love. Without the Holy Ghost there would be no Church, for He is her soul and quickens her, He is her heart and gives her the pulse of unity. His coming is the birth of the Church in the world.

It is peculiar that the Nativity of Christ, the festival of the sanctification of human nature, the "Mother of all other feasts," as St. Chrysostom calls it, should be less ancient than the festivals of Easter, the Ascension and Pentecost. The uncertainty of the day of our Lord's Nativity is said to have been the cause of this. It is supposed that it was first established in Rome on the 25th of December, in order to give a Christian meaning to the heathen festival in honour of the returning sun, by fixing on that day the rising of the sun of Christianity. But before the middle of the fifth century the feast of Christmas had passed from the West over the whole of the East. The fast of the four weeks of Advent, to prepare the sinful world for the merciful coming of the Lord, shows in what high honour it was held.

New feasts were added in the course of later centuries, when the Church was able without restraint to develope her own proper life, thus completing more and more the circle of holy recollections. But the feast of the Epiphany is exceedingly ancient, the feast of the appearance or manifestation of the Lord, which is kept on the 6th of January, and is dedicated to the joint commemoration of the three events by which He made Himself known to the world: the Adoration of the Magi, who were led to His crib by a star; the Baptism in the Jordan, when the heavens opened above Him; and the marriage at Cana, when He worked His first miracle. The love and piety of the faithful also by degrees assigned their proper places to the feasts of our Blessed Lady. The Emperor Justinian, as early as the year 542, commanded that the feast of the Purification of the Blessed Virgin should be kept on no other day than the 2d of February. A few hundred years later we find on the 25th of March the feast of the Annunciation of the Blessed Virgin, or more properly the Annunciation of our Blessed Lord. To these were joined other solemnities on days commemorating events of importance to Christianity: such as the remembrance of St. Peter as Bishop of Rome, which is kept on the 18th of January under the name of St. Peter's Chair; the day of the death of the Apostles Peter and Paul on the 29th of June; the nativity of St. John the Baptist, who shares with our Blessed Lord and His most Holy Mother, the distinction of His birth into the world being honoured; whilst for other saints and martyrs it is the day of their entrance into heaven, namely, the day of their death, that

c

is kept. In short, our calendar, which we carelessly glance at merely for the sake of the dates, or because we have something to do on this or that day, consists in reality of nothing but memorials of the supernatural life upon which our daily life should be moulded and arranged.

But as the vocation of a Christian is not to be fulfilled by a trifling and superficial joy, but by the supernatural rejoicing of a heart entirely resting in God, and a life wholly consecrated to Him, it was necessary that zeal for this sanctification should extend over all the aims and objects of life. Earnest prayer, devout attendance at the public worship of God, careful fulfilment of the precepts of the Church as to fasting, almsgiving, and various mortifications, were only fruits of the fervour which was an essential element of striving after perfection. An ardent spirit of penance laid the foundations of perfection in the minds of Christians, for it led through the compunction of repentance to humility; and humility is the soil, dark, trodden under foot and apparently insignificant, out of which springs the richest harvest. To become a Christian does not mean to become on a sudden inaccessible to sin. No! certainly not. The tempter entered into the desert with the Divine Saviour to endeavour to arouse sensuality, pride, and ambition even in Him. To become a Christian means to receive through the Sacraments, and first of all through Baptism, grace to fight with sin and power to overcome it. A Christian is still a man; and poor, weak human nature is not always willing to conduct this battle with that vigour and constancy without which victory is unattainable. Thus he falls—falls through his own fault, through his rejection of grace, which is always ready to come to his succour with divine assistance; and he falls out of the realm of salvation into that of evil. The more horror of sin there is in a soul, the more susceptible is it of the stings of conscience, and the more clearly will it perceive after its fall the loss of its happiness, and cry out for salvation from the abyss. Then God hears its cry of distress, and stretches forth His fatherly Hand and leads it to the sacrament of penance, the sacrament of mercy as it should properly be called; which is likened by the Fathers of the Church to the plank which saves from shipwreck.

The necessity of confessing one by one to the priest all grave sins without exception, secret or public, was universally maintained, and looked upon as the groundwork of salvation. This necessity rested upon the Christian faith in the priest's power of binding and loosing, which has its immovable foundation in the Holy Scriptures. "Peace be to you; as the Father hath sent me, I also send you." When Christ had said this, He breathed on them, (the Apostles,) and said to them, " Receive ye the Holy Ghost; whose sins you shall forgive they are forgiven them, and whose sins you shall retain, they are retained."[1] He chose for this action the time after His Resurrection, when He had ordained His Apostles and disclosed to them the deeper signification of His mission and of their succession to it. The power which the Father had given to the Son, of the remission of the sins of men and their sanctification, the Son gave to His Apostles, and in His Apostles to their successors also, because the need of remission of sins and of sanctification never ceases upon the earth. This power is one of the graces of the priesthood, and ceases with it as a flame expires when the wax is consumed. The Catholic priest alone can with the power of God remit sins.

The earliest teachers of the Church affirm this necessity of the confession of sins. Tertullian compares those who are unwilling to submit to this duty

[1] John xx. 19-23.

with the sick who die miserably, because out of false shame they will not show the hidden wounds of their body to the physician. The great St. Cyprian, Archbishop of Carthage, (A.D. 258,) says, that the mere thought of saving one's life by sacrificing to idols is sinful, and therefore to be confessed to the priest. St. Pacian, Bishop of Barcelona in 370, warns all against the attempt to deceive the priest, or to confess imperfectly, and blames those who have indeed fully confessed their sins, but who will not submit to the penance imposed upon them. St. Chrysostom, Patriarch of Constantinople, (A.D. 407,) holds it up as an especial dignity of the priest that he possesses power not over bodies as the princes of the world, but one which extends even to heaven, for what he does on earth by means of the power of absolving and retaining is valid in heaven. St. Ambrose, Archbishop of Milan, (A.D. 397,) defends the exercise of this power against the heretics, as an office committed to priests. St. Basil the Great, Archbishop of Cesarea in Cappadocia, (A. D. 379,) writes: "It is with the confession of sins as with bodily infirmities; we show the latter only to the skilful physician, and confess the former to those alone who can heal them." And St. Gregory, Bishop of Nyssa, (A.D. 300,) speaks thus: "Show boldly to the priest what is hidden, and discover to him the secrets of thy soul. He will have care alike for thy healing and thy reputation."

Confession of sins was made in various ways; sometimes publicly either before the assembled clergy and people, or before the clergy alone, and sometimes privately to the bishop or to a priest. Crimes which were known either by their nature or through chance, and had given public scandal, generally required public disclosure. Hidden sins were also frequently made manifest, sometimes spontaneously, but generally by the advice of the priest to whom they were first privately confessed, when he judged such humiliation to be desirable. This publicity, however, was urged upon none to whose interests as a citizen it would be prejudicial. The public declaration of the gravest sins, such as apostasy, idolatry, murder, or impurity, was invariably followed by public penance, as was also secret confession at times, according to the advice of the priest. The practice of penance was not the same at all times and in all places; it was most severe in the second century and at the beginning of the third. It was then thought a favour for a great sinner even to be allowed to begin his penance. It was looked upon as a slow and painful process of healing, which was to work a serious and lasting conversion, and to give the sinner the opportunity even in this life of making the most complete satisfaction possible, and of purifying his soul from the smallest stains of sin. It was not only to work upon the sinner himself, but others also were to be deterred from sin, and filled with the deepest dread of it, by the example of such heavy penances. Therefore permission to do penance and thereby to reconcile themselves with the Church and to receive her Sacraments was only given to those who demanded it humbly, urgently, and perseveringly. Until they had obtained it, their names, if they had committed any great sin, were struck out of the rank of the faithful, and they could never take part in the public offices of the Church. The penance began generally on the first Wednesday in Lent, with prayer and the imposition of hands by the bishop and the whole of the clergy. The penitent appeared in poor apparel, with his hair shorn, and ashes strewn upon his head, and with bare feet. If he were married, his wife must give her consent to his undertaking to do public penance, for as long as it lasted he must not only abstain from all pleasures, but live as a stranger in his own house. Prostrate on his face on the ground he received the sentence pronounced upon him by the laws of the Church, which was to try and purify him, often **during a** course of years, with practices of penance, **mortification**, and humiliation. If he had to go through all the four states of penance, he began by placing himself outside the church in the courtyard, and imploring the faithful who entered, to plead for him with God and the bishop. In the second degree he was allowed to stand at the doors of the church in the portico and there to be present at the prayers, but not at the Mass of the Catechumens. The third degree was called the beginning of penance, the two former being only preparations for it. The penitent was allowed to enter the nave of the basilica as far as the ambo of the lector, to be present at the Mass of the Catechumens, and to leave the church with them as soon as the Mass of the Faithful commenced. Immediately before his release from the third class he received anew the imposition of hands from the bishop, and listened on his knees to the prayers which were offered specially for him. As a penitent of the fourth class he was allowed to take part in all the prayers and celebrations of the Church, as well as to be present at the entire sacrifice of the Mass, but not to bring any offering or to receive communion. These were permitted only after the complete performance of his penance, with the solemn approbation of the bishop.

No ordinary dispositions would have sufficed to lead men to such repentance and humble resignation, and induce them to tread so heroically under foot all pride and self-love. But this holy spirit of penance diminished very much in the fourth century, and the inclination to submit to these severe punishments gradually decreased. Therefore the public accusations and penances ceased, and likewise the special office of penitentiary priests, who used to hear the confessions of the penitents, prescribe to them the degree and manner of their penance, watch over their conduct, and determine the time of their transition from one class to another and finally of their being admitted to holy communion. From that time penitents were allowed to confess to a priest of their own choice, and it rested with their own consciences to acquit themselves more or less faithfully of the penances which he imposed. Pope Leo the Great (A.D. 461) propagated this custom, and by means of established rules and laws prevented its exercise being left to the arbitrary discretion of each priest; and from that time secret judicial confession, which enables the priest to decide upon the remission or the retaining of sins, has remained in full use in the Church. The hearing of confessions was in the first instance the right of the bishops; but as they themselves were not sufficiently numerous to supply the demand for confessors, they bestowed the necessary jurisdiction upon the priests of their diocese, and in later times upon the monks also. For this reason priests can now hear confessions only in the diocese to which they belong, and in no other without the permission of the bishop of that diocese.

THE BOSPHORUS AND THE NILE.

WHEN the Eternal Word became flesh, uniting humanity to His Divinity, He became visible, and entering upon His own proper dominion over mankind, He began that battle of the work of redemption in which He was to triumph by dying for all, as well as for each individual. Henceforward, the community which He founded on the groundwork of the Christian faith, and which received for its inheritance the prosecution of His work of redemption amongst men, was to be visible and militant. The work was to be carried on in each individual human soul, for whom our Blessed Lord held in readiness as allies in the warfare all the powers of the supernatural world, and above all, Himself. For as the body is not satiated for ever after having eaten once at the table of the king, but daily feels hunger and seeks to satisfy it, so the soul is not saved for ever by the Saviour having died for her, but that for which He died, sin, must die also daily in her. This is her warfare. All and each of us must wage this warfare which penetrates inexorably into the whole of our earthly life. Its purpose is the deliverance from evil; its aim, the triumph over evil; its reward, the never-ending enjoyment of eternal good.

But, in this battle, so important to man, and to the community of men which is joined together in the visible Church by the confession of one and the same faith, all do not fight with strength, perseverance, and good will. The work of redemption never ceases; neither does the revolt of the spirit. Many, perhaps the majority, fall, and some desert. But the fallen and the deserters can raise themselves again into the freedom of the children of God.

In the opposing ranks of the enemy stands the spirit of evil, and it creates through sin, a bondage which entails new sins, so that those who enter it become the bounden slaves of the Evil One, and by their unbridled passions corrupt their hearts and pervert their minds. The history of mankind during the four thousand years between Paradise and Calvary contains the account of this slavery. The same slavery in another form has continued through the centuries after Calvary, and even in the midst of the visible Church herself. Those of her children who fall, fight not for the Spirit of God but against Him; they are not living, but dead members of the mystical Body of Christ; but so long as they do not separate themselves of their own accord from the revealed faith upon which the visible Church is built, and reject her teaching, the Church will wait with forbearance for their conversion because that faith can save them even in their last hour, and God has reserved to Himself alone the right of separating the chaff from the wheat in the day of judgment.

Two paths which lead to widely different ends are pursued even by those within the Church; the paths of grace and of nature. The one leads in strife, through ways of probation and of perfection, to union with God, the other leads into the broad career of self-seeking. The impulse towards both lies in each man who is born in nature and born again of grace; and each has his free choice which path to follow.

In times of great and general calamity, when the paltry joys of this transitory life are as it were encompassed by thorns and bitterness, and none can find secure rest or enjoy real refreshment, because all are threatened with dungeons, with ill-treatment, with poverty and banishment, with martyrdom and death; the mind turns more easily towards heavenly things, and the most frivolous natures are impressed with the nothingness of the goods and pleasures of earth. It is not, then, so difficult to despise riches and comforts, honours and distinctions.

But when the tribulation is past, and the first burst of joy which follows a happy and unlooked for deliverance is over, then many who have a secret affection for earthly things fall into a state of lukewarmness and spiritual debility, in which the desire of supernatural goods is soon extinguished. They make homes for themselves in the world, and seek to be comfortable and peaceful, and to recover all the ease and pleasure of which they had been so long and painfully deprived. If the religion which had hitherto been oppressed and persecuted comes to be supreme, to be preferred and praised, if it acquires power and consideration, and the outward glory consequent upon possessing mighty protectors, it no longer works upon its former followers in all its purity, but becomes intermingled with baser motives and considerations of human respect. These considerations were to many of its new followers of the first importance, so that if the religion did not correspond to their private wishes and aims they troubled themselves very little about it.

This was the case from the time that Christianity was introduced by Constantine into his imperial city of Byzantium. The spirit of the world produced all those effects which it generally causes in those who follow its inspirations rather than the drawing of the Spirit of God. Immoderate ambition and thirst of power, haughtiness and pride, avarice and sensuality, vanity and self-love, presumption and arrogance, took possession even of the Christians, because, as has been said, each one has the free choice whether he will serve Christ or Lucifer. The danger was the greatest on the throne and round about it, and within the limits of the imperial influence, because there the temptation to worldliness was the strongest. The magnificence of the imperial court, the splendour of the establishments and buildings of the city, the marvellous beauty of its situation, and its pleasant climate, all tended to produce the same effect. Everything was there congregated which could dazzle and captivate the senses.

In sailing from the agitated and stormy Black Sea into the Bosphorus, which winds between the coasts of Europe and Asia into the Propontis, (the Sea of Marmora,) there arise in succession pictures, as it were, from a magic mirror, each growing more and more beautiful, to the point where the ancient Byzantium sits enthroned upon her seven hills, like the queen of two regions of the world. The city forms a triangle, one side of which is washed by the waves of the Propontis, another is bounded by the Golden Horn, the harbour formed by a deep bay of the Bosphorus; and the third faces the land where, beyond the uplands of Thrace, lie the Balkan Mountains. On this side was the golden gate through which Constantine and his followers made their triumphal entries. But Byzantium sank gradually lower and lower; and many centuries before the Turk metamorphosed it into Stamboul, the golden gate was walled up, lest the people of the West, the Latins, should enter as conquerors through it. On the extreme point of the land arose the palace of the Emperor Constantine, a gigantic and splendid building, with innumerable apartments, halls, corridors, porticoes, baths, and gardens, which could accommodate six thousand inhabitants. It was surrounded by walls and towers, and formed a small city within the larger one. This most beautiful spot is now called the "Point of the Seraglio," and bears the palace of the Turkish grand seignior as it formerly did that of the first Christian emperor. Its pavilions, cupolas, and minarets, built of white stone, glitter in the sun's rays; and its fantastic architecture is chequered and overshadowed by the thick foliage of large plane-trees and the dark branches of majestic cypresses. The whole European coast of the Bosphorus, with its deeper or shallower bays, rises into hills from the water's edge, and these hills are covered with a luxuriant abundance of wood. Oaks, planes, walnuts, cypresses, chestnut and maple-trees, hang from the slopes over the meadows which border the shore, or dip their branches into the very waves The Asiatic coast is not everywhere so luxuriant, being here and there formed of bare and bleak mountains; but, on the other hand, it possesses a jewel of its own, the **Bithynian Olympus**, whose snowy peak glitters in the rays of the evening sun.

Above this confusion of palaces, houses, and towers, there rose the gigantic dome of the grand edifice which Constantine had erected in honour of the Divine Wisdom become man, the cathedral of Sancta Sophia, "that wonderful building in which even now the dogma of Christianity, interwoven with the fervent mysticism of the early ages, and penetrated by the glowing faith of the Fathers of the Church, is still quite unmistakable."[1]

A prodigality of riches was expended upon it, and the Emperor Justinian made further additions, when the building had suffered from an earthquake. It is said that on that occasion a holy relic was built into the walls between every tenth stone. The doors were made of cedar, inlaid with ivory and amber; the walls were covered with holy pictures and histories worked in mosaic and let into the marble. The marble pavement shone as brightly as a looking-glass. Pillars of porphyry, alabaster, verd antique, and granite, formed galleries above the side aisles. Silver lamps in the form of boats, in which the light was ever burning, hung from the roof. Trees of silver, with lights for fruit, sprang out of the marble floor. The canopy above the ambo bore a cross of gold of a hundred pounds' weight, ornamented with diamonds and pearls. Above the screen which shut off the choir, were twelve columns overlaid with silver, and between them silver statues of our Blessed Lord, His most Holy Mother, four prophets, and four evangelists. The altar stood in the choir upon a base of gold,

[1] Orientalische Briefe, Sept. 1843.

and the front of it was a mass of precious stones, pearls, and gold, pounded into pieces, and melted together. The bishop's throne was overlaid with silver and gilt, and golden lilies surrounded the silver canopy. Immeasurable riches were stored in the treasure-chamber: 6000 candlesticks of pure gold; seven crosses of gold, each weighing one hundred pounds; 42,000 chalice veils, embroidered with pearls and jewels; twenty-four copies of the Gospels bound in gold, each of two hundred pounds' weight; chalices, thuribles, and vessels innumerable and of indescribable costliness; 950 ecclesiastics performed the services in this House of God. Such was Sancta Sophia, the pride of the emperor, the joy of the faithful, the treasure-house of art, the jewel-casket of Byzantium, until the 29th day of May, in the year 1453, when Sultan Mohammed II. rode into it on horseback, and exclaimed, at the foot of the altar, in a voice of thunder, " There is no God but God, and Mohammed is his prophet." Then the Divine Wisdom had to give place to a human delusion, and the Lamb of God to disappear before the " Kismet," or fatalism, of Islam. Then the holy sign of the Cross was effaced wherever it did not happen to be overlooked; and the mosaic pictures on the walls and dome were plastered over with whitewash, which contrasts coarsely and glaringly with their marble frames. But there exists, even to this day, among both Christians and Mohammedans, a saying which expresses the belief that Islam will not always reign here supreme. It is as follows:—" When the Turks took possession of Constantinople, a pious priest was saying Mass in the Aja Sophia.[1] At the moment of the consecration, the bearer of the evil tidings entered the church, and the priest prayed with great fervour, ' May God preserve the holy Body

---

[1] Aja, from the Greek *agia*, holy. The Greeks call the Blessed Virgin the " Panagia," the all-holy.

of the Lord from profanation.' Suddenly the wall enclosed both Host and priest, and they will both reappear unharmed on the day in which Constantinople shall be recaptured by the Christians."

Constantine prepared his own grave in the Church of the Twelve Apostles. This church, where the head of St. Andrew was venerated, was also built with lavish magnificence. It was adorned with porphyry statues of the twelve Apostles, at whose feet Constantine desired to be buried, in order clearly to express his reverence for their sanctity, and his confidence in their intercession.

The profane buildings of the city were all in h same style of exuberant grandeur: wherever the eye turned, it rested upon marble, porphyry, and bronze. The marble was furnished by the quarries in the neighbouring island of Proconnesus in the Propontis, which gave to that sea its second name of the Sea of Marmora. The porphyry, alabaster, and granite came from Egypt and the Levant, and the timber from the immense forests in the Bosphorus, and from Taurus in Bithynia. In this respect also the situation of Byzantium was unusually favourable. The Forum of Constantine, which was surrounded by halls and courts of justice, containing many porphyry statues, had for its centre, like the Forum of Trajan at Rome, a column of porphyry eighty-seven feet high, encircled with golden laurel leaves, and surmounted by a statue of Constantine. It is now a ruin, destroyed and calcined by fire, whose remains can hardly be kept together even by cramps of iron, and which is shown to travellers under the name of "the burnt pillar." In the great circus, where the chariot-races were held, Constantine assembled the most celebrated works of art out of the temples and public places of the most opulent cities of his empire. The four bronze horses, the work of Lysippus, which now stand over the porch of St. Mark's church at Venice, and which formerly adorned the port of Athens, were among its chief ornaments. Rome alone was obliged to contribute sixty of her finest statues, Egypt one of the most magnificent of her obelisks, made of a single piece of rose-coloured granite sixty feet high, and Delphi gave the memorial of the victory of Plataea, three snakes entwined together, bearing on their heads the farfamed Delphian tripod. In one word, the riches, the art, and the splendour of the whole world were laid under tribute to Byzantium, nor were Constantine and his followers less careful for the wellbeing of the city, than they were for its glory and its magnificence. He erected enormous granaries, in which the corn of Egypt was stored, and afterwards distributed gratis to the people; noble aqueducts, which brought water from the mountains of Thrace ; numerous tasteful fountains, which distributed the water into all parts of the city, and baths luxuriantly furnished, and free of access to all. In short, with all these tributes from Rome, Greece, and Asia, there entered into Christian Byzantium a certain luxurious element, derived from heathenism, which was all the more dangerous to Christians, because it was so novel. Hitherto they had hardly been allowed to live, and now they were transplanted into the midst of all the enjoyments of life, with the full security of being able to avail themselves of them. And the great mass of the people chose rather to live in luxury, than to tread the "narrow way which leads to eternal life."

However, amid this mass, there were always holy and noble souls, who were not dazzled by earthly goods, nor taken captive by earthly happiness; and some saints, the favourites of God, were found even amongst those born to the purple. For if the kingdoms of light and of darkness meet in every human breast, their limits will not be clearly defined in the general working of the world. The threads of life cross and touch each other, and a gold thread may be interwoven with the black ones.

Thus was fulfilled in Byzantium the prophecy which Isaias spoke to Jerusalem, the type of the Christian Church:—" Thus saith the Lord God, Behold, I will lift up my hand to the Gentiles, and will set up my standard to the people. And they shall bring thy sons in their arms, and carry thy daughters upon their shoulders. And kings shall be thy nursing-fathers, and queens thy nurses: they shall worship thee with their face toward the earth, and they shall lick up the dust of thy feet."[1] Isaias also prophesied another blessing for the kingdom which Christ should found, and this was fulfilled in the desert, on the banks of the Nile:— " The land that was desolate and impassable shall be glad, and the wilderness shall rejoice and flourish like the lily. It shall bud forth and blossom, and shall rejoice with joy and praise: the glory of Libanus is given to it, the beauty of Carmel and Saron. For waters are broken out in the desert, and streams in the wilderness. And that which was dry land shall become a pool: and the thirsty land springs of water. In the dens where dragons dwelt before, shall rise up the verdure of the reed and the bulrush. And a path and a way shall be there, and it shall be called the holy way: the unclean shall not pass over it, and this shall be unto you a straight way, so that fools shall not err therein. No lion shall be there, nor shall any mischievous beast go up by it nor be found there, but they shall walk there that shall be delivered. Everlasting joy shall be upon their heads; they shall obtain joy and gladness, and sorrow and mourning shall flee away."[2]

[1] Isa. xlix. 22. 23.   [2] Isa. xxxv. 1–10.

A greater contrast can hardly be imagined than that between the smiling shores of the Bosphorus and the peaceful and monotonous banks of the Nile. The Bosphorus is all motion and variety; the sea with its ever-changing play of colours, with its ships and its boats, with its storms and its calms; the projecting and retreating coasts, with their hills and woods, rocks and green meadows, the abundance of light which spreads over the scene such a magnificence of colouring, that nowhere else do the waves look so blue, the foliage so green, the islands so purple, the snowy mountains so rose-coloured, the dwellings and houses so dazzlingly white, or the morning clouds so brilliant; while yet they all blend and melt into one another through a thousand shadings. But in the Nile there is a calm repose and uniformity in its whole course from south to north, from the Great Cataracts on the borders of Nubia, (the ancient Ethiopia,) past Assouan, (formerly Syene,) by Thebes, Memphis, and Cairo, till it empties itself into the Mediterranean Sea, not far from Alexandria, forming the Delta at its mouth. The entire landscape, from the twenty-second to the thirty-first degree of latitude, is perfectly level, and of only two colours, the yellow sand of the desert, and the verdure of the fields. The Lybian mountains in the west, smoothly shaped, and the Arabian ones in the east, gently undulating, all without points or peaks, lie outstretched on either side. And the palm, that peaceful tree, stands upright and motionless with its coronal of leaves, like a slender column with a capital, and introduces no disturbance into this majestic repose of nature with which the solemn sublimity of the ancient works of art, of the temples and the pyramids, perfectly corresponds. What value it has in the eyes of European merchants or agriculturists, whether the soil could be turned to account or cultivated,

D

are questions which belong to a different province. The peculiarity of Egypt, and Egypt is nothing more than the broad bed of the Nile, with its characteristics of solitude, uniformity, sadness, and silence, is attractive and grand, grand as the mysterious form of the sphynx which lies embedded in her sand. This great uniformity is caused by the Nile flowing almost in a straight line during its entire course through Nubia and Egypt, from south to north, by the absence not only of other rivers but of even a single tributary stream, and because the hills both on the right and left banks lie very nearly in the same direction as itself. It is only on the borders of Nubia and Upper Egypt, above Assouan, that the river has to force its way through a high bank of granite which crosses the desert from west to east, whose quarries would now supply as fine materials of syenite and red granite, as they did in the days of Constantine, if they were not disused. There the Nile forms what are called the Lesser Cataracts, which are not, however, waterfalls, but only rapids formed between cliffs and massive blocks of stone, round the islands of Philæ, Elephantine, and Bidscha, with their magnificent ruined temples. Assouan lies under the twenty-fourth degree of latitude, and below it the quiet course of thd Nile is never broken.

Its regular year y overflow is no devastating and destructive inundation; towards the end of June it slowly begins to rise, sometimes more and sometimes less perceptibly, but never suddenly or quickly. Through its rising the canals are filled which are dug from its banks into the country, and from which smaller canals and furrows branch out so as to spread the water as far as possible over the soil and render it fruitful. In the early part of October the Nile has generally reached its height, and has overflowed m many places so far as to form immense ponds. Then the water is stationary for some time, and is carefully and providently carried by sluices from one place to another. Then follow quickly, one after another, the sowing, the growth, the ripening, and the harvest. Towards the end of the winter the Nile retires back into its bed, and in April and May universal drought again prevails. Without the artificial system of canals from the Nile, and without its regular rising, the cause of which science has not hitherto discovered, all vegetation would cease, and the cultivation of the country would be impracticable, for it possesses neither streams nor rivers, and very few wells of tolerable water. Rain hardly ever falls: at Alexandria, only about ten times in the year, at Cairo three times, in Upper Egypt perhaps once in ten years. In days of yore this system of irrigation was much more perfect and more widely spread than it is at present; Egypt was then the granary of the Roman Empire, and had seven millions of inhabitants. Now, it counts only two millions and a half, and yet it supplies with corn the two holy cities of Islam, Mecca, and Medina. Its desert-like character, however, was even then conspicuous, the moment cultivation ceased. Deserts surrounded villages and even towns, but the largest lay between the right bank of the Nile and the Red Sea, in the province of Thebais. It was principally there that the second prophecy of Isaias was to be fulfilled. Byzantium became the representative of the sensual element which pervaded, and still pervades Christianity, and which may be disguised under the semblance of refinement, genius, prudence, or knowledge. The Thebaid became a general expression of the spiritual element of Christianity, whose fairest fruit is the state of perfection.

THE ANCHORITES.

The state of perfection is a thing which the world finds it very hard to understand, and yet which is very easy of comprehension when we reflect that the Divine Founder of Christianity was Himself perfect, that He requires His perfection to be imitated, and that by the gift of His grace He renders this imitation possible.

The anchorites were not merely lowly Christians who retired for a time into the forests and the wilderness, lest they should not be able to endure the tedious torments of the persecutions, which had been in force since the middle of the third century, under Valerian and Decius, and for fear they should fall away from the faith; not merely pious Christians, who fled for ever into solitude from the dangers and attractions of the world; not merely a counterpoise to the sensuality of those who were full of pride and self-love, evils which quickly grew up when the world was once more at peace, and the fear of bloody edicts had passed away; but they were the representatives of the supernatural aim of Christianity, and had received their direct authorisation from the words of our Blessed Lord: " Be you therefore perfect as your heavenly Father is also perfect." As the natural man feels himself impelled to wish for the goods and pleasures of earth, and claiming to share in them as his right, calls it happiness; so is it the right of the spiritual man who lives according to the laws of grace, to be allowed to despise these things. The former feels himself drawn to the world by a thousand allurements, and bound to it by a thousand ties, and this bondage is pleasant to him; but to the latter it would be painful, because a higher union would suffer if he were to turn his soul towards the world and its happiness. He does not say, "I will renounce and sacrifice everything in order to drive the world from my thoughts;" but he feels no desire for it, and therefore has nothing to renounce; the world is nothing to him. Neither does he say, "I will now think only of God and eternity and never more of men," but his soul is so filled with God and heavenly thoughts, and images, that it finds nothing in earthly things to attract it; nor does he say, "Now I will suffer for the love of God;" but he loves God, and if suffering comes, he regards it not, for it is a part of love; and for him there can be but one sorrow, not to love God. This is the fire of love which Christ Himself brought down from heaven, making the Holy Ghost the source of this new love, and saying of it, "What will I but that it be kindled?"

He who lives in a state of grace, can also lead a perfect life in the midst of the world, sharing in its joys and its happiness, so long as he "possesses them as though he possessed them not;" that is to say, when his heart is not attached to them. This is shown by the history of the rich young man in the gospel. When he asked our Blessed Lord what he should do to have everlasting life, Christ simply answered, "Keep the commandments," for the commandments are from God, and they sanctify life because they remind man of his holiest duties, protect him from his strongest passions, and remove the possessions of others from his grasp. But the young man had imagined and desired something higher than this. Then our Blessed Lord said, "If thou wilt be perfect, go sell what thou hast, and give to the poor, and come, follow me." Thus He did not command, but He recommended a higher perfection—evangelical poverty. In like manner, He reinstated marriage in its original sanctity and indissolubility, and added to it a new dignity by the seal of the sacrament; but nevertheless, He still more **highly praised virginity**, which has no thought but for the kingdom of heaven; and He adds with holy foresight, "He that can take, let him take it." Thus again He counsels, but does not command a higher perfection than that of marriage—evangelical chastity. And He gave, lastly, a third counsel, not so much by word as by deed—that of unconditional obedience; for He, the Son of God, most humbly obeyed not only His heavenly Father, but in His most sacred Humanity, the least of men, His creatures, and even those that were His enemies.

The Church has learnt from her Lord and Master to give the three evangelical counsels, as they are called, to those who can only find contentment in the most perfect deliverance of the soul from the fetters of the transitory goods of this world. Who can doubt that there are such souls? In all men, without exception, there exists a secret longing for something better, often misunderstood, and unconfessed. All men fell in Adam; and all desire to regain their purer state. In some this desire is so strong and so overpowering, that they have no other wish but to place themselves, as far as is possible here on earth, in that state, and to live according to the conditions of their original nature, in the likeness of God. There is surely many a Christian who, even if it were only for fleeting moments, has experienced this longing, and the unspeakable peace and joy which accompany it. Why could not this longing be lasting in the few who fostered it with all the powers of their soul and supported it by all the capabilities of their mind?

In consequence of the sin of Adam, an indescribable corruption invaded all the relations of life, poisoning and perverting them. Originally, man loved his Creator and all creatures in Him, but sin changed a self-sacrificing love into the venom of selfishness, and the love of the creature supplanted the love of the Creator. Originally, man possessed in God all the riches of the exuberant earth in their fulness, but sin destroyed this happy community of goods; and man, having learnt self-love, wished to possess property also, and prized it so highly that the more he had, the more he desired. Originally, man's will reposed on God; he was the organ of the Divine will; but sin brought him into continual rebellion against God, and his will, which when it is in union with that of God, participates in the power, wisdom, love, and bliss of God, sank when he turned away from God into weakness, wickedness, misery, and self-will. That one drop of sin flowed through humanity in these three wild destructive torrents—self-love, covetousness, and self-will: from them spring all the desolation in the lives of individuals and of nations, all the wreck of the moral, spiritual, and material laws. Then the Incarnate Redeemer came and crushed the triple head of the serpent, self-love through chastity, covetousness through voluntary poverty, and self-will through obedience. And as He willed to continue His life here below in His mystical body the Church, He added, by the three evangelical counsels, a member to this body, which continues, or at least strives to continue His glorified life on earth, and which is at the same time an ever-present remembrance on the part of humanity of its former higher condition, namely, the state of perfection; and a never-ceasing expression of the desire to return to it. He, the Divine Saviour, and the Church through Him, well knew that human nature, by reason of its earthly tendencies, is strongly attracted to the rich and broad lowlands of life, and that grace will have no other effect at best upon the majority of men than that of teaching them how to use, and not to misuse the goods of earth; therefore He, and the Church with Him, willed to keep open the path to ideal heights, to enable those to tread it whose natures incline to the ideal, because to keep them back from such heights would be to defraud them of the rights bestowed on them by Christ himself.

The Church has proceeded in this matter as she ever does with heavenly wisdom and discretion; that is to say, by inspiration. Earthly things belong to the great mass of mankind, and she sanctifies their goods and their enjoyments; but for those to whom the Holy Ghost has dealt a larger measure, she praises the heights of a life of renunciation. Since the first Apostles left their homes and their goods to follow our Blessed Lord, to this hour she has ever prized more highly voluntary poverty for Christ's sake than the noblest use of the goods of earth. And ever since the Apostle St. Paul wrote to the Corinthians, she has held the marriage state to be holy and indissoluble, but less high than the state of virginity for Christ's sake. And since the Son of God, obedient even unto death, died on the Cross, and daily obediently offers Himself anew on Christian altars, she has placed humble obedience for the sake of Christ higher than the wisdom of ruling well over empires and kingdoms. These three holy counsels ever silently preach that through Christ the triple head of the serpent is to be trodden under foot. The Church has upheld these heavenly maxims with a firm hand, in every century, unwavering through all the assaults and wars which from the beginning were waged against them, for this in common with all her other teaching has been opposed by error. Some heretics rejected marriage for all mankind without exception. Others condemned second marriages. Some even considered marriage to be instituted by the devil. Those who held this morbid and exaggerated doctrine attacked the simple and wholesome teaching of the Church with the reproach that it was not sufficiently strict, whilst others, sunk in sensuality, waged war against virginity, and accused the Church which upheld it of requiring from mankind what was impossible. But the Church requires from men only what Christ himself has required, to " keep the commandments." Beyond that she only advises what He Himself has counselled: "And then follow me." And if she were not to require the one and to counsel the other, she would lie against the Holy Ghost who is within her. That she cannot do.

The secret conviction that to obtain a higher good, the lower must be renounced, the belief that an especial blessing rests upon renunciation, is a mystical instinct which pervades even un-Christian nations, if they are not kept in spiritual blindness by complete barbarism. This instinct betokens a common descent, which has faintly inherited and transmitted the tradition of the fall, and of the redemption to be hoped for.

To regain some precious lost good, to purify self by penance and mortification in order to become worthy of this good; this is the idea of the Divine mysteries of redemption through the Incarnation of God which exists in many nations, but which, without Christian revelation, is frequently misunderstood and distorted. What we read of the fearful penances amongst the tribes of Asia, in China, Thibet, and Hindostan; of the great lawgivers of ancient countries who retired into deserts in order to withdraw from all exterior things, and to abstract themselves in contemplation that the truth might unveil itself before them; of the wise women and virgin priestesses to whom supernatural powers were subject at the price of renunciation; all this speaks of one universal attraction to something ideal. This tendency towards the ideal must be very strong in mankind, to have kept its place notwithstanding the fall. The Essenes, a Jewish sect, who called themselves the disciples of the prophet Elias, acted upon this idea. They had renounced all intercourse with the remainder of the Jewish people, and lived in great numbers in the neighbourhood of the Jordan and the Dead Sea, practising celibacy and community of goods, and cultivating the ground. The Therapeuts in Egypt were similar to them, and led a contemplative life in community. The custom was general also amongst the Jews of the Old Testament for parents to consecrate their children, and for young men and maidens to dedicate themselves for a stated period to the Temple. They were then called Nazarites, that is, consecrated to God; and they lived under supervision in special buildings in the Temple, where they performed minor services, were instructed in the Holy Scriptures, and observed certain practices; for instance, to drink no wine, never to cut their hair, and others of the same kind. The feast of the Presentation, on the 21st of November, marks the day on which, according to very early tradition, the Blessed Virgin Mary was brought to the Temple by her parents as a child, and, being dedicated in an especial manner to God, became a Nazarite. Parents who separated themselves from their beloved children, and children who voluntarily withdrew from their families, hoped thus to become pleasing to God, and to participate in His choicest blessings. The idea of an accepted sacrifice appears everywhere, though dimly and under a veil.

But when the true Victim had been sacrificed, when the Lamb of God had been slain, the mist was cleared away, and all became plain. There is one sacrifice, namely the pure sacrifice which the prophet Malachias foretold daily from the rising of the sun even to the going down; and every Christian must henceforward offer himself up in union with this sacrifice.

The life and death of the faithful of the first centuries show how thoroughly they comprehended this, and acted upon it. They all looked upon themselves as dead with Christ, and buried with Him in baptism, as the Apostle St. Paul expresses it. All led a life more or less mortified and penitential, in which those chiefly excelled who, whether priests or laymen, were endowed with especially ardent dispositions, who gave their possessions to the poor, practised works of mercy, often living through humility upon the work of their hands, and who became, particularly in times of persecution, a support and a stay for all who were in need of advice, consolation, or encouragement. There were also, in those early times, great numbers of virgins consecrated to God. A virgin who had taken this resolution, declared it publicly and solemnly in church, took the vow of chastity, and received from the hand of the bishop the veil and a golden head-covering called the mitrella. She lived with her family, but in retirement from the world, for she was "veiled," that is, hidden in Christ; and if any one of them ever had the misfortune to marry, she became, according to the expression of St. Cyprian, "an adulteress to Christ;" branded and excommunicated by one of the canons of the Council of Chalcedon, while her husband was threatened by law with death; for there must be no frivolous trifling with the Most High.

Let each one prove himself, let him weigh his powers, let him not overrate himself, but humbly draw back from higher things rather than press forward uncalled. Before he makes his choice, he has the right to choose his path, and he is in duty bound to do so with conscientious consideration. After his choice, he belongs no longer to himself, but to those to whom he has solemnly vowed fidelity; whether it be to God, to whom the state of chastity is affianced, or to man, the spouse who has been chosen for the marriage state. There rests upon each choice a corresponding blessing, and the especial grace of God; but in return for this, the fidelity, and together with it the honour and dignity, of the man, is pledged to God, for He is the receiver of the vow. Whosoever breaks it, breaks a covenant with God, cancels his engagement with God, and becomes in both cases the enemy of God; for the vows differ only in this, that the one, that of virginity, is offered directly to God, and the other, that of conjugal fidelity, indirectly. The heresies which deny any weight or binding power to the former have very logically proceeded to reject the ever-binding power of the latter, and have been reduced to declare that marriage can be dissolved; and, so far as it lay in their power, have trodden under foot the sanctity of their pledged word, and the moral order which God has established for the earthly happiness and the eternal salvation of mankind. Earthly possessions and the ties of marriage were the first fetters thrown off by those Christians who were called to the state of perfection, in order to be able to give themselves up unshackled to a higher spiritual life. As by so doing they renounced all claims to earthly prosperity, they were called the Ascetics, that is, the renouncers. They remained in their own position in the world, because, in those early times, the world offered them nothing but death; and because a martyr's death for Christ, which leads instantaneously to inseparable union with Him and to the vision of God, was the happiest thing which could befall a Christian.

But the times altered and the world became full of dangers, especially in the middle of the third century. The persecution had long been ended, and external repose had breathed a soft and lukewarm spirit into Christianity. The faithful had entered into manifold relations with the heathen, had suffered themselves to be infected by their lax and easy principles, and becoming feeble and worldly, had loved riches and comforts, grandeur and possessions, and in short had set their hearts upon these transitory treasures. Now, when a kind of persecution was raised under the Emperor Decius which had hitherto been unknown, and which had in view to exterminate Christianity by forcing its professors to apostatise rather than by putting them to death, the inward corruption of many was exposed, and denials of the faith and apostasies were unhappily of frequent occurrence; although these were far outweighed by the heroic courage and faith of the true confessors. This fearful example produced important results. If the world was so dangerously attractive, that its neighbourhood caused infatuation, and that intercourse with it paralysed the higher powers of the soul, how much wiser would it be to withdraw out of reach of its enervating influence, and to live at the greatest possible distance from it! Such were the thoughts of many souls that were mindful of their eternal salvation, and longed to escape from the dangers of pride and sensuality which abound in the world. Others who, solitary in spirit, had ever followed an unworldly aim, felt themselves all the more powerfully attracted to a hidden life with God as this attraction became in the course of time more general. It was particularly frequent in the East, amongst nations of rich and fertile imagination, which, when it is purified and controlled by the faith, supports the soul in its efforts to ascend, by keeping a sublime pattern constantly before the eyes. The Christian ascetics who retired into solitude from the tumult of the world were first seen in Egypt as hermits or anchorites. They were the fathers of the later religious orders which were multiplied under various forms with divers rules and constitutions, with or without vows. They became, notwithstanding their solitude, the civilisers of their time. By their intercourse with God, they had imbibed such abundant light, that they enlightened both their own and future ages. They were living guides to heaven, because the things of earth had never misled them, because their gaze was fixed with untroubled clearness upon the Author of all being, and in His light they comprehended the connexion of all things. The Evangelist St. John, the holy solitary of Patmos, says of the Eternal Word at the beginning of his Gospel, "As many as received Him, he gave them power to be made the sons of God."

Children in their father's house are masters at the same time. The joyful father in the Gospel says to the eldest son, "All I have is thine." This was the case with the anchorites. They brought the spiritual life to wonderful perfection.

To have, and to desire nothing earthly, is not sufficient for union with God, not even when a man makes himself poor in order to share poverty with Christ. Not to be earthly, that is the inexorable condition; and this abstinence from all that is earthly can be attained only through daily mortification of the will, the inclinations, the desires, and the passions. The body is in itself no hindrance to familiar intercourse with God and with spirits, nor to the sight of them; in paradise man saw God and spoke with Him. But when man separated himself from God by sin, he lost his heavenly privilege; and as formerly the soul spiritualised the body, because through its union with God, it had dominion over it, so now the body materialised the soul, after it had lost its supremacy and become subservient to the senses. Whomsoever men serve, by him will they be guided; they will obey him alone, and to him they will look for enjoyments and rewards. The soul followed its new mistress so blindly in its thoughts, desires, and purposes, that it could no longer say, " The Lord He is God," for it had no other Lord but the evil inclinations which embodied themselves and extorted worship under a thousand idolatrous forms. To such extremes had the soul gone, to such low depths had it fallen. It had voluntarily turned away from heavenly things to follow sensual enjoyments, of which it obtained abundance in return, but it lost in equal measure its capacity for spiritual things. Then the Redeemer came, who took upon himself as man the sins of sensual mankind, and caused Himself to be nailed to the cross for their expiation, giving them simultaneously a pledge of redemption, sanctifying grace, which connected them for ever with their Redeemer. This strength continued to dwell in His followers, and being the fruit of His crucifixion, it impelled them, as He had lived a crucified life, to lead a life of suffering out of love. This mystery of the Cross is to many a folly and a scandal, and they neglect it altogether; to others it is a painful necessity which they imperfectly obey through fear of hell; but to many it is the ladder to heaven by which they attain here below the object of their desires, and by climbing to a greater or less height, reach a more or less perfect union with God. For suffering out of love causes outward uniformity with the Incarnate God, and restores the inward image of God. If man wishes to recover his supernatural prerogatives, which sanctifying grace enables him to do, he must courageously embrace suffering out of love, that is, the crucifixion of self, the mortification of sinful nature, the death of the sensual man. When this is accomplished, the redeemed can see God; for God says, "Man shall not see Me and live."

To enter into this death depends not upon the deeds or the strength of man. Out of the many who lovingly embrace the mystery of the Cross, only very few reach the last and highest steps of the heavenly ladder, although they have faithfully fought their fight. Such great graces flow freely out of the hand of God; and that time may truly be called happy in which they are poured in the greatest abundance over souls. The best school for the crucifixion of self is to be found in the state of perfection.

Sin had penetrated into the soul through sensuality, and become its master. Therefore sensuality must be combated step by step as a fortress is reduced by famine in order to expel the enemy. All the indulgence, the effeminacy, and the refinements of material life, and all enjoyments flattering to the eye and the ear, all the many results of culture and civilisation—work upon the soul as damp air upon the strings of a harp; they relax and soften it. The body becomes accustomed to require so much, and to consider so many things as necessaries, that until all of them are gathered together no thought can be bestowed upon higher wants. On the other hand, a different system arises which begins by striving first to satisfy the highest needs. Because they are the highest, they are also the most comprehensive, and the more they spread the less room do they leave in which the lower can flourish, so that the latter are forced by degrees to wither away and die. Our Blessed Lord had said to the Jews, "You are from beneath, I am from above." There must therefore be one member of His Church which should ever bear witness that the Lord is from above. Our effeminate ideas find as great, or perhaps still greater, difficulty in forming a conception of the extreme mortification of the sensual man and the complete government of the will, which was practised by many of the anchorites, as in realising the torments suffered by the martyrs. For, on the one hand, the sufferings of the martyrs were not so long—a few days or weeks, at the utmost some months, and the struggle was over; and on the other hand, their only choice was between a mortal sin, the denial of the faith, and martyrdom. Therefore they chose death, as every good Christian must do. But the anchorites led, of their own free will, a life of the most painful austerities, daily and hourly renewed during twenty, thirty, forty, and even more years, without the alternative of any mortal sin. They became like "Jesus, full of the Holy Ghost, led by the Spirit into the desert."[1] And as the martyrs in Jesus suffered joyfully their bloody torments and died rejoicing, so the anchorites bore their unbloody torments joyfully in union with Him, and led a happy life. The sharp and prickly thornbush of asceticism bore for them the beautiful flower of mysticism, and their life resembled the cactus of Ethiopia, whose thorny branches produce the enchanting flower which only opens its fragrant golden cup at the quiet midnight, and is called the queen of the night. In the ancient holy anchorites we see how the mortified man can restore himself to his original state in paradise, and even here below regain his privileges; how he can partially attain to the goal of the blessed spirits, and become able to see God; and how, as our Lord said, streams of living water shall flow from those who believe in Him. But penance precedes the kingdom of God, as the great anchorite St. John Baptist announced to men.

The histories of the lives of these wonderful men have been preserved for us partly by the great doctors of the Church who had been their disciples, or the scholars of their disciples. St. Athanasius, St. Jerome, Theodoret, Bishop of Cyrus in Syria,

[1] Luke iv. 1.

and Rufinus, the learned priest of Aquileia, occupied themselves in visiting the actual spots and collecting witnesses and accurate information. Other less renowned, though no less trustworthy men, followed their example; so that we possess a collection of lives of the anchorites which is no less sublime and edifying than the acts of the martyrs. It is undeniable that the miraculous aspect of many of these lives is legendary. For a legend in the religious world is only a subjective completion and picturing of the objective truth. So has the Church, and with her all reasonable people, ever held it to be. She allows it to rest like the husk upon the fruit, but prizes the inner kernel of truth according to its worth. Amongst the old Florentine painters there is one called Sandro Botticelli who painted pictures of incomparable ideal grace; but the Mother of God and the Infant Jesus have always golden hair, not only gold-coloured, for he dipped his brush in liquid gold and painted their hair with it in order to express the beauty and the glory which surrounded them. No one will on that account deny the worth of Botticelli's pictures, nor will they believe that the Mother of God and the Divine Redeemer, in His most sacred Humanity, had threads of gold on their head instead of hair. It is the same with the legendary form of many historical deeds in the lives of the saints. The cause of miracles is in God, and the saints perform them because they stand in the midst of the kingdom of God which for them has already arrived. It is only a small territory, and is entirely encircled by the huge kingdom of this world in the middle of which we are placed. It is not demanded from us to scale the lofty heights of holiness from whence the streams of grace pour down in miracles. No one can require a dwarf to clothe himself in the armour of a giant. But it would be ludicrous in the dwarf to assert that because he could not handle the giant's armour, no one else was able to do so; and, moreover, that giants did not exist. What can he who has not fought them know of the giant combats of those mighty ones? Human nature is so pliable, so capable of accommodating itself to persevering asceticism, that we cannot set bounds to its powers of endurance according to our sensual feelings of comfort and discomfort. And if thousands remain on this side of the usual boundary, and if ten, yea or if only one pass over, it shows that the boundaries are for the thousands but not for the whole human race. In the actual condition of his nature corrupted by sin and born again in Christ, man can only stand, as it were, above or beneath himself—above himself through sanctifying grace, or beneath himself through sin. Those ancient heroes received from grace the wings for which the great soul of David longed, "the wings like a dove to fly and be at rest," to rest in God. Oh, how can he measure the strength which abounded in them, the light which illuminated them, the liberty which elevated them, who not only has never attempted such a flight, but has never once even felt the wish to attempt it!

O ye ancient solitaries, ye living temples of the Holy Ghost in the desert, ye are less known and less renowned in the world than your lifeless neighbours, the temples of Luxor, Thebes, and Baalbec. Every child can tell of the Pyramids, one of the seven wonders of the world over which your eyes looked up to heaven, but no one speaks of you who are the living wonders of the new and redeemed world. A thousand songs speak and sing of the statue of Memnon which stands on the borders of your desert, and which is fabulously said to have sounded when struck by the rays of the morning sun, but no voice praises you who sang day and night the hymn of the glory of the Creator in His creatures. Deeper than the hieroglyphics in the sands of your home are you buried in the forgetfulness of the world; but yet the key is not lost which opens and explains the sublime mysteries of your existence,—faith in redemption through the Incarnation of the Son of God.

THE DESERT.

IN order to attain to the high spiritual life of the ancient solitaries, an extraordinary recollection and withdrawal of the activity of the soul from temporal things and from trivial occupations was necessary. To understand the gentlest word of God all the sounds of men must have died away, and in order to be able to turn steadfastly and tranquilly to Him alone, the dissipating tumult of the manifold agitations which stir the world must be hushed. For this reason it was that the desire of solitude led men towards the deserts of the East, to Mesopotamia, Syria, Palestine, and Egypt. Here human dwellings were necessarily confined to certain spots, because in them alone man's physical existence was possible, and hence those giant cities of the East, as Nineveh on the Tigris, Babylon on the Euphrates, Thebes on the Nile—Thebes, the ruins of whose temples are so colossal, that beside them the Coliseum is dwarfed, and St. Peter's appears diminutive—Thebes, where, in the single hall of Karnak, there are 122 columns of 27 feet, and 12 columns of 37 feet in circumference. These and other towns took advantage, as it were, of their fortunate situation on large rivers, to spread themselves out far and wide, and to gather together in themselves a numerous population. As far as their jurisdiction extended, in their gardens, their plantations, and all that belonged to the supplies and requirements of a large and brilliant city, there reigned the most flourishing cultivation. But wherever the hand of man arrested for a moment his labour, and where the water of the river did not penetrate, there the characteristics of the desert instantly asserted themselves. Such is the great Syrian desert, from Anti-Lebanon to the Euphrates, at the entrance to which lies Damascus, with its vast circle of green orchards, in which walnut-trees, apricots, olives, pomegranates, and figtrees thrive in indescribable profusion, watered by the seven branches of the Barrada, a small river which rises in the caverns of Anti-Lebanon. Only ten paces from its banks begins the desert where the sand lies in heaps. The sands are equally overpowering in what is called the Lesser Arabian Desert, between Gaza and Cairo, which extends over the peninsula of Suez, and can be traversed with camels in eleven days' march, averaging eight hours a day. Nothing is to be seen but sand from the Mediterranean Sea to the line of hills which stretches from Arabia to Egypt. It is not always level, but sometimes lies in waves, and there is even a whole range of hills formed of loose sand, so deep that the camels sink up to their knees in it. A little moisture may collect in the rainy season in hollows at the foot of the hills, where isolated groups of palmtrees stand in dark contrast with the dazzling yellow sand, like tufts of black feathers. There is but one single water station with pure water in this desert, at Catya, and that is also a palm-grove. Beyond this there begins an interminable plain, with firmer soil, here and there covered with prickly bushes, all dry and gray, which lasts till you reach Lower Egypt and the irrigation of the Nile. There you can stand, as it were, with the left foot in the desert and the right in a paradise. To the right you have citron and nabektrees, acacias, sycamores, **palms, with reddish-coloured doves perched upon their waving branches**, fields of sugarcanes, maize, and cotton, all of the brightest green; to the left, the dry, hard soil, which of itself would not bear one blade of grass. And that which works this striking contrast lies midway between them, — a small canal, which could be crossed at one stride, and from which still smaller channels diverge like little rivulets. The soil is so fertile that it only requires a few drops of water and some grains of seed to become clothed with the most magnificent and luxuriant vegetation. Lower Egypt, especially where the two arms of the Nile form the Delta, is abundantly watered, and therefore exceedingly fruitful, and the desert-like character is driven back. But at Cairo it reasserts its full rights. Before the eastern gates is gravel strewn with many-coloured pebbles and shining quartz, first level and then undulated as far as the "petrified forest," where, by some convulsion of nature, large trees, palms and sycamores, have been dashed to the ground, covered with a deluge of sand, and turned into stone. Before the western gates are gardens, terraces, plantations, fields, and fruit-trees in abundance as far as the Nile, bearing on its bosom Ronda, the island of flowers. Cairo, the Egyptian Babylon, as it was formerly called, is situated midway between these two opposite poles of nature. Across the Nile in the boundless desert stands the city of the tombs of the ancient kings of Memphis, and the Pyramids tower above the horizon in various groups, while the actual Memphis, the residence of the Pharaohs, is now one vast region of verdant fields, interspersed with scanty palm-groves and innumerable villages.

In ascending the Nile the cultivation recedes and the desert advances, although 50,000 water-wheels (*sakieh*) turned by oxen, and assisted by countless shadoofs, are in motion night and day to supply the country with water. The shadoofs are holes dug to receive the water which men pour into them with leathern buckets, and from whence it flows through the trenches. But all these arrangements do not suffice, for there are not enough inhabitants to cultivate the earth. The lower grounds on the borders of the Nile sometimes become morasses, overgrown with rushes, the haunt of buffaloes; and by the side of fields where corn, rape, and beans grow to the height of a man, there lie tracts of the most fertile land perfectly waste for want of hands to drain the marshes and to till the ground. But what life there is, is of an attractive, pastoral character. "The evenings in Upper Egypt and Nubia are of matchless beauty. It is so hot in the daytime, and the sun's rays are reflected so dazzlingly from the water, the desert sands, and the calcareous mountains, that you are unwilling to leave the cabin of the boat in which the voyage up the Nile is performed. Towards evening you come out to inhale the mild and salutary air. The sun sinks behind the Lybian hills, which cover themselves with dark blue shadows, while the rays of light play upon the Arabian hills as upon a prism, and deck them with the fleeting hues of flowers, jewels, and butterflies. Single heights resemble large fiery roses, while the more extended ones seem like chains of purple amethysts. Date palms, in groups or garlands, or in less graceful straight rows, here and there a single nabek-tree, with its slender branches, or a stiff dom-palm, and the *Acacia nilotica*, sprinkled with millions of yellow blossoms, emitting a tropical fragrance, intertwined with blue and violet creepers, whose long wreaths hang in every direction in beautiful confusion,—all this is reflected in the still waters. The perfume of spring fills the air, a nameless balmy scent which our fields and woods also give out, but in June, and not in January. Fields of beans, lupins, rape, vetches, and cotton, are in full flower; wheat and barley are shooting up vigorously, forced by the dark rich mould of the gardens, and enticed by the warm sunshine. Flights of wild doves greet you with their cooing from the branches of the acacias and the palms. Aquatic birds sit together in swarms on the sandy banks, here white as marble, there raven-black, and chirp or scream forth their monotonous song, which they might have learnt from the uniform murmur of the waves. At times a large heron flies across the river, or a pelican dips into it with her heavy flight, in pursuit of fish; or an eagle soars slowly and peacefully higher and higher into the clear sky, as if he wished to see whither the sun had gone. For it has set in the meantime, and the red glow of evening, which illuminated the whole western sky, has cooled down into a pale blue. But see, there rises in the south a second ruddy glow of a rich purple colour, which reddens anew the fading hills, and lures forth at the same time the first stars. The glorious Venus shines in the west, the bold hunter Orion mounts slowly behind the Arabian hills; later on, low in the south-east, appears Canopus, which is never seen in Europe. Then you travel, as it were, between two skies. The Nile, now widened into a large lake, now contracted to a narrow band, is changed into a dark firmament, full of softly trembling stars, which blends into the real heavens. The large and peaceful stars look down from above, and have none of the incessant twinkling which they have in our clear winter nights, as if they were trembling and shivering with cold. On the banks there is yet life for some time longer. Fires gleam in the villages, for the position of the hearth is in front of the door. Bleating flocks of sheep and goats are driven home; dogs bark, asses bray, children shout, the water-wheel creaks as it turns. The men at the shadoof sing regularly, " Salam ya Salam," (Peace, O peace,) while they fill the buckets in the Nile and empty them into the channels which carry the water farther. Loud voices and cries, and the songs of labourers returning from the fields, are heard on all sides. The watcher in the lonely bark passes his time and drives away sleep by beating the darabookah, a kind of drum. At length all is hushed, and the freshness of the night settles down upon the water." [1]

These pictures are not to be seen everywhere upon the Nile. Sometimes, especially in Nubia, the vegetation on its banks dwindles down to a narrow strip of bean-fields, which scantily feeds the population of a poverty-stricken village. Sometimes it disappears altogether, when walls of rocks or boulders line the banks.

In Nubia the desert is increasing to such an extent, particularly on the Lybian side, that the gigantic temples of Abusimbil are gradually disappearing in the sand. At the Great Cataracts of the Nile, within the tropics, in the twenty-second degree of latitude, the desert somewhat resembles chaos before the Spirit of God had divided the elements. It is a plain, boundless as the ocean, of tawny sand, out of which rise dark blocks of limestone. These blocks, and the undulations of the uneven sandy soil which the wind raises here and there, and even the tops of the distant mountains, which are seen like clouds on the extreme verge of the horizon, make no variety in this immense plain. You seem able to see right into the heart of Africa, but not the slightest trace of waterfalls is to be detected.

The Nile has apparently disappeared. You are taken slowly some distance upon a camel to where the blocks of stone seem to cluster together more

[1] *Orientalische Briefe*, January 1844.

thickly. You climb one of them, and stand as it were upon a cliff, and thousands of similar cliffs are strewn to the southward as far as the horizon, like dark islands in the vast sandy sea of the desert. But that which surrounds them is water and not sand—a broad, shapeless mass of water, which dashes and curls wildly and confusedly round them, as the force of the torrent impels it. Such are the Great Cataracts of the Nile. It does not look like a river, nor like a lake; it is a waste of waters, whose course through the immeasurable plain is determined only by a slight depression of the ground, being bounded by the desert on the east and west. There is nothing here defined and circumscribed, or possessed of colour or form. Dull monotony and sullen confusion reign supreme. The yellow sand, the muddy waters, and the black stones, roll and tumble about together. There is no separation or division; all goes headlong, always on and on, since the earth has had her present form, and always will go on as long as she keeps it. Over this aspect of nature man has no power. He cannot guide such waters as this, nor govern this waste of moving sand and rocks. It is the most melancholy and insuperable of all wildernesses, at once in restless fermentation and of chilling stiffness, surpassingly curious, and unlike all other scenery. For a league farther the waters rush downwards. Then, near the village of Wadi Halfa, the rocky islands and obstructions come to an end, and the Nile gathers itself into its appointed bed, and becomes a river.

At Assouan (in the twenty-fourth degree of latitude) it forms the Lesser Cataracts by falling over masses of granite, which are here thrown across the whole country, split and sundered by chaotic forces. The falls and rapids are higher and more picturesque, because the Nile is pent up between steep rocky banks, and because the islands of

Philæ, Elephantine, and Bidscha, with their noble ruins, rise out of the midst; but the desert is, if possible, more frightful still. The sand is dazzlingly white, and so loose, that it is necessary positively to wade through it. The granite lies upon it, partly in blocks, partly in shattered pieces, and the eye grows weary of having neither bush nor blade of grass, nor even the tiniest piece of moss in the crevices of the rocks to rest upon.

Such is the nature of the Egyptian desert. It reaches from the right bank of the Nile to the Red Sea, a breadth of from five to six days' journey for a camel, and from the Cataracts to the neighbourhood of Cairo, where it joins the Arabian desert. Its centre is the Thebaid. It would hardly be possible to find on the face of the earth a spot better calculated to become the home of a soul estranged from the world, or which would better aid it to trample the world under foot.

One peculiarity of these deserts is the number of holes and caverns which are found in them. Limestone is the framework which supports the sand, and which rises out of it in the manifold forms of mountains and peaks, hills and rocks. The mountains of Palestine, Lebanon, Anti-Lebanon, and the Arabian mountains of Egypt, are all limestone. Time, the atmosphere, and the rain, easily form caverns in it, which, enlarged by human labour, are still made use of in Syria as dwellingplaces. The holy grotto at Bethlehem was a similar cavern. Mount Olivet, near Jerusalem, and the valley of Joshaphat, which reaches thence in intricate windings to the Dead Sea, as likewise the hilly desert of Mar Saba, which separates the Dead Sea from Bethlehem, are all perforated with caves like the cells in a beehive. In the first Christian centuries they were inhabited by solitaries; in those before the Christian era, they were used as graves. Hence it is often related in the lives of the anchorites, that they lived in tombs. These rocky sepulchres were nowhere more plentiful than in Egypt. The ancient Egyptians were a peculiarly serious people, with a fanciful thoughtfulness. The utter sadness of the unredeemed is impressed in forcible characters upon their temples, their colossal monuments, and their sphynxes. Life and death, soul and body God and man, even the whole of nature—the mysterious desert, the unintelligible Nile—all was a problem to them. They therefore spoke in figures, as is shown by their hieroglyphics; and they made idols with the heads of animals, and enigmatical statues, such as the sphynx, with the body of a beast in repose, and the features of a woman. They had a mysterious and strong yearning for the divine things which were to come, and an obscure idea that godly things were near to man. But as they had not revealed faith, which alone gives a higher knowledge, they sought to satisfy their longings by deifying almost everything which surrounded them, either because it was of use to them, or because they feared it, as the bull, the cat, the onion, or the crocodile. They had also a kind of dim suspicion of the immortality of the soul, and the Christian dogma of the resurrection. They believed that the souls of the departed tarried 3000 years in Amenthes, (the kingdom of shadows,) and then returned to earth to be reunited to their bodies, and to begin a new life. In order, therefore, that the soul might easily recognise its own body, and find it in the best possible preservation, they embalmed the corpses in the peculiar form of mummies, laid them in roomy stone sarcophagi, and placed these in sepulchral halls, which were most secure and indestructible when hollowed out of the rock. The magnificence of the tomb was in proportion to the riches and rank of the dead man. None certainly surpassed the

Pyramid of King Cheops, a tomb nearly the height of St. Peter's at Rome, in which nothing was found save one single sarcophagus. There are very many sepulchres in the hills of Upper Egypt, particularly near Thebes, in the valley of Assasiff, and in the rocky dale of Bab-el-Melek. The former are very much defaced by being made the habitation of the peasants, where little children share the space with fowls, donkeys, and bones of mummies. But the latter are very well preserved, because they are situated in the burning desert, a whole league distant from the Nile. They are called the tombs of the kings. Each tomb forms a spacious dwelling with a flight of steps, vestibules, halls, side-chambers, corridors, all hewn out of the rock, and painted from top to bottom with figures of the gods, scenes out of the region of shadows, and the lives of warriors, husbandmen, and artisans. One chamber is painted entirely with weapons, another with vases and vessels in incredible variety, another with musical instruments, another with tables, chairs, and sofas, covered with purple cushions and tiger-skins. Another with various kinds of fruits, many with representations of the judgments and worship of the gods. And all this expenditure of labour and art is buried in utter darkness with the mummy; for the whole sepulchral palace is as it were inserted into the cliff, and has no light, save from the entrance door. In each of these palaces, again, there is but one sarcophagus. Without having seen one, it is hardly possible to form an idea of the colossal and mysterious grandeur of such a tomb. It is hewn out of the bare rock with its steps and halls, its columns and chambers, and then with the utmost labour worked upon with chisel and brush, only to disappear with its mummy in the double night of death and oblivion, for large blocks of stone were rolled in front of the entrance to guard it from profanation.

What a contrast with the subterranean burial-places of the early Christians, the Catacombs! There also was the protecting darkness, there also labour, toil, and care, but only the reverence for the lifeless body which was due to it as the temple of the Holy Ghost, and as a member of the mystical body of Christ.

The sun of Christianity, however, changed the gloomy darkness of these ancient Egyptians into light, and in place of the mummies who occupied the tombs as bodies without souls, the solitaries entered into them, who might almost be named souls without bodies; for St. Macarius bitterly complains, "This wicked sinner, my body, would not consent to be entirely weaned from all nourishment." Formerly they sought by the semblance of life to make the dead live; now this earthly life appears to them in comparison with the eternal life, as a kind of death, and entering willingly into this death, they lived like the dying or like the blessed.

PAUL OF THEBES.

"And he was in the desert, and he was with beasts, and the angels ministered to him."—ST. MARK i. 13.

As John the Baptist, "the voice of one crying in the wilderness," became a herald of the Gospel, confirming his preaching of penance by his penitential life in a garment of hair, with locusts for his food—representing the transition from the kingdom of penance to the kingdom of God, treading and pointing out the purgative way which leads to the unitive way; so the silent anchorites became public heralds of Christianity, and announced after their fashion the marvels worked by Divine love. Because they possess the love of God, their life is unspeakably happy in spite of its deep seriousness; truly philanthropic in spite of its supreme contempt of the world; influential in the widest circles in spite of its strict retirement; giving indirectly a higher aim to earthly affairs in spite of its complete withdrawal from them; for the heathen gazed with esteem upon these apparitions, the Christians emulated them with veneration, and the whole world had an example before its eyes of the heights to which man can attain when he is not encumbered and chained down by self-love, avarice, and self-will. Like a beautiful rainbow, which seems a bridge betwixt heaven and earth, so were these peaceful lives raised above the discordant and troubled lives of their time. And the more the spirit of the world strove to become the lawgiver and ruler of that age, so much the more did these solitaries cause the chanting of psalms to rise and the spiritual powers to shine forth, which are above all time.

Their patriarch is Paul. When the great bishop St. Cyprian at Carthage, and the holy Archdeacon St. Lawrence at Rome, suffered martyrdom, in the middle of the third century, there lived in Upper Egypt, near Thebes, a young man of the name of Paul. He had received from his parents, who were dead, a good education and considerable property; he understood the Greek language, was well versed in other knowledge, and was, moreover, of a gentle disposition and pure heart, and above all filled with the love of God and with attachment to the Christian faith. The persecution violently raged in Egypt as elsewhere, and tortures were employed that were exquisite and wearying, but not mortal. Mistrustful of his human infirmity, the youth withdrew from the dangerous proximity of the great city, where bad examples were rife, and from the house of his married sister with whom he lived, to a small farm which he possessed close to the boundary between the habitable land and the desert. His sister had the misfortune to be married to a pagan husband, and this man resolved to denounce his brother-in-law to the Roman governor, impelled either by hatred to Christianity, or by the covetous desire of his possessions, or by the delusion of thinking he thereby fulfilled a duty towards the authorities. In vain the unhappy wife endeavoured to dissuade him with prayers and tears; he was inflexible in his resolution. But her sisterly love enabled her to give her brother a secret warning of the impending danger, and he speedily fled from his farm into the desert which stretches away to the Red Sea, vast and wide, and intersected by masses of stone and rocky heights. There he was safe, and he determined to make a virtue of necessity, and to await the end of the persecution in some cavern in the hills. Whilst he was searching for one with pure water in its vicinity, he got farther and farther into the desert, for pure water is somewhat rare in those parts. There are, indeed, small lakes here and there, but their waters are so brackish that they excite thirst rather than allay it, and are, moreover, injurious to health. Paul was not deterred by the futility of his search, but patiently prosecuted it, accepting with resignation the many privations it involved. He came at last to a face of rock with a large cavern at its foot. He entered it, and remarked that the back of the cavern was closed by a great stone. With great exertion he rolled away this stone which lay before an opening through which he passed, and found himself in a tolerably spacious, open place, surrounded by rocks, in the centre of which grew a splendid palm tree, whose branches formed a shady roof. Close by, there bubbled up a spring of water, as clear as crystal, which, however, flowed only a few paces before it was sucked up by the sandy In the hollows of the rocks which surrounded the place, Paul found an anvil, a hammer, graving tools, and other similar utensils. Ancient writers assert that it had been a workshop of coiners of false money in the days of Queen Cleopatra, and deserted some centuries before. The retired and peaceful spot exceedingly pleased this lover of holy solitude. It seemed to him as though God had prepared it for him, and guided him thither. All was collected there which was necessary for human life; clear water, fresh air, a protecting roof for shelter, the pleasant fruit of the date-palm for food, and its leaves for clothing. What more could one in love with holy poverty require? Paul was twenty-three years of age when he took possession of the little oasis.

The storm of persecution subsided when the Emperor Valerian was taken prisoner by the Persians. Everywhere fugitives came back to their homes and families, but Paul returned no more. Long years of unbroken repose passed away, Christianity grew powerful in the Roman empire, and penetrated into the very palace of the emperors, but Paul returned no more. Then the persecution of Diocletian burst forth like a devastating fire, and swept away another generation. Paul was like one dead, and his remembrance was blotted out from amongst mankind. The friends of his youth and his relatives were dead, and the new race knew him not. A new world was formed, Christianity conquered and became dominant, and the whole heathen world fell in ruins; but Paul, unmoved by the overthrow and resurrection of altars, by the ebb and flow of human races, by the wars or peace of kingdoms, by the triumph or the sufferings of the Church militant, lived on under his palmtree as if he belonged already to the Church triumphant; lived ninety years without seeing a single human face or hearing the human voice. But in compensation he saw other visions, and other conversation refreshed his soul; the contemplation of the perfections of God, and intimate intercourse with Him. In proportion as he released himself from temporal things he approached nearer to eternal things, and they so fully satisfied his aspirations, and took such complete possession of the highest powers of his being, that he felt no wants; he wanted nothing, and desired nothing; he lived hidden with Christ in God. What can be wanting to him for whom God is sufficient?

Man is endowed by nature and grace with extraordinary activity; his corporal and spiritual passions are constantly excited. His body must be supported by food and sleep, and if it is indulged it desires to be cherished, it requires enjoyments and comforts, and the more its desires are satisfied the more they increase. The passions of the soul, also, are violently excited by intercourse with others: love and hatred, hope and fear, joy and sorrow, wishes, endeavours, cares, expectations, and disappointments, career wildly through the human heart like the waves of the sea, rising, falling, and rising again, and filling it with a burning desire for some good, the acquisition of which is to bring rest; and as soon as it is attained, fresh restlessness begins. The higher capabilities of the soul, the thirst for knowledge and science, the strong desire for eternal things, cause violent efforts and mental struggles; and man would be utterly perplexed and distracted were he to attempt to satisfy all these wants, and to attend equally to those of the body, the heart, and the mind. He often, therefore, surrenders the attempt, and neglects the higher part of his nature to devote himself to the lower. But no sooner does the body cease to be subject to the soul than man falls straightway into dissipation, for he pursues fleeting earthly atoms, in the place of eternal unity, his true goal.

Paul acted not thus. He reduced his wants to their narrowest limits, being content to neglect all inferior things, and he allowed his body so little that it lost by degrees the power of taking more. The smallest quantity of food and drink, a few dates, and a little water, sufficed him. The roughest clothing, made of palm leaves plaited together, tormented unto death the sensitiveness of his flesh. He defended himself against sleep, in which men pass nearly a third of their lives in unconsciousness, as against a tyrant; and since he was determined not to be drawn away from the loving and admiring contemplation of the everlasting Good, his body was forced to content itself with the least possible measure of sleep. Thus did he put to death the inferior or sensual nature, as he had learned from Christ in the desert. But this is not enough to procure for the soul the full liberty of the life of grace; the intellectual nature which stands midway betwixt the two, in connexion with both, and which draws nourishment from both, must also be overcome, in order to put an end to all the influence which the inferior part exercises over it, by which its best and noblest powers are enfeebled and degraded into passions. The purgative way requires also the asceticism of the heart. All those attachments, affections, and interests, all that need of sympathy, interchange of thought, and excitement, are indeed permitted, but they easily turn the soul from God to men, and through men to the world and its snares. Their nature must be changed, their earthly tendency broken off. The current of feeling must not flow solely round father and mother, round wife and child or friend; but the love of God is to become so powerful that from it, as from the deep source of many streams, there shall spring the love of creatures without preferences and without exceptions. If we are commanded to show more love by word or deed for one than for another, the fulfilment of that command is a duty, and then it is the duty which is chiefly loved, and not the creature. Where the emotions of natural affection and friendship may coincide with the love of God, they are to be closely watched and rigidly separated, in order that the heart may learn to be raised up by the grace of God, and to love nothing but God and all things in Him. Christ loved His most Holy Mother, His Apostles, His enemies, His murderers; poor sinners as well as saints. So Paul loved mankind; he embraced them in God. There was room for all in his heart, because his inferior part had been put to death, and because he had overcome both his sensual and spiritual nature, and casting off the bonds of avarice and self-love, "the lust of the eyes and the lust of the flesh," had crucified the old man. The redeemed man had begun his new life. And yet he might at any time have made shipwreck on the rock of self-will, "the pride of life," if his will, which from childhood upwards had been so pure, had not still further purified itself by self-government in obedience to God. If the hope of working miracles, and thereby shining before men, or the wish to delight in his own excellence and eminence; if, in short, heathen pride had driven him to such self-control, the mirror of his will would not now reflect the amiable and omnipotent will of God, but it would shadow forth the image of the ancient serpent which had led him to this point. But his will was where his love was, with God. He cared not to look into the future to know what was concealed, nor to command the beasts of the wilderness. He wove his garment of palm leaves with the same equanimity as if his life of penance had not invested him with the wonder-working powers of the Redeemer. Sanctifying grace was so strong within him that he never even remarked the immense and persevering sacrifice of the natural man which he practised. A mighty and vivifying power dwells in suffering out of love, for it has its origin and participates in the Divine sufferings, and Christ wrote this new law with His Blood. It was marvellously exemplified in Paul. As he had subdued his sensual nature, he abrogated the laws of nature round about him in the power of his union with God.

But the remembrance of this holy old man was not to disappear out of the recollection of men. He was a hundred and thirteen years old; his end was approaching, and he knew it and rejoiced. About the same time, Antony, another celebrated solitary, had a temptation to pride; it seemed to him that he was the most perfect anchorite in the whole desert. His soul had been ever since his youth the scene of spiritual combats, of struggles between the heavenly hosts and the demons of darkness. If the latter urged him violently to evil, the former gave him counsel and help to withstand. He was now ninety years old, but his strife was not yet over; the demon of pride sought to poison his soul. Then he had a vision in sleep which revealed to him that a patriarch of solitaries lived in the depths of the desert, who was much more perfect than himself, and that he was to go in search of him. Antony arose and set forth to go wherever it should please God to lead him. In the desert where he lived there is neither road nor path, for the track of the caravans does not pass through it, and as far as the eye can reach, nothing is to be seen save blocks of stone emerging out of the sand, and in the sand the footprints of wild beasts. As Antony continued his pilgrimage, infernal delusions rose up before him, and monsters obstructed his path. Accustomed as he had long been to this warfare, he marked his forehead with the sign of the holy cross, and passed on. The monsters disappeared, but the first day had come to an end, and Antony knew not whether he was in the right road or not. The second day passed in like manner in the silence of the scorching desert. The fear of succumbing was far from Antony's thoughts, for his mortified body was accustomed to every kind of privation. But his fear was great lest he should be found unworthy to see that holy solitary, after whose exalted model his heart was inwardly longing. Therefore he watched the whole of the second night in earnest prayer, and as the third day broke, he perceived at last a living creature; a thirsty she-wolf came running from afar and disappeared panting and gasping in a cavern in the hills. After a short time she reappeared and ran away. Therefore Antony concluded that there must be a water-spring in the cavern, and he followed the track of the wolf. But the cave was empty. When his eyes had become accustomed to the darkness of the place he perceived at the farthest end a small crevice through which the light of day was shining, and he drew near to it. But Paul heard footsteps approaching, and instead of opening the door of his territory he closed it more securely with a large stone, in order to try the patience and the humility of the newcomer. Then Antony prostrated himself on the floor of the cave before the closed door, and begged for admittance. "Thou knowest," said he, "who I am, and wherefore I come. I am not worthy to see thy face; but it is my fixed determination not to leave this spot until this happiness is granted to me. Thou dost admit wild beasts, dost receive them with friendship, and give them to drink; wilt thou repulse men?" Thus the holy old man of ninety prayed and entreated from daybreak till the sun stood high in the heavens. Then Paul at last opened the door, and smilingly said: "Do people ask for favours with threats? Thou sayest that thou wilt die here, and dost thou wonder that thou art not admitted?" And the holy old men greeted one another by name, embracing each other like affectionate brothers, and giving each other the kiss of peace; and they sang together psalms of praise to God. Then they both sat down upon a stone, and Paul said to his guest: "Antony, thou seest now before thee the man whom thou hast sought out with so great trouble, and who will shortly be dust and ashes. Was this old worn body and this white hair really worth thy efforts?" But Antony knew what a treasure of holiness was concealed in that infirm body, and rejoiced to have found him out. Then Paul began to ask how the human race was at present constituted—who governed the nations—if there were still any idolaters—if people continued to build new houses in the old cities. And as they thus conversed of things both serious and cheerful, a raven came flying to Paul's feet and gently deposited a loaf of bread. "How good God is!" exclaimed the holy old man. "For sixty years a raven has daily brought me half a loaf. Now that thou art here, my brother Antony, behold Christ has doubled the provision for His two soldiers." And they thanked God with joyful piety, and sat down under the palmtree by the little stream. But it was honourable to break bread, because Christ had done so at the Last Supper, therefore a reverential strife arose between the old men: Paul wished to give the honour to the guest, and Antony to the aged patriarch. And their desire to eat was so slight that evening drew near before they had agreed to break the loaf between them, each one holding it at the same time, and keeping the piece which should remain in his hand. Then they bent over the spring and drank a little water, and immediately betook themselves to prayer, in which they spent the whole night.

The next morning Paul said: " My brother Antony, I have known for long that thou wert living in the desert, and God had promised me that I should see thee before I died. Now the hour of my deliverance is at hand, and He has sent thee to me that thou mayest cover my body with earth. See how good He is." But Antony entreated the holy old man with many tears— " Remain a little longer upon the earth, or take me away with thee." " Thou must not seek what is agreeable to thee," replied Paul. " It would indeed be a happy thing for thee, and I could desire it for thee, to be already allowed to follow the Divine Lamb; but thy life and thy example are still necessary to the brethren, therefore wait patiently. But thou shalt bury me like a dutiful son, and I beg of thee, if thou art not afraid of the labour, to fetch the cloak which the Bishop Athanasius gave to thee, and clothe me in it for my burial." The holy old man was perfectly indifferent as to whether he should be laid in the earth with or without a covering, but he wished to spare Antony the sorrow of seeing him die, and perhaps also to testify that he had persevered, living and dying, in unity of faith with Athanasius, who was at that time persecuted by the Arians. Antony was amazed to find that Paul knew of Athanasius and the cloak; and revering in him the all-penetrating eye of God, he kissed his hands silently and tearfully, and betook himself homewards in order to fulfil the last wish of the holy old man. Antony was himself of a great age, and nearly worn out by fasting and watching, but he hastened with youthful vigour, and without allowing himself any rest, to his mountain of Colzim on the Red Sea. Two of his disciples who had long lived with him, and whose delight it was to render him little services of love, came joyfully to meet him, and exclaimed, " O father, where hast thou been all these days?" Instead of answering, Antony smote his breast, and said, " O miserable sinner that I am, how falsely do I bear the name of anchorite! It belongs not to me. I know it now, for I have found Elias in the desert, and John in the wilderness; I have seen Paul in paradise." Then he hastened into his cell and brought out his cloak. The disciples sought to question him more closely, but Antony said: "There is a time to speak and a time to be silent." And thereupon he returned as expeditiously as he had come, in the hope of finding the holy old man still living. But he had a vision the next morning which showed him that Paul must have left this earth, for he saw the heavens open, and hosts of angels receive his glorified soul. Then Antony fell upon his face, strewed dust upon his head, and exclaimed: "O Paul, wherefore dost thou depart without taking leave of me? I had never bidden thee farewell! Ah! how late have I found thee, and how soon do I lose thee!" Antony performed the remainder of his journey rather flying than walking, and when at last he reached the cave he had the joyful delusion of thinking that Paul still lived, for under the palmtree, and in the spot where he was wont to pray, the holy old man was kneeling. But he was dead, and Antony perceived it when he knelt down beside him and could hear no sound of breathing. Even in death the holy patriarch expressed the chief thought of his life, " Let us adore the Lord to whom all live."

With tearful eyes and tender reverence, Antony enveloped the corpse in the cloak, whilst he recited the psalms and spiritual hymns which were in use at Christian burials. But he was grieved not to find anywhere a spade or other instrument with which to dig a grave. He reflected whether it might perhaps be the will of God that he should pass the remainder of his life in this cavern, or whether he should return to his monastery to fetch the necessary tools. But two lions put an end to his doubts. They came bounding towards him out of the depths of the desert with flowing manes. For a moment Antony was frightened; but he immediately lifted up his heart to God, and calmly awaited them. They did not take any notice of him at all, but sprang towards the corpse, bent down at its feet, wagged their tails, and growled gently. They then began to scrape up the sand with their claws, and to make a long and deep hole. Antony was pleased with the wise animals, which were such accomplished grave-diggers, and which had probably, like the she-wolf, often allayed their thirst at Paul's little stream. The grave was soon ready; and the lions then approached Antony with reverential gestures, bent down their heads to his feet, moved their ears, licked his hands, and behaved like two little dogs caressing their master, and seeking for some acknowledgment from him. He understood that they wished him to bless them, and he broke out into songs of praise, because even the irrational animals acknowledge the omnipotence of God. "My Lord and God," he exclaimed, "without whose will a leaf cannot fall from the tree nor a sparrow from the roof, give to these beasts what thou knowest and wilt." Then he motioned to them with his hand to go away; and when the lions had obeyed, he devoutly took the corpse of the holy Paul in his arms, laid it in the grave, and covered it over with earth. Antony took for his own the solitary legacy of the great anchorite, the fearful penitential garment, which Paul himself had made and always wore, a web of palm-leaves, which are generally used only for baskets and mats. Antony returned with this treasure to his cloister, and related the whole occurrence to his disciples. On the great feasts of the year, Easter and Pentecost, he himself put on this garment of one who had so perfectly practised Christ-like poverty. St Jerome, who describes this life, concludes thus:—"I beg of thee, O my reader, to remember the poor sinner Jerome, who, if God were to give him the choice, would prefer to clothe himself in the mantle of the holy Paul with his merits, rather than in the purple of kings with lands and vassals." As mysticism is the reflection of the Gospel in the lives of the saints, how wonderfully mystical this life must have been, between whose innocent beginning and peaceful end lie ninety years, to be described simply by these words, "And he was in the desert, and he was with beasts, and the angels ministered to him."[1]

ST. ANTONY.

"He went about doing good."—ACTS x. 38.

In the latter half of the third century, during the long interval of repose between the persecutions of Valerian and Diocletian, Christians were at liberty to order their lives according to the teaching of their faith; and many in the East devoted themselves to an ascetic life, which each one led by himself in the solitude of the country, outside the villages or towns containing their homes. They spent their days in holy contemplation, severe penance, and complete mortification, diligent in labour and fervent in prayer, in joyful remembrance of the Lord's promise that he would recompense an hundredfold those who for His sake

[1] Mark i. 13.

should forsake their families or possessions; and that, instead of a dream of happiness and a transitory love, they should receive happiness and love a hundredfold. But it was not yet the custom to withdraw into the remote desert. Paul had done so because it offered him a safe refuge, and he had then become captivated by the attraction of perfect solitude. Antony came into the world in the year of Paul's flight A.D. 251. His rich and noble parents were pious Christians, and lived at Coma, in Upper Egypt. He was brought up under their own eyes with great care, obeying them willingly, seeing no one but themselves and his relations, and he was happy and contented in his father's house. He found no pleasure in the usual pastimes of children, or in dainties and sweetmeats. He never attended the public schools, so he was unlearned in worldly knowledge. A decided impulse urged him towards the contemplative life. He was nowhere happier than in church, never failing to accompany his parents thither, and giving them no trouble by his restlessness, as other children do. He attended to the services with the greatest thoughtfulness and devotion, and listened so carefully to the reading of the Holy Scriptures that he learnt them by heart, and at the same time let their fruits ripen in his youthful mind.

His parents died within a very short time of each other when he was eighteen years old, and left him a double charge, a little sister, and considerable property in land. He managed everything most conscientiously; but his thoughts were bent in a very different direction. Six months might have passed away, when one morning, on the way to church, it struck him that not one of the Apostles hesitated to leave all at the first word of our Blessed Lord, and that later many of the faithful sold their possessions, and laid the value at the Apostles' feet. Immediately after, he heard read in church the story of the rich young man in the Gospel to whom our Blessed Lord promised perfection and a heavenly treasure if he would give what he had to the poor.[1] Then he could resist no longer, for it seemed to him as though this had been written in the Gospel solely for him, and was now read aloud in church for him alone. He sold his estate, which was very beautiful and fruitful, divided the proceeds amongst his poor neighbours, with the exception of a small sum, which he laid by for his sister, and lived for some time very contentedly, because he believed that he had understood and fulfilled the will of God. But God had a higher end in store for him. Another time he heard read in the Gospel the words of our Lord, "Be not solicitous for to-morrow." The joy of perfect freedom from all temporal cares then impressed him so deeply that he immediately sold his furniture, his clothes, and every thing he had, gave the money to the poor, and formed, at the same time, the resolution to dedicate himself to an ascetic life. Of him it might indeed be said, "He that can take, let him take it." There lived at Coma a few holy virgins. Antony gave his sister into their charge, to be brought up in all good ways, and, making over to them his modest fortune, he went to live, according to the custom of other solitaries, in a cave not far from his former estate, in order to think of nothing but the salvation of his poor soul. At a little distance from him lived an aged anchorite, who had adopted this form of life from his earliest youth. Antony begged him to teach him how to comport himself in complete solitude, and the old man willingly consented. To work and to pray without intermission, this was the chief part of his teaching, as it composed the life of Jesus in the carpenter's workshop at Nazareth. Antony therefore plaited coverings out of reeds,

[1] Matt. xix. 21.

and mats and baskets out of palm-leaves and fibres of bark, and sold them. He spent the price of them in alms, and in procuring his very few necessaries. Whilst his hands worked he fixed his thoughts on the contemplation of Divine things, on the eternal truths of the Christian faith, on the Passion and Death of Christ, on the teachings and precepts of the Apostles, on the events and narratives of the Gospels, or on the infinite perfection of God, and His grace and love for men. As Antony had never loaded his memory with worldly knowledge, nor sought other instruction than that of the Holy Scriptures, they had impressed themselves so deeply upon him that he knew them by heart; and therefore his memory and his holy meditations supplied to him the place of books. Every Sunday he repaired to Coma to church, listened with profound attention to the holy lections, refreshed himself at the Holy Sacrifice, and returned invigorated to his little hermitage. This simple and spiritual life implanted in his soul the most happy equanimity and repose. The brilliant prospects of his youth, his rank and birth, possessions or kindred, never occupied his thoughts. All the faculties of his soul were directed towards the end of the way which he now so resolutely trod. With fervent zeal he strove after perfection; and if he heard of any master in asceticism, he sought him out, as a diligent bee gathers together the juices of different flowers, and prepares her honey from them. He submitted himself with childlike humility to the solitaries whom he visited for this purpose, and served them like an obedient son. He admired sincerely in each one his most striking virtue—here cheerfulness of heart, there kindness, there patience—in one, fervour of prayer—in another, severe fasting and watching—in a third, imperturbable peace. And when he had gained for himself all their virtues and graces, he returned to his solitude filled with these noble and admirable images, turning them over in his mind, and endeavouring to practise in himself all that he had seen singly in others. For a pious emulation possessed him; and though he envied no one, he wished to be behind none in virtue. Thus he soon outstripped them all, but all loved him, the old man near him, as well as the solitaries who lived at the greatest distance from him. To some he was a humble and loving son and disciple; to others an affectionate brother; and his perfection was so great that it seemed to turn to the advantage of all the others. The Christian inhabitants of Coma rejoiced to see him in the distance or at church, greeting him with respect, and calling him a favourite, and a true servant of God.

The original enemy of all good, who succeeded in deceiving the first man in Paradise, attempts to deceive every man who strives in earnest to regenerate his fallen nature, and to change a son of Adam into a child of God. He did not approach the Saviour on his way into the desert, but only when he imagined that through His severe penances He might have become proud, and therefore feeble. He proceeded in the same manner with Antony. In the beginning he left him alone, for the first fervour of men in a new position consumes like fire all obstacles, but it is often followed by a certain interior exhaustion, and then if a will armed with faith does not spring into the breach, men easily lose the fruits of their former exertions, and abandon their first love.

The tempter began gradually to lay his snares around Antony, and his indefatigable attacks and the untiring resistance he met with show the heights of virtue to which Antony had raised himself; for the evil spirit need hardly tempt tepid and negligent souls; they give themselves up to him of their own accord, following their evil nature instead of combating it. At first he represented to the holy youth the weariness of this arduous life, and the terrific effort that would be required to walk for perhaps fifty or sixty years along the thorny path of abnegation. Then arose apprehensions for his sister and for his own health, for he was of a delicate bodily constitution; and after that thoughts of the life in the world which would have been within his reach through his rank and riches. A thick darkness seemed to settle down upon the bright region of his holy thoughts, but he defended himself against the powers of darkness by holy prayer and firm confidence in the Passion and Death of our Blessed Lord. Then Satan sent him a whole array of evil and wild temptations, through which he imagined that he would surely subdue him. But Antony armed himself with unconquerable faith in the future judgment and eternal punishment, because it is written, "No unclean hath inheritance in the kingdom of God." By continual prayer he refreshed and increased his faith, and rendered ever present to his memory the value of the soul, which can be bought by nothing short of the Incarnation of Christ, and the exceeding height of holiness to which men are called and enabled to attain by this deed of divine love. By strict fasts and painful vigils he made his body participate in these spiritual combats, and put to shame all the efforts of the evil one. The ancient serpent, who imagined himself equal to God, was brought to confusion by the delicate youth; and despite of his power over flesh and blood, was vanquished by a man of flesh and blood, because the Incarnate Saviour strove in him, as the Apostle St Paul says in the first Epistle to the Corinthians, "Yet not I, but the grace of God with me." At length the enemy acknowledged that Antony always repelled him from his thoughts and kept unpolluted the purity of his soul, so he appeared to him in the form of an ugly negro boy, and said, " I have been overcome by thee, and yet have deceived and overthrown so many." " Who art thou?" asked Antony. " I am called the spirit of impurity," was the answer. " Then I will no longer fear thee," said Antony, " for I see by thy colour and thy form how abominable and how feeble thou art. The Lord is my helper, and I despise my enemies." And continuing to sing psalms he praised and thanked God, and the evil one disappeared. This was Antony's first great victory, or rather the victory of Him who hath condemned sin in the flesh, and hath commanded us "to walk not according to the flesh, but according to the Spirit."[1] Antony was not, on this account, allured to a false repose. He knew the cunning of the enemy, and that he never lost an opportunity of discovering and profiting by a weak moment, and what unremitting watchfulness is required to oppose him. He only became the more determined to tread indefatigably the narrow way which leads to heaven, and to bring his body thoroughly into subjection, as the Apostle St. Paul had done, lest conquering on one side he should be subdued on the other. He undertook a still more severe form of life than hitherto, and the habit of suffering made him feel pain no longer hard. At times he watched the whole night through in prayer. He generally ate every day a little bread and salt with some water after sunset. But sometimes he took no food for two, three, and even four days. His couch was a mat of rushes, often the bare earth, and his clothing a penitential hairshirt, for he knew that the closer the wings of sensuality are clipped the more easily can the soul take her flight. He said, " When I am weak, then am I powerful."[2] With the Apostle St. Paul, who had gone through all

---

[1] Rom. viii. 4.   [2] 1 Cor. xii. 10.

G

these struggles for the consolation of his followers in the faith and in suffering, he never dreamt of reckoning the value of the ascetic life according to the time of its duration or by its outward penances; but he prized it according to the amount of the love and the interior efforts to serve God. He therefore considered himself always as a young beginner, because every day he began anew to love God, and daily incited himself to fresh desires, looking constantly forward and never backward. Always to be such as we should appear before God —pure of heart and ready to obey Him in all things, and Him alone: this was the object of his endeavours and of his daily warfare.

The great prophet Elias was his model, and he therefore sought a more complete solitude, at a greater distance from Coma. He found a cavern formerly used for burial, which exactly suited him. He begged one of the anchorites to bring him bread and water on certain days, and shut himself joyfully up in his sepulchre. Here he had to undergo fearful assaults of the enemy, who maltreated and tortured him so violently that he lost speech and consciousness from the pain and exhaustion. These bodily vexations often occur in the lives of the saints, and chiefly in those who are the most gifted with extraordinary graces, and favoured with visions and revelations. It is as if these wrestlers for heaven were to experience also the full power of hell. One day the brother came into the sepulchre with bread and a jug of water, and, to his sorrow, found Antony lying apparently lifeless on the ground. He lifted him carefully on to his shoulders, and, with many tears, carried him to his former abode, and called together his friends and relations. The neighbours assembled in sympathy, for all had heartily loved Antony. They spent the evening mourning and weeping by the supposed corpse;

but as it grew late, some went away, others grew drowsy one by one, and the anchorite alone kept watch. At midnight Antony came to himself, and sitting up, found himself, to his astonishment, in the midst of all the sleepers, who lay around in profound repose; he beckoned to the anchorite to come to him, and begged him to wake no one, but to help him to return to his peaceful sepulchre. This he did. Faint with the effort and with his wounds, Antony remained in his solitude after the faithful brother had left him, without help, without nursing, without succour, and falling to the ground from exhaustion he offered up a fervent prayer, and then exclaimed with a loud voice, " Behold, O ye enemies of God, here is your enemy Antony again! I shrink not from fighting with you; lay hold of me constantly with all your power; for I know that nothing can separate me from the love of God which is in Christ Jesus our Lord." And then he began to sing the 26th Psalm, " Ii armies in camp should stand together against me, my heart shall not fear."

This holy and undaunted courage in demanding new combats in such a state of weakness, frailty, and suffering, brought upon this second Job a furious assault from his enemy. The devils assailed him in crowds under the form of wild beasts, in order to inspire him with fear of death, and so to drive him out of his solitude. But Antony bore all these terrors with calmness; and keeping himself by humility firm in his confidence in God, he combated his adversaries with fortitude. " Has the Lord God given you power over me?" he said; " well then, here I am, tear me to pieces; but if you have not this power from Him, how dare you undertake maliciously to terrify me?" And he made the sign of the holy cross, which was his resource in all dangers and anxieties, because the cross has effaced them all.

Then the enemy vanished, and a heavenly light filled the sepulchre, and flooded Antony's body and soul with a stream of unutterably sweet consolation. All his wounds were healed, all his weakness had disappeared, and not a trace was left of the misery of the natural man. This light amid the thorns of his sufferings was like that fire in the thornbush, the veil behind which God concealed Himself, and Antony sighed out from the depths of his heart, "O my Saviour, where hast Thou been hitherto? Wherefore camest Thou not sooner to my assistance?" and a Divine voice spake out of the light, "I was always with thee, I have ever watched thy strife, but I awaited the issue of the battle. Because thou hast not given way, I will henceforward always help thee to conquer." Stronger than ever, and clothed as it were in holy armour, Antony raised himself up and looked upon that promise as a summons to advance more resolutely than before, and to give himself up more unconditionally than he had hitherto done to the guidance of God.

St. Jerome says: "O blissful solitude and seclusion, thou art the true Arabia Felix upon earth, for in thee are formed the precious stones of virtue, of true life, and of the evangelical counsels, with which the heavenly Jerusalem will be built, the city of the great King Jesus Christ. Solitude, silence, prayer, and a penitential life are, as it were, the four elements which make a man of good heart and will, holy and blessed." This Antony also believed, and his deeds were not at variance with his faith, but as he believed, so he lived. One day he visited the aged hermit in the neighbourhood of Coma, and telling him that he intended to withdraw entirely into the desert in order to offer himself up more perfectly and uninterruptedly to God, he proposed to him to do the same. But the aged anchorite objected that this was not customary amongst the ascetics, and that, without a special vocation, no one should venture on such a novelty. Antony, however, recognised this vocation in himself, and taking a friendly leave of the pious old man, he departed alone to the Thebaid desert, and to the Arabian hills on the Red Sea. On this journey he had once more temptations to overcome. He was now a man in the full vigour of life, five and thirty years old, of great virtue, of lofty mind, fervently loving God, and firmly resolved to climb even to the topmost step the ladder of perfection. Such a man has a great future before him if he perseveres. But what sacrifices were involved in this perseverance! What battles were to be fought! Who knows whether on the way to this new Calvary, the image of the world with the noble and beautiful things which it contains amongst its dross and rubbish, did not once more rise up before his mind and seek to infatuate him with its captivating delusions? It is certain that he twice actually found treasures of great value in his path with which he could have betaken himself to the world. The first time he threw away the Satanic deception, the second time he passed over all the gold as quickly as if he had been treading upon live coals, and so reached the mountain. On a solitary height he found a ruined watch-tower which seemed to him sufficiently inaccessible to choose it for his dwelling. There were indeed many serpents and scorpions living in it, but they retired before Antony, as if they acknowledged his authority, and he immediately built up the entrance with stones. He was now established in his impregnable castle. There he remained imprisoned for twenty years without letting any one enter. He had arranged that one of his hermit companions should bring him every six months the small quantity of bread that he needed. The bread which is eaten even now in those parts keeps very long without spoiling; but it becomes as hard as stone, so that it has to be broken with a hammer. This was his only nourishment, and he caused it to be thrown in to him over the wall; never even speaking a single word to him who brought it. But whilst Antony so entirely forgot the world, the world did not forget him. He fled from it and it sought him out. First came his friends in order to convince themselves that he was able to endure such severe penance, and that he was not pining with want and sickness. They heard him in the peaceful night singing psalms and holy hymns, which comforted them exceedingly, although he would not allow them to enter his castle or to speak to him, and they had to pass the night outside. But sometimes things were less peaceable inside, and sounds of wrangling and threatening voices were heard, so that those outside thought that robbers or murderers had got in to him by means of ladders. But if they peered through the crevices in the ruined walls they saw no one but Antony; and as the noisy tumult still continued, they were terrified, and called out despairingly and mournfully to Antony for help as if some evil were going to happen to them. Then he approached the entrance, and consoling and quieting them, begged them to go home and to have no more fears for him. "It is only the faint-hearted who fear the devil," he said, "therefore it is in them alone that he can inspire fear. Sign yourselves with the sign of the cross, and go in peace." Thus his spiritual combat continued without intermission, and ever gave him occasion for new victories and higher peace in God, so that he led not only the ordinary double life of the spiritual and material man, but a double life in his spirit, in which the highest powers of his soul, his pure will, and his pure love, rested recollectedly upon God as it were upon an inaccessible rock, and were not disturbed by the battle in the valley which the lower spiritual powers, the memory, understanding, and imagination, had to engage in.

The descriptions which his friends gave of the extraordinary events which were taking place could not fail to attract great attention, and to cause curiosity in some, and sympathy or affectionate confidence in others. The idea gained ground amongst all, that a man so wonderfully endowed could not but have a purpose to fulfil in his time. Increasing numbers crossed the desert with the hope of seeing him, hearing him, or speaking to him. But Antony remained unseen and unheard. Even the noise of the spirits round about him seemed gradually to have died away. The stillness of the desert or of the grave surrounded his castle. But when his visitors were seized with the painful apprehension of his being dead, he began to sing psalms in a clear and pleasant voice, "The Lord is my helper, I will look down upon my enemies;" or, "Let God arise, and let His enemies be scattered;" or else a song of triumph and of heroic faith such as sometimes emerged from the sea of tribulation and bitterness which encompassed the royal psalmist.

Twenty years passed away in this complete abnegation of all earthly things, during which the Holy Ghost himself fashioned this "preacher in the desert," to be such as his age required, and as the Church was in need of. The stormy fermentation of the time was working in all souls, and all did not understand how to tame and regulate the powerful elements. Men came forth from darkness of mind into the full light of the truth; and if the great minds gazed with peaceful eye upon the divine ray, others, the arrogant and the inquisitive, were blinded instead of being enlightened. Mental excitement universally reigned; and, as often happens at the beginning of new and great epochs, a powerful impulse lent to the feeble and the indifferent a certain elevation above ordinary things. Weak characters formed themselves upon the example of the stronger ones, without possessing their strength—became imitators instead of followers—became shallow where others grew deep and firm. All these things were very apparent in the favourite attraction of the day, the ascetic life, and gave it a bright side and a dark side. Many of the ascetics possessed indeed the dispositions necessary for this life, but yet only embraced it exteriorly, laying all the value upon privations and mortifications, and continual repetitions of prayers, whilst they neglected their souls. Others placed perfection in singularity, and thought themselves better than others, because they had chosen this vocation, without caring how they fulfilled it. Some only wished to be unlike other men, and became repulsive instead of sublime, rough instead of simple, fatiguing themselves with privations, in which they reached surprising heights, and yet remained inwardly in bondage, because their soul did not ascend with them. Then gloomy dejection or obstinate pride took possession of them, and they ended sometimes by falling away, not only from their vocation, but even from virtue and from the faith. To others, solitude became the first step towards thoughtlessness and indolence both of mind and body. Many had the right dispositions, but they had not the straightforwardness and power of a Paul, an Antony, and other great ascetics, and therefore they were in need of guidance which would give them a decided training and a certain aim, so as to prevent them from drying up and withering away. And they themselves felt the want of it. They longed for a model, for a master. It was as if they divined the important place they were to occupy in the future history of the world, and in the development of the human mind. In order that the monastic life should unfold itself into a perfect blossom, a perfect monk must first live, who should represent in himself, at least in outline, an ideal for this state, whose agency was to be felt throughout the world.

It was for this the Holy Ghost had moulded Antony. For this He had impressed the Holy Scriptures so deeply on his memory, that they were now become as it were his own interior. For this Antony had had to unlearn the language of men, that he might speak as if with a fiery tongue. For this he had imbibed so much from the Divine Spirit and from heavenly mysteries, that he was filled to overflowing with unusual graces, and able to become the centre of a new and influential sphere of life. For this he had to die to nature in order to enter as one fully reconciled to God into the mysterious realm of grace. For this end, faith, a divine virtue, the most persevering and sublime act of the purest will, had prepared the ground upon which the gifts of wisdom, counsel, and knowledge shone in all their brightness.

The desert had now a well-known road through it, made by the numbers of people who flocked to Antony and sought for consolation or instruction from him. Notwithstanding his humility, which made him in his own eyes the least and the most unworthy of all, he believed at length that he ought not to refuse them this spiritual alms. The renown of his discernment, his power, and his virtue, spread far and wide, and grew so great, that people began to bring the sick, the crippled, and the possessed to him, that he might heal them. At the same time, the numbers of those who asked to become his disciples in the spiritual life increased also; and some ascetics who were his friends urged him to leave his solitude on account of these manifold needs of others. Antony, without hesitation, acknowledged this also to be the will of God, and returned amongst men as though he came from heaven. The twenty years of stern mortification had passed over his exterior without leaving a trace behind them; his face had kept its old sweetness, his figure its former beauty. He appeared neither weakened by repose nor consumed by austerity. He had not grown morose in his tower, for he had not lived like an unwilling slave in outward fetters, but he had given himself up voluntarily to the captivity of the gentle and sweet yoke of Jesus. An amiable sweetness was expressed in his features, his words, and his gestures; but he was never moved by cheerfulness to open laughter, nor did too deep a sorrow for the sins of the world ever cloud his brow. His spirit was so pure, so entirely released from every distracting thought, that nothing could disturb his peace. The praise and admiration of men made him neither proud nor bashful—it did not affect him in any way. And as the hidden life of Jesus was reflected in Paul, so was his public life in Antony, which may be again expressed in these few words of the Evangelist St Luke, "He went about doing good." Like two monuments of the exceeding love with which our Blessed Lord fulfils His promises when men obey the inspiration of the Holy Ghost, these two holy men stand as it were at the gates of the monastic life of all ages, and point to the one thing on which rest the power, the efficiency, the greatness, and the beauty of this life: the imitation of Jesus, or suffering out of love.

It shone forth in Antony with exceeding grandeur. The graces of the Death on the Cross, and the glory of the-resurrection in Christ, immersed his whole life and works in the power of the Incarnate God, who conferred upon him the "perfect gifts which are from above, coming down from the Father of lights," that he might "walk as a child of light," and exercise a child's rights after he had fulfilled the duties of a child. So long as the kingdom of heaven suffered violence, Antony had bravely borne his part therein,—that part of which it is written, "To every one that hath, shall be given." And now there was given to him the absolute power which follows from perfect obedience, the exaltation consequent upon voluntary humiliations, and the glorification which is the reward of perfect self-denial, according to the immutable fundamental law of the order of grace. The Divine Father of this regenerate soul had been liberal in His gifts to him; and as He Himself had lived amongst miracles—which, however, were no miracles to Him, the Author of life and the Creator of nature, but only the overflow of His divine power—so the miracles which Antony worked blossomed, as it were, of their own accord around him, because Divine power went out from him in whom the image of God had been restored. The lame walked, the blind saw, the sick were healed, the possessed were delivered, the mourners comforted, the wavering were strengthened, and the infidels believed. Many of his audience became his disciples, and left the world, renouncing their possessions and their joys; and the desert began thenceforward to bloom with lilies, according to the prophecy of Isaias. With overflowing love, Antony exhorted all men to prize the love of God beyond the best joys of earth, because God has promised us the unutterable bliss of eternal life, and has purchased it for us through "His own Son, whom he hath not spared, but delivered him up for us all."[1] An indescribable contempt for earthly things was enkindled in all hearts by his words, and still more by his example; and to the anchorites, in particular, he became the pillar of fire, which showed them the way of their vocation through the darkness of the night in the

[1] Rom. viii. 32.

desert. They collected around him once in great numbers, and begged that he would give them a clear rule of life which they could observe amid the dangers and temptations of their state. He spoke thus:

"The Holy Scriptures contain, indeed, sufficient instructions, but still it is well for us to strengthen one another in the faith, and to learn by communication with each other. Do you, my children, say to your father what you know of good, and I, your elder, will impart my experiences to you. Endeavour, above all, not to fall back from what you have begun, nor to sink under your burden. The first precept for each one must be, to keep his progress as constantly in mind as if he had only just begun. That he may not grow weary of this, let him ever compare the shortness of this earthly life with eternity. How wonderful is the immeasurable liberality of God! Here on earth things are sold according to their value, and exchanged for their equivalents. But we procure the promise of eternal life for very little; for if we live as ascetics for a hundred years, we take possession of a glorious place in the kingdom of God, not for a hundred years, but for eternity; and for this transitory earth we receive heavenly bliss,—for a perishable body a glorified one. O my children, for mortal things we inherit immortal ones. The sufferings of this world are not to be compared to the glory which shall be revealed in us. Therefore, when you embrace the ascetic life, never rate highly what you have forsaken; never believe that by such choice you have done anything great. If the whole world were yours, and you renounced it, it would still be less in comparison to the heaven you receive than if for one penny you gained a hundred pieces of gold. What is a little gold, some cultivated ground, or a miserable house? You could not any way take them with you to heaven; and a Christian should set value on those goods alone which he can never lose,—on intrepid faith, on love, knowledge, justice, mercifulness to the poor, meekness, and hospitality. If we do this, we prepare for ourselves a dwelling in heaven, as the Evangelist says. In this endeavour the Lord Himself is our helper. The slave never says, I worked yesterday, therefore I need not work to-day. Neither must we imagine that because of the work which is past, God will excuse us from the present work. Ah, no! He would be wroth with our slothfulness. In order that we may not become slothful, let us be mindful of the words of St. Paul, 'I die daily.' If we live as though we died daily, we shall never sin. We shall be angry with no one; we shall forgive all men, and shall never have an impure thought. Therefore look onwards, my children; look upward, and not backward, like Lot's wife, who died in the act of doing so.

"Our Blessed Lord Himself says, 'No man putting his hand to the plough and looking back, is fit for the kingdom of God.'[1] Such looking back implies nothing less than a falling away from your vocation.

"Secondly, I beg of you, my brethren, not to imagine virtue to be something impossible or fearful,—not something very distant which must be fetched from afar; oh, no! it lies within us. Its germ is implanted in the human mind, and awaits our good will to expand. The Greeks travel over land and sea to seek for knowledge and wisdom. We need not do that in order to find a holy disposition and the kingdom of God; for our Blessed Lord says, 'Lo, the kingdom of God is within you.'[2] Who can doubt that purity of soul, if it does not soil itself with the stains of sin, is the fountain and source of virtue? Virtue lives in the spiritual life, and dies in the sensual life, in

[1] St. Luke ix. 62.   [2] St. Luke xvii. 21.

which the soul turns herself away from God, and follows her own lusts. Virtue and vice do not come to us from without, but from a pure or impure heart. May the Creator, therefore, find His work as He formed it in the beginning; and let us not, my brethren, lay waste what God in His munificence made so beautiful.

"Thirdly, my brethren, let us constantly remember that we must, according to the testimony of the Apostle St. Paul, 'put on the armour of God, that we may be able to stand against the deceits of the devil. For our wrestling is not against flesh and blood; but against principalities and powers, against the rulers of the world of this darkness, against the spirits of wickedness in the high places.'[1] Even Satan and his angels were created by God good and not evil. But of their free will they revolted; they chose rebellion, and were precipitated from heaven. Then the merciful God destined for men the heavenly thrones which they had sinfully lost, and therefore they foster feelings of raging envy and hatred against us men, and lay many snares for us. They deceived our first parents in paradise, and they practise their cunning upon all the children of Adam. The heathen worship of idols is their work, for they find therein assistance in their endeavours to make men lose heaven. They spoke out of the mouth of the idols, and answered by the oracles; and the heathen living in the blindness of an unredeemed state, and in the sinful lusts of their heart, gave credit to them, and were subject to them. But now, since the glorious coming of the Lord, their idols and oracles grow more and more dumb, and the Lord has delivered us from them, for He said: 'Begone, Satan, for it is written, The Lord thy God shalt thou adore, and Him only shalt thou serve.'

[1] Ephes. vi. 11, 12.

Since Christ has crushed their power, we need no longer fear them. We have indeed good weapons against them in the faith and a pious life. For this reason the devils fear indeed all pious Christians, but most of all the ascetics, with their fasts and vigils, their prayers and their confidence in Christ, their humility and meekness, their elevation above vainglory and cupidity. The evil spirits know that Christ said to His own: 'Behold I have given you power to tread upon serpents and scorpions, and upon all the power of the enemy, and nothing shall hurt you.'[1] But it was not in vain that our Blessed Lord immediately added: 'Yet rejoice not in this, that spirits are subject unto you; but rejoice in this, that your names are written in heaven.' For this is an artifice of Satan; he strives to make us proud, by showing us hidden things, in order that we may boast either to ourselves or to others of the gifts of prophecy and knowledge, as if they were fruits of our own holiness. Therein lies a great danger, for in consequence of the sin of Adam men are easily incited to curiosity and pride. Even supposing that the father of lies could speak and foretell the truth, what would it profit us to know future things a few days earlier? No one of us will be judged because he did not know such things, nor will any be saved for having known them. We enter into the glory of heaven by the fulfilment of the divine commandments, and by the transgression of them we fall into eternal punishment. No one must undertake the ascetic life for the purpose of acquiring the gifts of prophecy or of miracles, but with the intention of becoming the friend of God by a holy life, and of obtaining the victory over Satan, with the Lord for his helper. But if any one earnestly desires a foreknowledge of future things, let him exert

[1] St. Luke x. 19.

himself to acquire a pure heart and a pure mind. I firmly believe that if a devout man remains in perfect innocence he will become very far-seeing and profound. Such a soul lays itself open before God, and He reveals Himself to it. Such was the spirit of Eliseus in ancient times, who possessed to so great a degree the gifts of prophecy and miracles. If the devils come to you with predictions, believe them not, for they lie. If they come and extol you with praises of your austere life, if they call you blessed, if they exhort you to increase your penances under the mask of holiness, if they even attempt to pray with you or to sing psalms, listen not to them, close your ears and eyes, your heart and soul, make the sign of the cross, and pray; pra perseveringly, trustfully, and peacefully, and they will take flight. Then you will see that they were no good spirits. Learn the discernment of spirits; it is not difficult. If angels approach you, their presence makes itself known to you by the quiet rest and peace you feel in yourself. If for a moment, through human weakness, you fear, yet at the same time confidence, joy, and delight will arise; for the Lord God is with them, the Author and Source of all joy. The heart becomes thereby completely plunged in contentment, and at the same time filled with supernatural light; but the soul, inflamed with the desire of heavenly goods, longs to burst the bonds of the flesh, and to hasten with the angels to the mansions of the blessed. The presence of evil spirits, on the contrary, announces itself to the soul by dejection and anguish, whilst the thoughts fall into disorder and confusion. Negligence, sadness, fear of death, dislike of the other ascetics, a perverse yearning for relations and friends, make their appearance, and with them evil desires, disesteem of virtue, and a weakening of holy resolutions. If you have been frightened by one of these apparitions, and it goes away, and in its place there comes unspeakable joy, courage, cheerfulness, renewal of spirit, safety of thoughts, love of God, then trust, pray, and be thankful, for help is come from above; the joy and firmness of soul betoken the vicinity of an angel.

"Neither must you, my brethren, take any pains to work miracles. If any one amongst you can cast out devils, or if he possesses the power of healing the sick, he must not pride himself upon it, nor must you admire him for it, or despise him who has not the power. On the other hand, you must all endeavour to lead a holy life, strive after perfection, and seek to gain that which you are still in want of. To work miracles is not our office, but God's—the work of His Divine Omnipotence, which He sometimes causes us to carry out. Therefore our Blessed Lord said to those who glorified themselves before Him for their miracles, but who were not filled with good dispositions: 'I know you not.' The Lord acknowledges not the ways of the unholy.

"I share my experience with you, my brothers, and therefore—not on my own account, God knows —I speak of myself. The devils have often praised and commended me, and tempted me in every way. I answered them: 'Nothing shall separate me from the love of Christ.'[1] Therefore it was not I that restrained them, but God. 'I saw Satan like lightning fall from heaven.'[2] I referred this to myself, my children. Learn to be courageous in your ascetic life. Listen! Once Satan came to me and complained that all Christians, and the ascetics in particular, abhorred him. I said, 'Wherefore dost thou disquiet them?' He answered, 'I do not plague them, they torment themselves; therefore they ought to be masters of themselves, and not to curse me.' I replied, 'Thou art a liar from

[1] Rom. viii. 35.   [2] St. Luke x. 18.

the beginning; but now for the **first time thou hast** spoken the truth. Christ **has enchained** thee.' I uttered the name of Christ with great faith, and Satan disappeared. You see, therefore, that you never need be afraid. Only be not sad, but always rejoice that you are of the redeemed. Think always the Lord is with us, what power can our enemies have? They come and take precisely the form of our spiritual life at that moment, they are the reflection of our thoughts. Art thou of an earthly disposition? then thou art their prey; that is the punishment of unholy souls. But if thou dost rejoice in the Lord, and dost meditate on eternal things, and occupy thyself with divine things, they can do nothing."

Thus spoke Antony, to the great consolation of the anchorites, and of those who wished to become such. They admired the grace which was given to him in the discernment of spirits; and one awakened out of a false delusion, and another burned with renewed love of his vocation; a third became clear as to whether he should become an ascetic or not; a fourth found himself armed against temptation. Each one felt his imperfections remedied, and his wants relieved. Thus Antony became their support, and the guide and centre of their spiritual life. The mountains and hills became peopled as with heavenly choirs, who, singing, praying, and teaching, took heed only to eternity, maintained concord and love amongst themselves, and laboured diligently in order that they might be charitable. Each one lived in his cell, which was almost always a cavern or a tomb. None disturbed or were burdensome to the others, and none perpetrated or suffered injustice. It was like an independent country of religion, entirely separated from the world. The cells lay dispersed here and there, and formed rather a village of cells than a monastic building. This sort of community was called a laura. **The first began at Pispir near the Red Sea, and soon after it a second on the Nile at Arsinoe.** Antony governed both. By living under one common guidance and government, they avoided the danger which is pointed out in these words of Holy Scripture: "Woe to him that standeth alone; when he falls there is no one to help him up." In this way the unformed life of the ascetics was gathered together into a more decided shape, and Antony was looked upon as the founder of the monastic life. In the midst of a barren land, there sprang forth the highest spiritual beauty, and it might be truly said, "How beautiful are thy tabernacles, O Jacob! and thy tents, O Israel! as woody valleys, as watered gardens near the rivers, as tabernacles which the Lord hath pitched, as cedars by the water-side."[1] Antony did not forget his own soul whilst thus directing the souls of others. He generally remained alone in his cell, and diligently plaited reed mats, an occupation which did not prevent him from praying interiorly. His whole soul was inflamed with a most ardent desire for heaven, and he was often heard to sigh with inexpressible longings, and at the same time with sorrow that his body still required food and sleep. He seldom ate with the brethren, and even if he sat down with them, it often happened that he became immersed in contemplation, and forgot to eat. He nevertheless constantly advised the brethren not to maltreat their bodies so much as to make them unable to work, which was contrary to the will of God, but at the same time to be careful that the body did not overcome the soul, but that the soul should keep complete mastery over the body, and should lift it up with her, as the Apostle St Paul says, even to the third heaven.

When Maximin Daia's persecution of the Chris-

[1] Num. xxiv. 5, 6.

tians was raging fearfully in Egypt, (from 305 till 313,) Antony said to his brothers: "Come to Alexandria; let us be present at the victory of the martyrs; perhaps we shall be crowned also, or it may be permitted us to accompany them to death." A martyr in will, he hastened with some of the brethren to Alexandria, and kept by the side of the holy confessors everywhere, in the courts of justice, in prison, and at the place of execution; but the destroying angel passed him over. The magistrates only issued an order, that no monk or anchorite was to show himself in the streets. All hid themselves or fled, with the exception of Antony. In white festal apparel he appeared the next day on an elevated place, while the confessors were being brought before the judge, and encouraged them. No harm came to him in consequence; at the end of the persecution he returned to the desert, and to his daily martyrdom of faith and suffering. His vigils grew even longer, his fasts more strict, his prayers more fervent, his desire to mortify himself more and more violent. He put on over his hair shirt another garment of rough skins, doubly painful in that hot climate,—but what was really painful to him was the concourse of people coming to him as to a worker of miracles. He feared the pride that might arise out of the great esteem in which men held him. They came from afar in their spiritual and bodily afflictions; no distance was too great, and no journey inconvenient; they complained of no trouble, and were deterred by no danger; sea and desert were no obstacles when it was a question of seeing Antony. And yet sometimes he would not admit them to his presence. But he helped them, nevertheless, by that wonderful power which God had given him, because he had given himself to God. A general in the army of the name of Martinian, came to him, found his cell closed, and most humbly craved admittance, because he wanted help for his daughter, who was possessed by the devil. Antony replied without opening the door, "Wherefore dost thou come to me for aid? I am an infirm mortal man like thyself. But if thou dost believe in Jesus Christ, the Lord whom I also serve, call upon God with faith and confidence, and thy daughter will recover." Martinian departed consoled, and his daughter was cured.

A man from Palestine, called Fronto, who had also been tormented by evil spirits, sought Antony out, and begged his prayers. Antony acceded directly to his wishes, and then said to Fronto "Now go, thou shalt be healed." The man would not believe it, and insisted on remaining longer with Antony; but he said to him, " Thou wilt not be healed here; but when thou settest foot on thy native land, the mercy of God shall attend thy steps." At length Fronto resolved to have confidence and to return home, and Antony's promise was fulfilled to the letter.

An inconsolable father and mother, whose daughter was fearfully afflicted with strange and painful illnesses, undertook the difficult and tedious journey from Tripoli in North-west Africa. But when they came to Egypt and heard how troublesome the journey was through the desert, and how Antony sometimes refused people admittance, they grew fearful, and begged some monks who were on the point of setting out to go to him and to intercede for them. They would await the result with the holy anchorite Paphnutius, who, in Maximin's persecution, had had both his eyes torn out for the faith. The monks departed and came to Antony. But before they could acquit themselves of their commission, he related to them all the circumstances, and added, "I have seen them in prayer, and the sick child has received, also in prayer, the assurance of her recovery.

Therefore, neither they nor any one else should come to me; for I cannot cure any one; God alone can do this, and He certainly will, in all places, if only He is rightly asked to do so."

Antony longed so earnestly for solitude with God, that he contemplated taking refuge in the Upper Thebaid. Whilst he was revolving these thoughts in his mind, a voice from above said to him, "Whither goest thou, Antony? What drives thee hence?" He knew which voices he should listen to, and which he should reject, and he answered, "I am going to fly into the Upper Thebaid, because things are here required from me which are too high for me." "Go not thither," said the voice; "thou shalt find rest in the farthest desert." "How shall I find it?" asked Antony. The voice was silent. But immediately after he met some wandering Arabs, (Bedouins,) who sometimes travelled about for reasons of commerce between their oases in the depths of the Egyptian desert. He asked their leave to go with them into the desert, which they willingly granted. He journeyed with them for three days and nights, and came to a spot which pleased him much. It was a cliff some thousand feet high, out of which a spring bubbled up and flowed away in a little rivulet. Though it was small, some beautiful palm trees grew on its margin. In the rock there was a cavern just long enough for a man to lie down to sleep in it. A hidden entrance led into a narrow, dark cleft, which opened again into two small caverns on the top of the mountain of Colzim, (now the mountain of St. Antony,) one day's journey from the Red Sea. Antony remained here, and made it a paradise of solitude.

The Bedouins gave him some bread, the palm-trees afforded dates, and the little stream pure water. Thus he had all he wished. The brethren no sooner remarked his disappearance than they spread themselves abroad in every direction to seek for information of him, and soon to their joy they discovered his place of abode. They wanted to take him back again to the lauras, but he said that the voice and the hand of God had led him hither. If they wished it, he would sometimes visit all the monks and the anchorites, and they might also frequently come to him, but this was the place of his repose.

They begged to be allowed to provide him every now and then with bread. He did not wish to impose this burden upon them, and asked them instead to bring him some grain, with a spade and a hatchet, and then he would provide for his own maintenance. This they did. And then Antony began to carry that out in practice, which his spiritual children, the monks of later centuries, have left behind them as an immortal monument, and for which they deserve the gratitude of men of all ages and dispositions. The holy old man with his own hands made the wilderness fruitful. He increased the number of palms by the side of the stream; he conducted the water through various little canals towards places which seemed to him favourable for laying out a corn-field and a small garden, which he planted gradually with vegetables, a few fruit trees, and one or two vines, not for himself, nor for his brothers or disciples, but for the sick and the needy who visited him. He did not succeed in all this without great exertions and trouble; but he was indefatigable, and fortified himself at his work by singing psalms. When he was quite tired out he sat down under a palmtree, and constantly praying in his heart, plaited baskets out of the fibres and leaves of the palms, which he gave to his disciples when they brought him olives and oil at intervals in order to strengthen his gradually failing body.

At first the wild beasts did his little plantations

a great deal of harm, especially wild asses. They were accustomed to drink out of the stream, and they came and fed upon his young corn and vegetables. Then he once gently took hold of one of these animals, and said, "Why do you eat what you have not sown? and why do you injure one who never did you any harm? go, in the name of God, and return no more." From that time they never troubled him again. The temptations of Satan, however, always continued, and the tried warrior of Christ could not lay aside for a single moment those spiritual weapons which he had recommended to his brethren. In this constant strife his soul underwent such purification that it attained to the prerogative of the souls of the blessed, and rose to the knowledge and discernment of all things in God. He saw things in their inward relation to one another, the consequences of things in their original cause—all time like a constant present—all space in its centre.

Once he rose hastily from prayer and said to two disciples who were near him, "Take a bottle of water, my sons, and go quickly in the direction of Egypt, for I have seen one of our brethren there in great danger of dying of thirst. Another is lying already a corpse upon the sand. Hasten!" The astonished disciples immediately set out, but had to take an entire day's journey before they found the dying brother and the corpse. Another time he sat in an assembly of several monks on the summit of his mountain, and conversed with them on eternal things. As he lifted up his eyes to heaven he saw a company of angels descend, and receive a soul which, departing from earth, rose to meet them. Antony contemplated this happy vision as if he were already glorified; and as to the glorified it is one and the same thing to see and to understand, he knew what this apparition signified, and after a short pause he said to his expectant hearers, " Our brother Ammon of Nitria has just departed this life and entered into eternal joys." Nitria was in Lower Egypt, near Lake Mareotis, at least thirteen days' journey from Colzim; and a very numerous community of monks was established there, amongst whom Ammon was greatly distinguished, particularly by his wonderful miracles, which caused him to be celebrated in all Egypt as a holy instrument of God. After a long time a message arrived from Nitria which showed that Antony had seen the precise day and hour of Ammon's death.

About the year 340, Antony had a vision of a less consoling nature. He sat buried in contemplation, sighed often and deeply, got up trembling from his work, threw himself on his knees, and remained very long in prayer. When he rose at length, the brothers in alarm begged him to tell them what had troubled him so sorely. Tears flowed from his eyes, and he mournfully said: " O my children, what have I seen! The anger of the Lord is poured out over the Church! She is falling into the power of men who resemble unreasoning beasts. I saw the holy altar surrounded by asses, who kicked against it, and overthrew the tabernacle, with what it contained; and a voice said, ' My altar will be desecrated.' " But then the loving old man comforted the desponding brethren again, and told them that God's wrath would abate, and the Church would shine forth with renewed splendour; only they must beware of the heresy of the Arians. Two years had not elapsed since this vision, before God's Church in Alexandria was visited with the stormy and cruel persecution of the Arians.

God gave him also other revelations for the good of souls. The brethren once asked him how it would fare with the soul of man when separated from the body? In the following night a voice awakened him and said, "Arise, Antony, go forth and behold." He obeyed; and issuing from his cell, he saw a giant standing upon the earth, whose head reached up to the sky. He also saw winged forms who were trying to rise from the earth above the clouds; but the strong arm of the giant sought to hold them all down. He succeeded with some, and dashed them to the ground, but not with others, who flew upwards. The giant and the fallen ones then gnashed their teeth, but the others rejoiced. The voice said, "Antony, bear this in mind." And he understood that Satan can only hinder those souls from ascending to heaven whom he has already here below made to fall, and that he cannot harm holy souls. These visions inflamed him more and more with perfect love, and he imparted them to the brethren in order to enkindle it in them, and give them a desire of suffering and mortification, with courage and perseverance in their strife. For his own part he received them as he did his temptations, resigned in God, without either wishing for them, or rejoicing in them, well knowing how dangerous the unusual ways of the spiritual life are to the pride of sinful nature. With regard to priests, he never forgot that through their holy ordination they belonged to a different order of graces from him, a simple layman. Although he had received the unction of the Holy Ghost to an extraordinary degree, and was, as a Christian, both priest and king, yet it never entered into his mind so to explain those words of the apostle St. Peter about the "kingly priesthood" as if he possessed now in the world the power and distinction of a king, or in the Church the absolute power of a priest. A Christian is, indeed, said to be a king; but it is in the kingdom of eternity, where a throne and a crown await him. He is truly called a priest, a sacrificer; but it is in a spiritual sense, because he daily immolates himself, and has no thoughts but for holy things. The "kingly priesthood" of each Christian consists in striving, with a sanctified soul, after the highest things. Antony's respect for priests never diminished. He received with humility the blessing of the bishops. If ecclesiastics visited him, or if he found himself in their company, he begged them to say the usual prayers, instead of doing it himself. He gave to young deacons the advice which they asked him for, but he sought to learn something useful from them in return, and rejoiced in it.

Meanwhile the monks gave Antony no rest; they would have him come down from his mountain and visit their lauras. He went to Pispir, to Arsinoe, and also to the anchorites who did not live in lauras, but in solitary cells, and came to the boundary of the inhabited country, near his old home. There he had the pleasure of seeing his sister again, who was already aged, and who had always remained in a state of virginity. She was now superioress of a society of virgins, who led an ascetic life in community, and formed the first convent of nuns. The concourse of people which flocked to Antony was indescribable. He healed them, exhorted them, comforted, converted, instructed, and prayed with them. And whilst he thus "went about doing good," and lovingly spread salvation and blessing around him, he was longing for his peaceful mountain in the desert, and thirsted as ardently for his wilderness as those whose hearts are set upon temporal things thirst after the world. Like one escaped from a great danger, he hastened joyfully back to his solitude as soon as his presence was no longer imperatively necessary. A distinguished person was once completely captivated by Antony's winning and salutary discourse, and begged him to give him a little more opportunity of edifying himself therewith. But Antony replied: "Indeed I cannot do it. As the fish belongs to the water, and dies on dry land, so the monk belongs to his cell. By remaining too long in the air of the world, he is in danger of spiritual death, because his resolutions and his efforts easily relax under its influence."

The Emperor Constantine heard of this great servant of God, and sent a letter to him in the desert from his golden Byzantium, with a humble request for good advice and prayers. His sons, Constans and Constantius, did the same. Antony was neither flattered nor surprised at these marks of imperial favour, and was unwilling to answer the letters, because, he said, he did not know how to write according to the forms of the world. But the brethren advised him to do so, for fear his neglect should offend the Emperor. "Then I will do it," said Antony. "But do not wonder or rejoice that the kings of this world should write to me; they are only sinful mortal men like ourselves. We should rather wonder and rejoice that God Himself should have written His holy law for us through His only-begotten Son." Then he answered the letters in the way that beseemed a holy and humble solitary, who has nothing at heart but the honour of God and the salvation of the souls of both kings and peoples.

His renown penetrated into the lecture-rooms of the heathen philosophers, as it had done into the palace of the Emperor. Two of them repaired to the mountain of Colzim. When Antony perceived the newcomers, he saw in spirit who they were. He therefore immediately asked them through the interpreter who accompanied them, "Wherefore do you wise men undertake a troublesome journey to an old fool such as I?" They answered that he was no fool, but a wise man. Then he replied: "It would not be worth the trouble to come to a fool. But if you believe that I possess wisdom, you should take pains to acknowledge it, and to follow my instructions. If I had come to you with such a belief, I should have followed your doctrines. Therefore, as you have come to me as to a Christian philosopher, do you become what I am, a Catholic Christian." The philosophers wondered at this simple and wise logic, and returned to their philosophical schools and systems. And other philosophers came again to him who thought him not wise, but extremely narrow-minded, because he could neither read nor write. They asked him a few questions, with great contempt for his ignorance. Antony answered: "Tell me, I beg of you, which is the oldest, understanding or letters? Did intellect invent letters, or did letters invent intellect?" As they answered that intellect had invented letters, Antony said, "Very well; therefore whoever possesses understanding has no need of letters." This answer pleased them very much; for he had such a refined way of expressing himself, and was, at the same time, so kind and cheerful, that no one could be angry with him, but all loved him. Nevertheless the philosophy of the heathen world did not yet consider itself conquered. Some of the most learned and experienced men in art and science travelled, as it were, to the end of the world, to enlighten this simpleton in the wilderness, and to prove to him the "folly of the Cross." He conversed more fully and seriously with these, reviewed with them their idolatrous doctrine, showed them its absurdity and revolting immorality; and then, having set before them the Christian doctrines, he said, "Either you believe what our Holy Scriptures say, or you do not. If you do not believe, you may not revile the Cross, for you do not acknowledge it at all. But if you believe, why do you stay beside the Cross, instead of proceeding to the Resurrection, to the Ascension? The very same Scripture bears witness to the shame of the Crucified, and the glory of the Risen Son of God. Read it with simplicity, and you will see that all that Christ has done and worked proves Him to be God, dwelling amongst us for the salvation of men." The philosophers discoursed at great length, and vainly beat the air with their sophisms. Then Antony smilingly answered, "You boast of the proofs which you produce, and require that we also should not honour God without proofs. Tell me, therefore, how is the true knowledge of all things, and, above all, the knowledge of God, attained? Is it a knowledge through demonstration, or a knowledge springing immediately from the power of faith? Which is the most ancient, knowledge through reason, or knowledge through faith?" The philosophers replied: "Knowledge through faith is the most ancient." "You have rightly answered," said Antony; "for faith arises from the direct application of the soul to divine things; and dialectics are only the science of making inferences about divine things by reflection and abstraction. He who possesses the strength of faith has no need of this art: it might even be superfluous to him; for we recognise by faith what you seek to arrive at by arguments, and you cannot even conceive what we acknowledge. Therefore knowledge through faith is surer and more sublime than your sophistical conclusions. Consequently our holiness rests not upon such wisdom, but upon the virtue of faith which is given to us by Jesus Christ from God. It follows from this that our doctrine is true: behold, without knowledge we believe in God, and recognise His Almighty Providence in His works.

"By this you may see how strong we are who lean by faith upon Christ, and how weak you are with your wordy and sophistical disputes, that you gain no one over to you from Christianity, and that you do not check the progress of the religion of Christ. Where are your oracles? Where are the Egyptian sorceries? Where the juggling of the magicians? When did all that cease? With the appearance of the Cross of Christ. Is not that wonderful? Your religion was never persecuted, but was quietly transmitted by inheritance; ours was persecuted, and yet flourishes more abundantly and fruitfully than yours. When was death ever so despised as on the coming of the Cross of Christ? When did the virtue of virginity manifest itself thus? Look at the martyrs who, for Christ's sake, despise death; behold the virgins of the Church, who, for Christ's sake, preserve themselves pure and unspotted in body and soul: they are an answer to you; they have arisen out of the power of the Cross of Christ. Your boasted fabric sinks to ruin, but the faith of Christ, which you despise and the emperors persecute, fills all the earth.

"Let this be enough to convince you that the Christian faith is the only true religion. For see! you have no faith, and are always seeking how to prove this or that. Believe, therefore, and then you will learn that it is not sophistry, but faith working through love, which is needed. If you only have faith and love, you will no longer seek for proofs, but you will consider faith in Christ sufficient by itself."

There were some persons then near Antony whom he was to deliver from their painful state. These were the possessed. This state, which is often mentioned in Scripture, was frequently seen in the first Christian centuries. The powers of darkness intrenched themselves in many forms and ways to maintain their supremacy and to resist grace. Redemption made the regenerated man not only figuratively a child of God, but actually a living temple of the Holy Ghost, in which, according to our Lord's promise, "He Himself and the Father made their abode," and transformed him again into the image of God. In opposition to this kingdom of light, of salvation, and of holiness, the ancient serpent sought to maintain his kingdom, and to set up his throne in the unredeemed sinful creature. And as by grace man is raised to the likeness of God, so without it he sinks to a resemblance of the evil spirit who abides in him. Possession took various forms, sometimes driving its victims into the condition of inferior animals, or into a perverted state of mind; sometimes appearing as mysterious and frightful bodily disorders, or as nameless pains and despondencies of soul. These afflictions, although unspeakably great for those subject to them, were still only an impotent revolt of the serpent against his Destroyer; they were ejections of his poison against the Heel that was crushing his head. Like other saints, the favourites of God, Antony received from Him the power of delivering the possessed from the evil spirit which tormented them, by the sign of the Cross, from which all graces flow, and by the Most Holy Name of Jesus, "in which every knee bows in heaven, on earth, and under the earth." He exercised this power precisely at the time when the wise ones of this world were seeking to convince him of their superior knowledge. But they were overcome, and confessed that they thought it an honour to have seen and spoken with this wonderful old man.

It very seldom happened that any one slighted Antony's warnings or admonitions. Emperors and governors, warriors and magistrates, bishops and priests, gentle and simple, ecclesiastics and laymen, all honoured him. The Arians alone despised him, as was natural, for they despised Christ. Arius the heresiarch taught that the Son was not of one substance with the Father, but only His first creature. The immediate consequence of this doctrine was the denial of the Holy Ghost; for the Holy Ghost proceeds, as the Catholic Church teaches, from the Father and the Son. Therefore Arius denied the chief mystery of the Christian faith—the dogma of the Holy Trinity,—and had thus ceased to be a Christian. But it is frequently the case with heretics, that although they are no Christians, and have nothing in common with Christianity, they add falsehood to apostasy, and assert that they are Christians—that they retain the essentials, and reject only what is not essential. Thus did Arius also. If he had plainly announced his doctrine in its forlorn nakedness, all men would have fled from such a skeleton. But he aimed at entrapping the shortsighted and the thoughtless: and he succeeded by asserting that the Son of God, although not equal to the Father, and only His creature, was nevertheless God. By this assertion he was not only heretical, not only unchristian, but he taught direct polytheism and idolatry, by adjudging divine honour and worship to a creature as well as to God. The passions of men made the faith a convenient mask; intrigues and factions, worldly dispositions and indiscretion, also sought under this head, as they always and everywhere do seek, the satisfaction of their own selfish ends; and thus Arianism became a scourge which, during two centuries, inflicted bloody wounds on the Church of God. Resistance to it occupied the whole life of St. Athanasius the Great, who was obliged to quit his patriarchal throne at Alexandria because the Arian bishop Gregory, powerfully protected and supported by the whole faction of the heathens and Jews of Alexandria, had obtained possession of the see of the Evangelist St. Mark. Athanasius, one of the greatest and most elevated minds, not only of his own, but of any age in the world's history, was an intimate friend, admirer, and disciple of Antony, and, princely as he was, wrote the life of this poor, ignorant, basket-making solitary, because he recognised in him a faithful imitator of Jesus. And Antony being really such, it was to be expected that the Arians should despise him, for no fellowship can exist between Christ and Belial. Holy and unholy souls, such as an Athanasius and an Arius, cannot have one and the same object for their reverence and their love.

A new kind of persecution of the Christians then reigned in Alexandria. Hardly thirty years had elapsed since the one carried on by Maximin Daia, before the wolf made a fresh incursion into the fold. This time it was in sheep's clothing and therefore one of those which our Blessed Lord had warningly predicted. Arianism was waging war against the Church. The Arian governor Philagrius joyfully received Bishop Gregory, whom an Arian synod at Alexandria had imposed upon the Egyptian Catholics as their patriarch, to their great surprise and sorrow. They turned away with horror from the intruder, and refused to surrender their churches to him and his followers. Then Philagrius excited, by the hope of booty, the Jewish and Pagan populace, which was very numerous in the great commercial city, to destroy and plunder the churches. In the year 341, in Holy Week, Christ was covered with shame and nailed to the cross in His people. Fierce and rapacious hordes, armed with swords and clubs, forced their way into the church of St. Quirinus, and fell upon the faithful, killing some, wounding others, carrying off many to prison, and giving themselves up to every kind of excess. They trampled under foot some monks who had come from the desert for the festival of Easter. They tore off the veils of virgins consecrated to God, and scourged them to blood. Women were beaten, and priests were maltreated and struck with rods, to induce them to deny Christ. The Sacred Hosts were scattered about, and birds and fir cones were offered up to idols on the altar of the Holy Sacrifice, whilst heathen hymns alternated with blasphemies of Christ. Pagans and Jews stepped into the baptismal font and perpetrated abominations, and, after burning the Holy Scriptures, they plundered the altar, and all the wine, oil, and candles they could find, and, lastly, tore down the rails and the doors. All this was permitted by Gregory; yea, on Good Friday, the outrages were renewed under his very eyes, and with his approval. For, as he entered a church with Philagrius, and the faithful shunned him with loathing, instead of asking for his episcopal blessing, he caused thirty-four persons to be arrested on the spot, publicly beaten with rods, and put in chains. Amongst them was a virgin who was reciting the Psalter, and who, during this shameful ill-usage, never laid down her book, nor lifted her eyes from it. Even on Easter Day many Catholics were thrown into prison, and Philagrius, the governor, punished the loud complaints of the faithful as if they were the perpetrators of crime, and treated them with outrageous cruelty if they demanded justice before his tribunal. In this manner Gregory took possession of all the churches in Alexandria, and the Catholics were obliged, in order to avoid holding communion with the Arians, to renounce all public worship, without having the consolation of being able to assemble silently in the houses as in times of heathen persecution. For Gregory's eager spies continually crept about, and instantly gave Philagrius information of such assemblies, which were then violently dispersed, and punished with imprisonment. Even the priests who took the Last Sacraments to the sick were watched, and, if possible, deterred from it.

After the Church in Alexandria had been suppressed, Gregory and Philagrius made a journey through the entire patriarchate with the same object, taking with them a worthy associate, Balacius, the commander-in-chief of the army. Bishops who had grown gray in their holy offices and cares were deposed, and condemned to mean public works. Bishop Potamon, the venerable old man, the holy confessor, whose eye had been torn out by the tortures of the heathen persecution, was beaten so heavily, that he died of his wounds. Anchorites and monks, priests and laymen, women and virgins, were arrested, scourged with rods, and then admonished to enter into ecclesiastical communion with the Arians.

Antony had very often begged the governors and judges to be gentle and merciful in their offices, to release prisoners, and not to deal too harshly with debtors; and as it was now a question of those who were perfectly innocent and defenceless, he wrote many times beseechingly to Gregory, but in vain. He wrote also to Balacius, who had caused virgins and hermits to be stripped and scourged. "I see the anger of God approaching," he said to him. "It is already nigh; in order that the eternal destruction which threatens thee may not overtake thee, desist from persecuting the Christians." Balacius laughed, threw the letter to the ground and spat upon it, reviled the messenger, and ordered him to say to Antony: "As thou art an anchorite, and dost interest thyself in them, I will punish thee also." A few days later, Balacius rode out with the governor, and was suddenly bitten in the leg by his horse so severely, that he died of the wound.

About this time Antony was tempted to think

that no one had ever yet been so faithful and perfect a servant of God as he. It is related in the life of St. Paul how Antony was enlightened upon this point, and came to Paul, and with what love these two holy patriarchs, who had been so unusually and lovingly guided by God Himself, greeted each other, to separate again directly after upon earth. Antony returned to his beloved mountain, and lived for thirteen years more, full of graces and blessings. He interested himself so deeply in all the suffering and the oppressed that it seemed as though he himself bore their sorrows. He was like a physician for the whole of Egypt. Every one repaired to the mountain of Colzim, as to a healing spring. All passions, pains, and miseries lost their sting near Antony; those who came in affliction, departed in joy; the disheartened poor came, and he taught them to despise riches; the sorrowful came, weeping for their dead, and he dried their tears; the angry came with hate and enmity in their hearts, and he pacified them; monks came with lukewarm souls and failing energy, and he raised them up, and strengthened them in renewed good resolutions; young men came flying from the seductions of the world, and he inspired them with contempt for it; maidens came, for whom the bridal wreath and marriage feast was already prepared; they saw Antony, and earthly love being extinguished by heavenly love, they prepared their souls for the marriage feast of the Lamb; the afflicted came, who were tormented by sickness or misery, by temptations or devils, by evil or sorrowful thoughts, by the thousands of interior and exterior calamities of which this earthly life is so full, and Antony could always give counsel, and procure relief. By means of his gift of discernment of spirits, he could narrowly observe the inward thoughts of each one, his ruling passion, his inclinations, and the motives that had brought him thither. He administered his consolations and his remedies accordingly, and none could deceive or mislead him. He attained to a very great age, and the approach of his death was revealed to him by God. He once more left his beloved mountain cheerfully and expeditiously, and appeared in the lauras, going through them all, examining and arranging everything; but the joy of the monks at his visit was changed into sorrow when he announced to them, with inexpressible serenity of soul, that he had come to them for the last time. "I do not think, my dear children," he said, "that I shall ever see you again in this world, for I am one hundred and five years old, and my human nature is inclining towards its end; grieve not, for I am journeying with great joy from a strange land unto my home; but constantly remember that you are to die daily, and that you must keep yourselves pure from all stains, in order to rejoice likewise over your return home to your heavenly country. The only means of keeping yourselves in this purity is firm faith in our Lord Jesus Christ, in the doctrines of the holy Catholic Church, and in the traditions of the fathers as you have received them from holy writings, and from my exhortations. Keep yourselves entirely apart from heretics, and the heterodox; flee from them whatever they may be called, whether it be Arians or Meletians, or any other name, for they are not in the truth nor in love. Be not confounded, nor fear if you see the powerful ones of this world, the princes and potentates take the false religion under their protection; theirs is only a human and earthly protection, and it will perish together with the falsehood it seeks to sustain."

The brethren broke forth in tears and lamentations, because he would no longer remain in the midst of them, and grant them the consolation of his presence and instructions to the last But solitude with God had been the persevering attraction of his life, and this supernatural desire led him back again to his mountain, around whose base a little paradise had grown up, created by his own industrious and blessed hands. The old custom was still in use at that time in Egypt of drying the corpses into mummies, and preserving them unburied in sepulchral chambers, or even sometimes in houses for many years. Antony abhorred this custom, which may so easily give rise to unholy practices. He had often spoken zealously against it, and he feared that the monks, out of a corrupt affection, might deny his body its rest in the grave, which has been sanctified by the Holy Body of Jesus. He therefore took a fatherly leave of them, and returned to his cell.

It was the custom that one or two young monks should live near those who were very old, partly to serve them in their illnesses and infirmity, and partly to benefit by their example and their teaching. Therefore, for the last fifteen years, two disciples had lived near Antony, and he had guided them in the spiritual life with great affection. Their names were Pelusian and Isaac, and the latter, being well versed in foreign tongues, was his interpreter. He summoned them to himself a few months later, when sickness came upon him, and made them his executors. He wished to be buried by them in a place which should be known to them alone, and to no one besides; "for I trust in God," he said, "that at the general resurrection my body will rise again, even without having been embalmed." To St. Athanasius he left one of his sheepskin garments, and the other to the Bishop Serapion, who was a brave confessor of the faith and defender of the Church; and his hair shirt he left to his two disciples. Then he said: "My little children, I am now going the way of my fathers—God calls me. I see that it is so. Never lose the fruit of your labours, be abstemious, persevering, courageous; the everlasting tabernacles await you; save your souls, O my children! Antony departs, and is no more with you." The disciples kissed him; lovingly and serenely he looked upon them once more, laid himself down, smiled, and died as he had lived, happy in Him in Whom he had believed.

Such was the end of this mighty one in the kingdom of God. During his long life, he was never ill, he never lost the vigour of his body, his upright posture, his active walk, the brightness of his eyes, or any of his teeth. Athanasius the Great wrote his life, in order to give to all monks an example of the perfection of their state, and at the same time to show them in what this perfection consists. In the preface, he says, "It has been a great advantage to me to think of St. Antony, for the mere knowledge of how he lived is a good guide to virtue." One example out of a thousand will show how right Athanasius was.

Thirty years after the death of Antony, who died in 356, three young men sat in a pleasant house encompassed by a garden at Milan. One was a celebrated teacher of rhetoric, another a professor of jurisprudence, and the third, who belonged to the imperial court, and was called Pontitian, was a Christian. The two others were only catechumens, and were by no means firm in the Christian faith. Pontitian had read the life of Antony, and was speaking to his friends about the renowned Egyptian anchorite, and about the monastic life which had been formed by him and around him; and they were amazed, for these things were new to them. Pontitian said moreover, "When I was at Trèves with the imperial court, two young men of my acquaintance went one day to walk in the gardens outside the town, and found in a simple and retired country house some men who were living a poor and retired life after the fashion of the Egyptian monks. They entered into conversation with them, went into their house, and found there the history of the life of St. Antony. One of the young men opening it read aloud some of it to his companion, and they were so taken with it, that they sat down and did not rise again till they had read the manuscript entirely through. But they arose renewed in spirit, and firmly resolved to forsake their possessions, their position in the court, their worldly prospects and their brides, and to join themselves to the poor in spirit who have the promise of the kingdom of heaven. Another friend and I had gone out with them; but having taken another path, we only began to seek them when the day was declining, and we found them at last in the little house with the good men, and proposed to them to return with us to the emperor's palace. But they imparted to us their intention to serve God alone without reserve, and, moreover, to begin from that hour and in that spot to do so, and they invited us to embrace the same purpose. We wished them success, and recommended ourselves to their prayers; but not feeling this sublime vocation in our souls, we returned to the palace with hearts bowed down to earth, whilst those two whose hearts were raised towards heaven remained in the poor little cottage with the servants of God. The noble maidens to whom they were betrothed no sooner heard of these things than they also dedicated themselves to God."

Thus Pontitian spoke, and then left the two men who had listened to him with the greatest attention. He was hardly gone when one of them exclaimed: "What is this? what have we heard? The simple rise up and bear heaven away with violence, and we, the learned, the wise, the educated, we fainthearted dastards wallow in flesh and blood!" He hurried into the garden, threw himself on the grass under a figtree, sighing and sobbing, and wept from the unutterable torture of his mind. The suffering of his soul which longed for God, whilst his passions chained it to the earth, flooded him with tears. "O Lord! O Lord! how long!" was his cry. "Shall I then always say tomorrow, tomorrow without fail? Why not today, why not now break with this earthly misery?" In this unspeakable oppression of heart it occurred to him that Antony had received as if God Himself had spoken them directly to him, the words: "Sell all whatever thou hast, and give to the poor, and thou shalt have treasure in heaven, and come follow me." And he arose, took up the book of St. Paul's epistles, opened it, and read in silence, "Put ye on the Lord Jesus Christ."[1] The night passed away, the day broke; he was saved, and converted to God on the spot, and his friend Alypius with him. And this convert was St. Augustine. He himself relates it in the Eighth Book of his Confessions, by which he in his turn has drawn thousands of souls to God, as Antony had drawn his. Antony, Athanasius, Augustine! What greatness, what genius, what sanctity and beauty of soul, what acuteness of mind and largeness of heart, what cherubic knowledge and seraphic love do these three names represent! What made them so great? Solely their mother, the Holy Catholic Church, who gave them the supernatural life of love, the love of suffering. With this love Antony prays, Athanasius combats, Augustine teaches, and the glory which rests on their brows is none other than the reflected light of the Holy Ghost who lives in the Church for evermore.

[1] Rom. xiii. 14.

ST. HILARION.

"Thou art mine."—Isaias xliii. 1.

As there were children amongst the martyrs, so there were also found children who embraced the martyrdom of the soul with supernatural love, and like thousands of others renounced the world for Christ's sake.

Amongst those who, thirsting for salvation, sought Antony in the desert, there once appeared a remarkably delicate and beautiful boy of fourteen called Hilarion. His home was in Palestine where it borders on the Lesser Arabian desert and the Isthmus of Suez. He was born in a place called Thabatha, near Gaza, the ancient city of the Philistines, and he was like a rose amongst thorns, for his parents were pagans. They were rich, and wished to do all in their power to give their son a good education, and develop his brilliant talents. The schools of Alexandria had a wide reputation; there they sent Hilarion very young to the house of a tutor, and he learned with zeal under his superintendence. But the spirit of heathenism, both in religion and in the world, was so repulsive to him that he never indulged childish curiosity by going to see the games in the amphitheatre. When and how grace led him to the Christian faith is known to God alone. The fruit of this grace was that he abandoned grammar and rhetoric, Plato and Aristotle, as soon as ever he heard of Antony, whose name at that time was renowned throughout Egypt. Hilarion penetrated through the desert to Antony, and immediately became his disciple and scholar. He laid aside worldly clothing, assumed the rough sack-like tunic and the scapular of sheepskin, and lived like the other anchorites. He also kept his eyes fixed on Antony, and observed how humbly he received every one, how lovingly he instructed the brethren, how austere a life he led, without ever deviating from his fasts, his vigils, and his prayers. These things pleased the holy youth extremely; but he disliked the constant influx of people who came to Antony with their many cares and necessities. He said to himself: "I did not leave the town to find again all this crowd in the desert. It may be very well for our Father Antony, for he has fought his fight, and receives in reward the grace to help others in fighting theirs. But I have to begin, and I must begin in the same way that he did."

With this determination he left the desert, after two months, beloved by Antony, and admired by all the anchorites, and returned to his own country. His parents had died. He divided the inheritance they had left him between his brothers and sisters, and the poor; and completely denuded of every earthly possession, he sought out such a place of abode for himself as should become one who had renounced all, to be the disciple of Christ. This extreme poverty was his joy. The seaport and commercial town of Majuma lay a few miles from Gaza, and from thence a long marshy district of the coast reached as far as Egypt, a d the mouth of the arm of the Nile forming the delta, beyond Pelusium. This is a swampy desert where there is no living thing save flies and gnats, and nothing thrives but reeds and rushes; and which is, it possible, still more desolate and dreary than the sandy desert which bounds it on the south. This was the place of Hilarion's choice. His relations and friends in Thabatha and Gaza warned him that this wilderness was at times very unsafe, on account of sundry robbers and murderers who roved about in the neighbourhood of Majuma in search of booty, and who plundered merchants and travellers, and then escaped into the desert, where no one dared to follow them. Hilarion's answer was, that he feared not murderers, but only everlasting death. Every one shuddered at this project, in one so young and so delicate in frame, and wondered at his fervour of heart, which, arising from his ardent faith, shone forth from his eyes, and cast a marvellous splendour over his countenance. But he put on a rough cloak, such as the peasants of that country wore, over his hair-shirt and scapular, took with him a slender provision of dried figs, and proceeded into the depths of the inhospitable desert, where he had the sea in front of him, and behind him an interminable morass. For protection against the storms from the sea, which were sometimes accompanied by torrents of rain, he built a kind of hut out of the clods of earth of the swamp, which he roofed with reeds, and plaiting a mat of rushes to cover the damp ground, he took possession of this hovel as though it were the antechamber of heaven. He was then fifteen years old. He began his warfare against the natural man with incredible valour. Fifteen dried figs daily, which he never ate till after sunset, were his only food; and as he was mindful of the apostolic saying, "If any man will not work, neither let him eat," he endeavoured to make a portion of the swampy land productive, that he might grow a few vegetables. Besides which, like the Egyptian anchorites, he plaited baskets, not out of palm leaves, which were not to be had, but out of rushes, whose brittleness made it an exceedingly troublesome work. He sought to keep his soul constantly united to God by prayer and contemplation of divine mysteries and heavenly things, and thereby to sanctify all his actions. The natural man is so inclined towards earthly things by reason of the fall, that it seeks everywhere to assert its claim to them. Hilarion experienced this also. Thoughts entered into his soul, and images appeared before his eyes, in which although he knew nothing of the world and its pleasures, he recognised temptations to evil, because they sought to disturb his joy in God, by promising him false joys. Then the holy youth was angry with himself, and smote his breast contemptuously, because it contained a heart of flesh and blood which dared to stir in opposition to the heavenly desires of his soul. In order to strengthen the energy of his soul, and to crush his inferior nature, he commenced a terrific fast. He ate a few figs, and drank a bitter juice which he pressed out of the grass of the marsh, only every third day, or even every fourth. Yet he never intermitted any of his laborious work, and he redoubled his vigils and prayers. His delicate body was wasted to a mere skeleton, but his spirit grew strong and overcame every infernal deceit. As soon as he had so accustomed himself to any bodily mortification, that through the pliability of human nature it had become a habit to him, he immediately invented some new torture. He lived in the way described above till his twentieth year; he then left his damp hut, collected stones with great exertions, and built therewith a sort of cell or cavern. It was indeed long enough for him to lie down at full length in it, but only four feet wide, and five feet high. It was impossible to stand upright in it, and it resembled a grave more than a cell. His nourishment consisted at this time of a few lentils, which he soaked in cold water. Afterwards he took bread with salt and water, then he lived for three years on raw roots and wild herbs, after which he returned to six ounces of barley-bread daily.

At the age of sixty-four, he made a fresh beginning with incredible zeal in the service of God, and in austerity towards himself; and abstained from bread to eat only cabbage mixed with some meal. Of this he never ate more than five ounces a day, and upon that he attained his eightieth year.

Hilarion's solitude was once invaded by robbers. These wicked men well knew that nothing was to be found there, but they came for the pleasure of frightening this poor hermit. But they wandered about in his neighbourhood the whole night, although they were very familiar with it, and did not find him till broad daylight, when he was quietly sitting in his poor cell, plaiting baskets and praying. "What would you do if murderers surprised you?" they asked him. "So poor a man as I am fears them not," replied Hilarion. "But they might kill you out of vexation at finding nothing." "They certainly might, but still I should not fear them, for I am quite ready to die." Such holy peace in this complete poverty and abandonment made so deep an impression upon these quarrelsome, bad men, that they felt remorse, and promised him to amend their lives.

Otherwise Hilarion was little disturbed in his solitude, although it was known in the whole of Palestine what an unearthly life he was leading, and how completely he was immersed in prayer. He knew the whole of the sacred Scriptures by heart; and when he had finished his daily psalms and hymns, he was accustomed to recite them slowly and devoutly as in the presence of God. Thus twenty-two years passed away, which were occupied in nothing but the longing for God. Single solitaries, or those who wished to become such, sought him out now and then, brought him his scanty necessaries of life, and received in return the baskets which he wove with such great trouble; but it pleased God to keep him during this length of time completely hidden. After this he received one day an unexpected visit. A woman of Eleutheropolis, in Palestine, came to him with the firm confidence that such a mortified soul must be more intimately united to God than other men, and could therefore pray more efficiently. Hilarion was not in the habit of receiving such visits in his desert, and was also determined not to have any concern with them; but the woman fell upon her knees, and cried out with a mournful voice, "Fly not, O father, and forgive my temerity! Regard only my necessity, and not my sex, although this sex brought forth the Saviour. I am in need of thy intercession." Then Hilarion kindly asked what her desire was, and she told him that her husband's heart was turned away from her, because their marriage of fifteen years' standing had not been blessed by children, so that she had a double grief; and she entreated Hilarion to assist her, and bestow upon her a spiritual alms. He comforted her, and encouraged her to trust rather to God, who has ordained the time and the hour for all things, than to the prayers of a poor solitary. The gift of consolation is a grace of holy souls; the woman returned, strengthened and rejoicing, to her native city, and gratefully praised Hilarion's intercession when her wish was afterwards fulfilled, and God gave her a son. At the same time, a still more afflicted woman had recourse in the deepest grief to Hilarion. This was Aristeneta, the wife of Elipius, the governor of Palestine, who had made a journey to Egypt with him and with her three sons solely to visit St. Antony. On their journey home, the three boys sickened at Gaza of such a dangerous fever that their recovery was hopeless, notwithstanding the exertions of the physicians and the most careful nursing of their parents. Aristeneta herself went about like a dying person between the deathbeds of her children. Then her maid-servants told her of the holy anchorite who led such a saintly life in the desert by the sea, that God took great delight in his prayers. Aristeneta arose and, with the permission of her husband, went to Hilarion, accompanied by a few retainers. She cried to him, even from afar off, "I beg of thee, for the love of Jesus Christ, to come to Gaza and restore my sons to life." Hilarion excused himself, and said that he went very seldom, and only from the greatest necessity, even into a quiet village; and that he never would enter a town, still less a large heathen city like that, full of idols and idolatrous temples. Aristeneta threw herself at his feet, and implored him, saying, "Thou shouldst come all the more, and glorify the name of Jesus, and put the idols to shame by saving my children." Hilarion still continually refused, because his humility shunned all ostentation; but Aristeneta remained on her knees, repeating only these words, "By the Holy Blood of Jesus, save my children!" and she wept so bitterly that her followers burst into tears. Hilarion, overcome by compassion, promised her at length to be in Gaza at sunset. He kept his word, and came, and prayed by the dying boys, who were immediately cured. They recognised their delighted parents, praised God, kissed Hilarion's hands with gratitude, and asked, in childish fashion, for something to eat. This sign that the power of God abode in his prayers spread Hilarion's name abroad in the world, and his hermitage became a place of pilgrimage. Heathens came, and returned believing; believers came, and returned no more to the world.

Up to that time there had been neither monasteries nor monks in Syria and Palestine. Hilarion became their founder, and, at the same time, a master of the spiritual life for all those, rich and poor, men and women, who thronged to him in crowds. The disposition in which he received them is beautifully described in a few words by St. Jerome, who wrote his life: "Our Lord Jesus had the aged **Antony in Egypt,** and in Palestine **Hilarion."** When the sick and suffering came to Antony, he was accustomed to say, " Why do you not go to my son Hilarion? He knows better how to help you than I do." The deserts and mountains of the Holy Land, of Lebanon and Anti-Lebanon, Mesopotamia, and Persia, became peopled by degrees with lovers of the ascetic life, with fervent penitents, with anchorites, some of whom lived in complete retirement, others in lauras in community, and who also afterwards were united together in enclosed dwellings called cloisters. Hilarion was their spiritual father. He travelled at times to all these brethren, and visited them in their cells and lauras, to keep watch over them, and to encourage them to make progress and persevere. He used to say to them, " The fashion of this world passeth away, and that alone remains and gives everlasting life which is purchased by the tribulations of this present life." These journeys resembled little migrations of nations, for nearly all the anchorites whom he visited accompanied him a part of his way, so that there were often about a thousand, or even two thousand of them together. Each one had to take a small provision of food with him, so as not to be burdensome to any one else. Yet this great crowd of men was at times a burden to those monasteries or lauras in which Hilarion took shelter. But the joy the brethren felt in receiving him by far outweighed the little discomforts they underwent. Hilarion was in the habit of writing down on paper the places where he would pass the night, and those which he should only visit by the way. There was one brother who, although he may have possessed many good qualities, had not made much progress in the virtue of holy poverty. He lived in his vineyard, and looked upon it as entirely his own property. The brethren asked

Hilarion to designate this vineyard as one of his resting-places, in order to cure the brother of his avarice. "No," said Hilarion, "wherefore should we be a burden to the brother, and an annoyance to ourselves?" When the penurious man heard this saying, he was ashamed of himself, and invited Hilarion and his followers to pass the night with him. Hilarion accepted the invitation. But before he had set out, the miser repented over and over again of having given this invitation; and he placed watchers all around his vineyard, with instructions to drive away the pious company with blows and stones, as soon as ever they approached the vineyard; which was accordingly done. The brethren were angry with the miser; but Hilarion laughed and passed by, remarking to some of his companions, that it is not avarice, but the blessing of God, which fills the barns and casks. Then Brother Sabas lovingly received the little army of three thousand men. He also had built his cell in his vineyard, and laboured diligently and carefully in it, but solely that he might give all the produce to the poor, living himself like a true ascetic on a little barley bread and vegetables. Although it was the greatest pleasure of this man, who was voluntarily poor in Christ, to give a rich harvest to the needy, yet he hesitated not for a single instant to exercise hospitality, and to invite the brethren to enter, and to refresh themselves with his grapes. Hilarion offered up a prayer with them, and then arose, blessed the vineyard, and let his flock feed therein, saying, "Do as you are permitted." They then continued their pilgrimage. At the vintage, the produce of this vineyard was much greater than usual, whilst that of the miser was much scantier.

Hilarion had a great dislike to all those ascetics who did not trust themselves with perfect confidence to the providence of God, but took too much thought for their nourishment, shelter, or garments. His opinion was, that in order to undertake the conquest of the kingdom of heaven, the soldier of Christ should be little encumbered with baggage. He expelled a brother who spent the proceeds of his garden sparingly in order to make a little store for himself, and who even possessed some ready money. This brother wished to be reconciled with Hilarion, and therefore addressed himself to his favourite disciple Hesichius, and brought, as a proof of his better disposition, the first crop from his garden, a basket of green peas. Hesichius showed them to Hilarion in the evening, but he pushed them away, and said that their smell was repugnant to him, for he detected covetousness therein. Then he asked who had brought the peas; and after Hesichius had named the brother, he said: "Put them in the manger before the oxen, and thou wilt see that even beasts will reject them. The hand which gave them is not free from cupidity." Hesichius obeyed, and the peas remained untouched.

Hilarion had received from God great power over all that was evil, wherefore persons possessed came to him from far and near, and he freed them by his prayers, from the spirits that tormented them. The promise of our Blessed Lord was fulfilled in this man of faith—"As thou hast believed, so be it done to thee."[1] Even the emperor Constantins sent a young Franconian, one of his attendants, with a numerous guard of honour from Byzantium to Gaza, that he might receive assistance from Hilarion. As it sometimes happens, by the especial permission of God, that those nearest to the saints honour them the least, so was it in this case. The inhabitants of Gaza were mostly Pagans, worshipping their idol Marnas, and hating Hilarion on account of his miracles, as an enemy

[1] Matt. viii. 13.

of this Marnas; but the imperial embassy frightened them, and to make amends for their former insults, many of them joined themselves to the guard of honour. Hilarion was walking in the open air, and reciting the psalms in a low voice, when this concourse of people came to meet him. He appeared so holy and attractive that they all fell upon their knees, and he gave them his blessing, and bid them return to their homes, keeping only the one possessed with him. The young man was in a terrible state, and was so drawn up that his feet hardly touched the ground, and all his limbs were dislocated. Moreover, he spoke in Greek and Syriac, just as he was addressed, although, when he was well, he only knew Latin and Franconian. Many times the indescribable fury of the paroxysms made him more like a wild beast than a man. Hilarion commanded the devil, in the name of the Lord Jesus, to depart from the young man, and he departed. The young man then insisted upon giving his benefactor ten talents of gold. But Hilarion showed him a piece of barley-bread, and said, " To him who lives upon this, gold and dust are alike."

He possessed also great power over wild animals. An unwieldy Bactrian camel had gone mad, and had trampled some men to death under its feet. Then thirty men led it, bound with strong ropes, to Hilarion, and ran away with the greatest possible speed, when the holy man ordered them to set the beast free. With outstretched hands he approached the camel, which was going to attack him fiercely, when it suddenly fell to the ground quite tamed.

Thus, as we have seen, Hilarion had passed his youth in the deepest solitude, and served God alone in peace. But afterwards he had been obliged to spend the whole of his mature manhood in constant intercourse with every kind of people, amidst their cares and necessities, their wants and infirmities, leading countless souls to the way of truth, and thousands to the paths of the highest perfection.

He had become the founder of the monastic life in the East, had called into existence innumerable cloisters, lauras, and cells, and in the midst of all these dissipating and dangerous works, in the midst of the praise and admiration of the best and noblest of his contemporaries, he had always in the depths of his soul glorified God alone, and not himself, never having had the slightest feeling of pride or of self-complacency.

He was now an old man of sixty-three; and, according to the ordinary opinion of mankind, he might have been at ease about his salvation. But he was not. He daily wept and longed with unspeakable desires for the peaceful life of his youth. As the brethren saw him in such grief, they pressed around him, and he mournfully said, " O my children, I have become quite worldly again, and I receive my reward already in this life. Where is the obscurity of my early years? Do you not see how all Palestine and the neighbouring lands honour me, how noble and wise men, pious priests, and holy bishops visit me, a miserable man? Where is my solitude? Do you not see how the desert has been changed into the world, and is filled with people who come to me with a thousand wants, as if I could help them, and as if any one were not a better instrument of God than I? Where is my poverty? Alas! under the name of monasteries and the care of the brethren, I have property and temporal possessions. Do you see, therefore, what danger my soul is in of becoming worldly, and of losing in eternity that reward of abnegation which the Lord has promised to us " an hundredfold?" Thus he lamented, and would not be comforted. But his disciples, and, above all Hesichius, affectionately watched his every step, lest he should secretly fly from them into some impenetrable desert. That he might at least do what he could, Hilarion began to proceed against himself with renewed severity, and to deprive his feeble and wasted body of the use of bread; and, at the same time, to expound still more fervently and profoundly to the brethren the Holy Scriptures, which were the sweet food of his soul. But anxiety about his eternal salvation never left his mind.

At that time he was visited one day by Aristeneta, whose children he had restored to life by his prayers many years before. These children were now men, and Aristeneta was living like many highborn ladies of that time, in complete retirement from the world, entirely devoted to arranging the affairs of her soul before she should have to render her account to the Eternal Judge. She wished to make a pilgrimage to St. Antony, and her first station was with St. Hilarion. She no longer brought with her the retinue and the luxuries of her former life; poor and simple, and with few companions, she begged for Hilarion's blessing on her journey. But he said, with tears in his eyes, "If I were not immured in the monastery as though it were a prison, I should long ago have taken flight to our father Antony in the desert. It is too late now; we lost him yesterday. Delay thy journey, for the news will soon arrive." Such was actually the case. Antony had departed, but he still lived in those who, like Hilarion, had found realised in him the ideal of their own aspirations, and who had formed themselves after his pattern not outwardly alone, but even in their most inward being. Hilarion now felt a still more pressing need of withdrawing himself from the great tumult of men. He was so weakened by fasting that he could no longer undertake a journey on foot; he therefore one day asked for an ass. He wished to go away. Quick as lightning the news spread abroad; and as if Palestine had been threatened with ruin, the people flocked to his cloister to detain him. "Let me go," said he, imploringly; "God does not lie. He shows me the desolation of the Church, the desecration of altars, the shedding of my children's blood. I could not bear to see such terrible things! Let me depart." They understood that God was manifesting future things to him, but nevertheless they watched him night and day. Then Hilarion declared that he would touch no food till he was allowed to depart; and as he kept his word, and neither ate nor drank for six days, they resolved, sorrowfully and mournfully, to let him go. Then he blessed the people, chose out forty monks who were active in mind and body, made them take a few provisions with them, and started with them on a pilgrimage to the mountain of Colzim. On his road he visited the monasteries of monks and the anchorites, and also two holy confessors, the Bishops Dracontius and Philo, whom the Arian Emperor Constantius had deposed and banished to Babylon in Egypt, the present Cairo. The entrance into the desert, which stretches as far as the Red Sea, began at the city of Aphroditon. There the deacon Baison had made the arrangement of having foreign travellers carried through the pathless and waterless desert upon swift dromedaries, which, accustomed to a quick trot, traversed the sands rapidly, like those now used in Egypt and Syria for pressing messages. Yet it was three days' journey to Colzim. But Hilarion shrunk from no exertion in order to see the place which Antony had sanctified, and to pray on the spot where the teacher of his youth, who had exercised such powerful influence over his whole life, and had drawn him to follow his example, had lived in the most intimate union with God, and where he had died. Hilarion arrived there on the anniversary of his death, and was joyfully greeted by Antony's two faithful disciples, Isaac and Pelusian. They had been eye-witnesses and companions of the last years and death of the holy patriarch, and could give Hilarion all the accurate details about him which he desired. They went with him over the little oasis, Antony's own creation, and related how the arid and savage nature of the place had been changed and softened under his blessed hand. Hilarion knelt down near the ledge of rock which had been the couch and deathbed of the holy old man, and paid respect to it by a devout kiss. The saints know best what is due to holiness, and what it is to be holy.

Hilarion returned to Aphroditon, dismissed his travelling companions, and left them in their monastery in Palestine, keeping only two disciples, with whom he went to a neighbouring desert, where he lived in such strict fasting and silence that he said he had only now begun to serve God. There had been no rain in this country for three years, so that the inhabitants could not irrigate the parched soil sufficiently for cultivation, and men and beasts were starving. It was generally remarked that all the elements were mourning the death of Antony. But when it was known that Hilarion was in those parts, the people, convinced that he was a friend of God, who could alleviate every want and trouble, thronged to him in masses; enfeebled men, wasted women, and dying children, pale with hunger and the pangs of death, cried aloud to Hilarion, as a follower of Antony, to ask God for rain. He did so, and was heard. But the grateful reverence of the people drove him once more from his cell, because he no longer found there the retirement and solitude which was his soul's most urgent need; and he proceeded to Alexandria, there to bury himself in the desert of Lower Egypt. During a visit which he made to a monastery in Bruchium, the port of Alexandria, he learnt that Julian the apostate, who had become emperor in the meantime, was very furious against him, and was causing search to be made for him in Gaza. He immediately saddled his little ass, and prepared himself for a journey. The monks implored him to remain, as no one would seek him there, and even if he should be found, they would all suffer and die with him. "Let me go, my children," he said; "you know not what God destines for us." He was hardly gone before the soldiers of the governor of Palestine arrived in search of him, and of Hesichius, with orders from the emperor to put them to death. So great was the antipathy of the powerful emperor to the poor hermit, of the apostate to the saint. The renegade emperor of the world acknowledged such power in this aged ascetic that he could not suffer him to live on the earth with him. And such has ever since been invariably the case; the imitation of Jesus in its greatest perfection, as ascetic souls in the Church have striven to practise it, is an object of hatred and of persecution to the apostates of all ages. This is a proof of its immense power, for what is powerless is always allowed to pass unmolested.

Whilst Hilarion concealed himself in the desert, the Arians and the heathens of Gaza, who had a natural sympathy with each other, making common cause, burnt down his cloister, laid it waste, and ill-treated and chased away the brethren. Amongst these there was a Judas of the name of Hadrian. He went to Hilarion, and sought to induce him to return to Palestine, under the pretext that he would greatly console the afflicted brethren there, while, in truth, all the faithful brethren rejoiced to know that the holy old man was in safety from his enemies. Hilarion was not deceived by Hadrian, but dismissed him.

and continued his wanderings farther, even beyond the sea to Sicily. On landing, he offered the captain of the ship, as payment for himself and his companion Zananus, the book of the holy Gospels, which he had written out in his earliest youth, and which he always carried about with him. But the captain having pity on these two beggars, would not take it, and let them go their way. Hilarion, rejoicing to be thought a beggar, left the densely populated coast and penetrated into the interior of the country, where he erected a cell of branches on the borders of a wood. Every day he collected a bundle of dry twigs, which Zananus carried to a neighbouring village, and exchanged for a piece of bread. Upon this they both lived very contentedly, entirely given to prayer. But Hilarion's light had been already put upon a candlestick, notwithstanding the pains he took to hide it under a bushel. Here, as well as in Palestine and Egypt, the suffering had recourse to this man of prayer. God accepted the intercession, which Hilarion could not refuse to those who asked it; the sick were healed, and reverence following upon gratitude, he was once more surrounded by a throng of men. In the meantime Hesichius, who had been separated from his beloved master, had sought him in all the deserts, monasteries, and ports of the East in vain. After three years he embarked for the Peloponnesus, and there he heard a Jew relate many things about a Christian prophet in Sicily who worked miracles and wonders, like a second Elias. He inquired his name and age, but the Jew had only heard of him, and never seen him. Hesichius immediately took ship for Sicily, and his first question there was about the worker of miracles, whom every one knew. When he learnt that this servant of God never accepted even so much as a bit of bread from those who wished to testify their gratitude to him by rich presents, but always answered with our Blessed Lord, "Freely have you received, freely give,"[1] Hesichius rejoiced, for thereby he recognised Hilarion, and he immediately rejoined him.

Then they travelled together through a strange country, whose language and people were completely unknown to them, to Dalmatia, on the eastern shore of the Adriatic Sea; a beautiful land, but often severely visited by earthquakes. One was then desolating the seaport town of Epidaurus. Whilst the earth yawned to swallow it up, and the hills crushed it in their fall, the sea rose with exceeding violence to such a height that the ships were dashed upon the rocks of the coast. The afflicted inhabitants fled, as if by inspiration, to Hilarion, who lived in a cavern amongst the mountains, implored him to save them, and led him to the sea-beach. Hilarion possessed the faith which removes mountains. He traced three crosses on the sand of the shore, and lifted up his hand against the waves, which raised themselves on high, stood still, fell backwards, and retreated slowly from the shore. St. Jerome, who wrote his life, and who was himself a Dalmatian, says, "The town of Epidaurus and the whole of Dalmatia speak of this miracle to this day, for mothers relate it to their children, that it may be perpetuated in the remembrance of the generations to come." Why is it so difficult for us to look upon miracles with the eye of faith? Do we, perchance, belong to those whom our Blessed Lord called "O ye of little faith," when He made a great calm upon the sea?

A country which Hilarion entered under such circumstances could never be the place of his abode. He went to the island of Cyprus, whose primate was St. Epiphanius, Bishop of Salamis, his countryman, and formerly his disciple. At his table a fowl was once set before him. Hilarion declined

[1] Matt. x. 8.

to partake of it, because, since he had borne the habit of an anchorite, he had never tasted anything that had had life. "And I," answered Epiphanius, "since I have worn this habit, have never suffered any one to retire to rest with anything against me in his heart, and I myself have never laid me down to sleep in discord with any one." "Forgive me, my father," replied Hilarion meekly, "thou hast followed a better rule of life than I."

He settled a few miles from Paphos, amongst the ruins of an abandoned idolatrous temple, and lived there two years, always praying, always working miracles, always seeking to escape from the renown of his own sanctity. Five years before his death he sent Hesichius away with the commission to greet the brethren in Palestine, and to discover a place in Egypt or Lybia, where he could await his last hour undisturbed. Hesichius returned, and advised the old man to remain in Cyprus, where he had found out a wild and solitary valley in the interior of the island. It was situated amongst the mountains, and was almost inaccessible, being enclosed all round by high and rugged rocks; but it had a clear stream, a verdant meadow, and many beautiful apple-trees. The whole place was also said to be inhabited by evil spirits. The old man was pleased at the thoughts of living and dying in such a wild solitude, surrounded by his ancient foes. Climbing and scrambling with difficulty, at times even creeping on their hands and knees, they reached the valley which Hilarion recognised as the place of his repose. He would have no earthly consolation, and sent back his beloved disciple to Palestine, with the permission to come to visit him twice a year, which he did. Hilarion laid out a little garden by the stream, and lived upon vegetables and water, as he had done in his youth. He never tasted the apples, but they rejoiced his eyes. No one dared approach him. Thus he gained once more his long-sought beloved solitude, and saw nothing but heavenly images, which the earthly eye cannot perceive. Shortly before his death, a paralytic person, the owner of this rocky wilderness, contrived to reach him, and begged so earnestly for his prayers, that Hilarion wept and implored God's mercy for him, and dismissed him cured. This had the usual consequences, but they no longer affected him. He became sick, and wrote his will, leaving to Hesichius his book of the Gospels, his hairshirt, and his poor mantle. Many pious people of Paphos visited him with great devotion. Nothing in him lived save his eyes and his voice; his whole body was already, as it were, dead. Once more the holy fear of God's judgment fell upon him, and he spoke to himself encouragingly: "Fear not, O my soul! depart, depart. Seventy years thou hast served Christ, and dost thou fear death?" Then a deep rest settled upon his brow, and he slept in the Lord, in the God who had called him so early, and had said, "Thou art mine."

PAUL THE SIMPLE.

"And a path and a way shall be there, a straight way, so that fools shall not err therein."—ISA. xxxv. 8.

In the desert inhabited by St. Antony, a peasant, sixty years of age, was wandering restlessly to and fro in great distress. His wife, who was young and beautiful, but very wicked, had deceived him and grievously offended God. He had surrendered to her his little house and all that he possessed, and hastened away without knowing what was to become of him. He was a simple, guileless man, who would not for the world have told a lie, or done his neighbour any harm. He was called Paul. For eight days he strayed about, helpless and full of anxiety. Then God suggested to him to forget all things else, and to think only of the salvation of his soul; and he arose and went straightway to Antony, and said to him that he wished to learn to be an anchorite. Antony replied that it was not possible at his age; he must serve God very piously some other way, for he could never bear the austerity of the ascetic life. " Only teach me what I have to do," answered Paul quietly, " and I will certainly accomplish it." " It is impossible," replied Antony; " thou canst not become an anchorite. But if thou art resolved to leave the world, go into a cloister where monks live together, that thou mayest, in case of need, find the care and support which thine age requires. Here thou wilt find nothing, for I live entirely alone, and only eat a little every third or fourth day." Thereupon Antony went back into his cell, and shut himself up in it for three days, and applied himself to his prayers and contemplations, leaving to Paul the choice whether he would take his advice or not. On the fourth day Antony emerged from his cavern, and, behold, Paul was still there. " My dear old man," said he kindly, " this is no place for thee." " My father," replied Paul resolutely, " I will die nowhere but on this very spot." Antony perceived that he had no victuals whatever with him, and as he did not yet know what spirit inspired the old man, he took him into his cell, gave him some bread and water, and said, " Paul, thou mayest be perfect and blessed, if thou wilt observe obedience." " I will observe it, only command," said Paul, simply. This childlike readiness to obey, at such an advanced age, much rejoiced Antony, and he immediately began to treat Paul as a soul endowed with great grace. He said to him, "Now go out, place thyself before the cavern, and pray till I bring thee some work." Paul went out, and betook himself to prayer. Antony left him standing the whole day and the whole night; and whenever he looked at him through a little crevice in his cell, he saw him standing immersed in prayer, so immovably on the same spot, that during the twenty-four hours he did not stir a hair's-breadth, careless alike of the scorching heat of the sun and of the nightly dews. Then Antony brought him some palm-leaves steeped in water, and said, "Plait a rope out of these as thou seest me do." It was troublesome and laborious work, but Paul did it with great diligence, and made a piece fifteen ells long. But when Antony saw the rope, he was not pleased with it, and said, "Thou hast twisted it too tightly; undo it, and plait it again more loosely." Paul unplaited all the fifteen ells, and then plaited them together again, which was extremely difficult, because the damp and moistened palm-leaves had got bent and crooked with the first plaiting. He had to practise this for seven whole days, without receiving food or drink, because Antony wished to try whether he would be patient under neglect, or was to be deterred by difficulties. Paul's courage did not fail him; he never complained by word or look, and cheerfully remained at his work. Antony rejoiced more and more; and, going to him after sunset, asked him. "Wilt thou now eat a little bread with me, my dear Paul?" "As thou willest, my father!" was the answer. They went into the cavern, and Antony brought out four little loaves, of six ounces each, one for himself, and three for Paul. They were so hard and dry that they required to be soaked in water. In the meantime Antony recited a psalm, and repeated it twelve times, Paul joyfully reciting it with him. Then the holy master said to his holy disciple,

"We will sit down, we will not eat yet, but ponder on the benefits of God." And as night had come on, he added, "The meal-time is past, let us make our thanksgiving, and retire to rest." Paul obeyed without hesitation. At midnight Antony aroused him for prayer, and on the evening of that day they first tasted bread. When they had each eaten a loaf, Antony, who never took more, said, "Take another little loaf, and eat it." "If thou wilt eat another, I will, but not otherwise," answered Paul. "I cannot, because I am a poor anchorite, and as such must live poorly," replied Antony. "Then I cannot either, because I want to become an anchorite," said Paul, quietly.

St. Antony taught as follows about obedience:— "Our Lord has said, 'I am come, not to do my will, but the will of Him who sent me.' This must be our guide. If any one wishes to become perfect in a short time, let him not be his own teacher and master, and let him not follow his own will, even when his will is not evil. For Christ's will was certainly not opposed to the will of His heavenly Father, but the reverse; and yet He would not do His own will, in order to teach us obedience, which consists, above all, in the complete renunciation of our own will. The Son of God could not have erred, if He had followed His own will, and yet He followed it not. How much less ought we, who with the best intentions often go so far astray, to act from our own impulses, if we wish to reach the highest perfection!" Antony exercised his disciples according to this doctrine, and Paul submitted himself with incredible humility and simplicity to such discipline. First, he had for a whole day to draw water out of the well, and pour it out again directly, then to tear his habit, to mend it, and to tear it again; and many times to pull baskets to pieces, and to plait them together again. Once Antony received a present of a vase of honey. He said to Paul, "Break the vessel, and let the honey fall upon the sand." And directly after, when his command had been fulfilled, he added, "Now gather up the honey, and put it into another bowl quite clean, and without any admixture of sand." If we consider how man is visited by God with innumerable providences and judgments, the reason of which he cannot fathom, and which frequently run counter to human prudence and sagacity, we shall deem that school wise and loving in which Paul was exercised to so great a degree in equanimity and resignation. And if we consider the proneness of every man to prefer his own will to all else beside, we shall praise God, whose grace renders possible such abnegation of our strongest inclinations, and love that man who received grace in such unspeakable purity of soul, and corresponded to it so faithfully.

After Antony had convinced himself that Paul was obedient to him in all the strictness of the spiritual life, he said: "See now, my brother, if thou canst trust thyself to live on, day after day, in this manner, I will keep thee by me." With exceeding cheerfulness Paul answered: "I do not know, my father, whether the difficulties are yet to come, and whether thou wilt teach and order me hard things; for all that I have hitherto done or observed in thee I can accomplish by God's help, and without very great exertion." After a few months Antony conducted this soul, so perfect in its simplicity, into a cell which was about a thousand paces distant from his own, and said: "Paul, in the name of Jesus, and by His grace thou art now become an anchorite; live in solitude, labour diligently, raise up thy thoughts, thy heart, and thy mind to Almighty God whilst thy hands are busy; eat not nor drink before sunset, and never enough to satisfy thyself; learn to struggle and combat with our ancient adversary the devil, and practise punctually all that I have told or shown to thee." Paul received this exhortation with the greatest attention, and followed it with equal exactness, for he looked upon it as given to him by God Himself. Antony visited him sometimes, and rejoiced over this simple piety, which had no suspicion of the height of its own virtue; and when strange brethren were with him, he often called Paul, that he might edify them, and serve them for a model. Once some very holy and enlightened brethren came to visit Antony, and Paul was sent for to serve them, which he most willingly did with humble joy. These saintly men conversed together upon divine things, and once happened to be speaking of the prophets. As Paul had never heard of them, he asked ingenuously, "Were the prophets before Christ, or was Christ before the prophets?" Antony almost blushed at this question, and said to Paul kindly, "Be silent, my brother," and Paul held his peace. The brethren remained three weeks with Antony, and Paul served them with the greatest care, but in such unbroken silence, that at last they said, "Why dost thou not speak to us?" Paul smiled sweetly, but did not answer. When, therefore, the brethren asked Antony the cause, and he could not at all recollect having ordered anything of the kind, he said to Paul: "Speak then to the brethren; wherefore art thou silent?" "Because thou hast commanded me, my father," answered Paul quietly. Then Antony exclaimed: "O my brethren! Paul condemns us all, for none of us observe and follow the inspirations of the Holy Ghost as carefully as he takes heed of each word that I speak to him."

Paul was precisely one of those "little ones" to whom God reveals His eternal mysteries. The sublime and sanctifying mystery of the obedience of the Eternal Son in the Incarnation was clear to him; not to his intellect, but to his heart. He obeyed because his God was obedient. "That is the highest degree of obedience," says St. Bonaventure in his "Golden Ladder of the Virtues."

According to the teaching of St. Antony, certain evil spirits ruled men through certain vices. If any one had fully subdued in himself and entirely rooted out any vice, such as pride, covetousness, sloth, or envy, Almighty God would sometimes reward his valiant struggle by deputing to him power over the demon of this vice in others. By humility and obedience, Paul so thoroughly conquered the old man in himself, that he quickly raised himself to the highest perfection. The power of God found no purer instrument than this simple old man, and therefore his prayers became nearly all-powerful over the devils and those possessed by them. Antony caused the most melancholy cases of this kind to be delivered by his beloved Paul, perhaps out of humility, for saints always vie with each other in this virtue. Once a youth was brought to him who was tormented almost to madness by the demon of blasphemy. He took him to Paul, and said: "Drive the evil spirit out of this soul, that it may be able to love and praise God." "Why dost thou not do it thyself, my father?" asked Paul. "Because I have not time," answered Antony, and then went away. Paul made a most fervent prayer, and then said, "Hast thou heard, thou bad demon, Antony commands thee to leave this soul?" But the youth only raved more wickedly and wildly against God, and against all that was holy. "Leave this soul, or I will complain of thee to Christ," repeated Paul. Still there were no results. He then went out into the burning noonday sun of Egypt, which is not unlike the Babylonian furnace, and, climbing a rock, he said, "Beloved Redeemer, Thou seest that I stand here; now I will not go away, neither will

I sleep, eat, or drink, till Thou hast delivered this poor youth from the evil spirit; for Antony has ordered me to ask Thee." And by this dove-like simplicity he accomplished the work.

With affectionate love and veneration, the brethren gave this favoured child of God no other name but that of Paul the Simple, as is related by Palladius, Bishop of Helenopolis, who remained for three years in the Egyptian deserts towards the end of that century.

AMMON, ABBOT OF NITRIA.

"Lord, who shall rest in Thy holy hill? He that walketh without blemish."—Ps. xiv. 1, 2.

IN a country house near Alexandria there sat a youth of two-and-twenty years opposite to a maiden, and explained to her the seventh chapter of the First Epistle to the Corinthians, which treats of the pre-eminence of the life of virginity over the state of matrimony, a superiority which the holy Apostle points out when he says: "The virgin thinketh on the things of the Lord: that she may be holy both in body and in spirit."[1] And "More blessed shall she be if she remain a virgin."[2] These two young people were in festal garments, and wore wreaths of flowers on their heads; this was their bridal dress, for they had just been married. The young man was called Ammon. He was of a rich and noble family, had lost his parents when a child, and had received an excellent education from his uncle, so as to be able to shine in the world in after life. But grace took possession of his soul so early and so completely, that the happiness and splendour of the world never had the smallest

[1] Ver. 34. [2] Ver. 40.

attraction for him. Riches, honours, enjoyments, and pleasures, repelled instead of alluring him. His uncle, who was otherwise an upright man, saw this with great grief, and imagined that marriage would be the best means of suggesting other thoughts to Ammon. Without asking him, he conclnded an alliance for him with the daughter of a distinguished man, and after all was settled, Ammon heard, for the first time, of the arrangement. Pure souls are safe in God's hands. Ammon submitted himself outwardly to his uncle, whom he tenderly loved and honoured.. But grace was so strong within him that it overflowed upon his bride; and the elevation of his soul was so great, that it raised her also above earthly things. After Ammon had imparted to her what the Apostle Paul, by the inspiration of the Holy Ghost, says about virginity, and what our Divine Saviour says of heaven in the nineteenth chapter of the Evangelist St. Matthew, there sprang up in the heart of the young maiden the flame of heavenly love, and they both agreed to remain in a state of virginity. Ammon would have wished to be able at once to follow the life of an anchorite, but he would not take this step without the consent of his bride; and as she did not know what would become of her if he left her, she begged him not to separate from her for the present. Ammon was content, and they then began a peaceful angelic life, which they led together for eighteen years. They inhabited a pleasant country house, surrounded by a large garden, and Ammon occupied himself diligently with its cultivation. He gave his especial care to a garden of balsam-trees, because those trees, like vines, require to be cultivated with great trouble, in order that they may exude their precious odoriferous gum, which is used for incense and for medicinal purposes. His wife superintended the household, worked diligently in order to clothe the aged and poor, visited and tended the sick, and sanctified these simple occupations, as Ammon did his, by a continual elevation of the heart to God. Twice a day they recited psalms together, and towards evening they united again in taking a simple meal. Their days thus passed in a peace which the world knows not and gives not, and their prayers were so efficacious that grace descended upon them more and more abundantly. The whole neighbourhood was edified by the conduct of these two earthly angels. Virgins who thirsted after the heights of perfection requested the counsel and prayers of this holy woman; men and youths who wished to secure their salvation turned to Ammon for instruction; and every soul that approached them in any kind of trouble left them consoled and strengthened. Although it is not named amongst His seven gifts, the gift of consolation is the work of the Holy Ghost, Whom our Blessed Lord calls "the Comforter."

One day Ammon's pious wife said to him, "My dear lord, it is now eighteen years since, by God's grace, I have followed thy salutary advice; if now thou wilt take mine, I shall be assured that thou lovest me heartily in God." Ammon replied that she might always be assured of that, whether he took her advice or not; and asked what it was. "I think," said she, "that thou, and perhaps I also, could do more for the salvation of the souls of others, if we lived henceforward separated from one another. Formerly thou hadst compassion on my youth and inexperience, and remainedst with me; but now that I have become thy disciple in the spiritual life, I think it only right that I should give thee thy full liberty, in order that thy great wisdom and virtue may be no longer hidden." With heartfelt joy Ammon blessed the goodness of God, and thanked his wife, saying, "That thought came from above, my dear sister, and since thou art willing, I will build a hut for myself in solitude. But do thou remain in this house, under the protection of Almighty God." He gave her all his property, that she might be unfettered in practising works of mercy; and before long, some pious virgins joined her, with whom she led an ascetic life, and they composed in reality, if not in form, a monastic community.

After taking leave of his wife, and promising to visit her once or twice a year, Ammon departed into the desert, where he remained twenty-two years. He was one of those rare men who possess such independent strength of mind, that whatever direction they take, they receive little from other men, but give them very much, and can arouse them to great things. Therefore his spirit did not urge him towards the universal pilgrimage of the day to Antony, but like Antony he sought first perfect solitude with God; and it was not till later that he visited the great patriarch, and formed an intimate friendship with him, as was to be expected from two holy souls united together in God. Ammon established himself in Lower Egypt, his native country. There, west of Alexandria, lay the great Lake Mareotis, half marsh, half water, such as are often found on the coasts of the Mediterranean, where they are not rocky. On the southern shore of this lake, which Palladius only reached after a journey of a day and a half, a great deal of saltpetre or nitre was dug up, and therefore that part of the country was called Nitria. It reached as far as a vast desert, which stretched out to Mauritania, in Northern Africa, but to the south may have extended even into the impenetrable centre of Africa. Limestone rocks, offshoots of the Lybian mountains, rose up in this desert, and formed the mountain of Nitria, which Ammon, in the first half of the fourth century, chose for his hermitage, and upon which Palladins, towards the end of the same century, found five thousand monks. In this desert Ammon fitted up for himself a cavern for a cell, and raised himself to the highest contemplation and knowledge of the truth. The powers which he imbibed from the fulness of divine light and divine love overflowed out of his soul upon the souls of others, vivifying, refreshing, and purifying them like the streams of water that descend from a high mountain into a valley. He had reached this intimate union with God by a different road from Paul of Thebes, from Antony, or Hilarion. He had not been able to withdraw himself from the world, and to fly into the unfrequented desert in his tender youth. His circumstances were such that everything was at his command which generally brings earthly happiness to men. But men who love God look at all things which they find around them only in the light in which they are seen by the eye of faith, and by keeping this view consistently and thoroughly before them, they make for themselves a new and rightful happiness. Whilst the faint-hearted call them indiscreet and eccentric, they alone are really of sound mind; and whilst men of the world pity them, they advance to the conquest of true felicity. And to that end they have a sure guide, the same that Ammon had, the unadulterated inspired Writings. "You shall buy as though you possessed not," is said in that wonderful Epistle to the Corinthians, which puts before us the ideal of perfection, and shows it to be attainable, yet without discouraging the great majority who do not wish to put it in practice. Ammon strove after it with all his might, and he was so filled with the prospect and hope of heavenly goods and eternal joys, that earthly and temporal goods were as little considered by him as if he had not possessed them.

He saw them with his eyes, and handled them with his hands, and was surrounded by them, and yet he had detached himself so completely from them, that now in the solitude of the desert he was no poorer than in his rich house.

Before long he became in Lower Egypt what Antony was in Thebais and Hilarion in Palestine, the teacher and the centre of the spiritual life. Those who sought salvation came in troops to the mountain of Nitria, and many remained with Ammon, and became anchorites. The mountain resembled a beehive, so perforated was it with cells, whose inhabitants nourished themselves with the sweet honey of holy contemplations. Their occupation was weaving linen, the produce of which Ammon employed partly for the support of the brotherhood, partly for the poor far and near, and partly for the entertainment of their numerous guests. Hospitality was practised to the utmost. When strangers came, the monks hastened to meet them, and singing psalms, conducted them first to the church, and then to the spacious hospice, where they washed their feet, brought them food and drink, and waited on them. A large house which was on the mountain, near to the church, was devoted entirely to guests. There they might live for years, if they so wished, and during the first eight days no work was required from them. But if they stayed longer, they had to work in the kitchen garden, or the kitchen, or the bakery, or in some other household labour, and also to observe the universal silence which was established at certain hours. If learned or scientific men came, they were provided with books and writings, in order to maintain themselves by their own kind of work, and they also had to accommodate themselves to the general way of life, so as to make no disturbance in the monastic rule. At regular hours, many times each day, the monks said certain psalms, and sang hymns and canticles, so that the whole mountain resounded with heavenly choirs. Every day also Ammon instructed them in the duties of the ascetic life, and explained to them the Holy Scriptures. On Saturday and Sunday they assembled in the great church, halfway up the mountain. By degrees, as many as eight priests were required for this numerous congregation and its spiritual necessities; but the senior one always offered the holy sacrifice of the Mass, and preached.

If any of Ammon's spiritual sons felt himself called to a life of unusually severe penance, and had first given proofs of his humility and constancy, he received permission to retire from the community life at Nitria to a greater solitude. Such anchorites pitched their tents ten miles further into the desert; and at the time that there were five thousand brethren living in community at Nitria, six hundred had retired into that part of the desert, which, from the number of their cells and huts, received the name of Cellia. These cells were so wide apart, that no anchorite could be either seen or heard by his next neighbour. Each one remained alone with his own work, which he took to Nitria once or twice a year, and received in exchange his necessary provisions. No one ever visited another to converse with him. No one spoke to another for recreation; but if any one of them was far advanced in the spiritual life, and knew that another was waging a terrible combat, he went to him to give him advice or consolation. The hermits of Cellia had a church of their own, which was situated in the centre of their desert, wherein they likewise assembled on Saturdays and Sundays. Some of them lived at a distance of three or four miles from it. There they met, but only as strangers come down from heaven, to carry on upon earth the occupation of the blessed, namely, to worship God. When the service was over, each returned home in silence. If any one did not appear, the others then knew that he must be sick and they visited him, but cautiously, and not all together. Suffice it to say, that if they lived outwardly apart, and without a single temporal consolation, they were inwardly united in the holy love of God and their neighbour, and in this union they were living members of the body of Christ, through Whom again they were united to their heavenly Father, and could say, with greater perfection than the Apostle Philip,[1] whose supernatural eye had not then been enlightened by the Holy Ghost, " It is enough for us."

The holy founder of this pious community was endowed with unusual gifts and graces, and could read the secrets of souls and of times as if from an open book. Some afflicted parents once brought their only son to Nitria in bonds and chains. He had been bitten by a mad dog, and now in his madness he sought to attack others. The parents told Ammon their trouble, and besought his intercession. "My dear children," replied he, "my poor prayers can do very little in this affair, but you yourselves can do a great deal." They asked how that could be; and he said, "You have robbed a poor widow of her cow; give it back to her, and our good God will take such pleasure in that act, that He will restore your son to health." Ashamed and penitent, but full of hope, they returned home, repaired their misdeed, and their son recovered. Another time two men assured him that they wished to do him a service out of love for God. " I am glad of that," said Ammon, on purpose to try them ; " I will give you an opportunity at once. Some one in your village has given us a large new cask, which we are in great want of, to keep water in for our guests to drink.

[1] John xiv. 8.

I beg of you to send it up here." They promised to do so, and left him. But one of them repented of his promise, and said to the other, "I shall certainly not send the cask up to the mountain; it would destroy my camel." But the other kept his word, although he had only a little ass, not without great trouble and labour to himself and his beast. When Ammon saw him coming, he went kindly to meet him, thanked him, and said, "See, it has done thy companion no good to take such excessive care of his camel, for in the meantime the hyenas have torn it to pieces." And when the man returned the next day to his village, he found his companion tearing his hair, because the wild beasts had devoured his camel during the night.

Once St. Antony sent a friendly greeting to the holy Ammon, with an invitation to visit him once more. Thirteen days' journey divided them, but Ammon arose without hesitation, and, accompanied by the messenger and his favourite disciple, Theodore, made the pilgrimage from the mountain of Nitria to the mountain of Colzim. They journeyed safely as far as the arm of the Nile called the Lycus, and there they sought for a boat in which to cross it. But it was an unpeopled country, traversed by no traders, and therefore no boat was to be found, and nothing was left for them but to swim across the river. The brethren prepared for this, but Ammon was unwilling to take off his clothes. He was softly lifted up by a supernatural force, and transported to the other side of the stream, being borne upon the water, as his Lord and Master had been. Antony received him with heartfelt joy, and said, " Thy tarrying will not be much longer amongst us, my brother, therefore I had a great desire to speak of eternal things with thee once more." They remained some time together, and refreshed their souls in each other's light. Then they parted; and when Ammon died soon after upon the mountain of Nitria, Antony saw his glorified soul ascend to the heavenly country like the "rising morning."[1]

ST. PACHOMIUS,

ABBOT OF TABENNA.

"Lord, what wilt Thou have me to do?"—Acts ix. 6.

As Antony may be called the creator of the monastic life, so was his younger contemporary Pachomius its lawgiver. The companies of anchorites had hitherto lived partly as hermits, and partly in community in lauras, without form or rules, and held together only by the powerful minds of their teachers, Antony, Hilarion, and Ammon. They now received from Pachomius laws and regulations by which they were joined together in a firm and lasting union. Pachomius was, properly speaking, the founder of the religious orders, of which the other three communities were the forerunners and models.

Pachomius was descended from a heathen family in the Thebaid, and was carefully instructed in the sciences of his country and his time. From his earliest childhood he was distinguished amongst his heathen companions by his innocent disposition and his pure morals. It was related of him that, when a young child, he accompanied his parents to an idol which spoke oracles; but it was dumb in the presence of this child, and the idolatrous priests declared to his amazed parents that no one was in fault but the little enemy of the gods, their son.

At the time that Constantine was carrying on

[1] Cant. vi. 9.

the war against his colleague Maxentius, he caused all the strongest youths in that part of the Roman empire which was subject to him to be levied as recruits, and to enter the army. This was the fate of Pachomius, who was then barely twenty years old. A whole troop of young people were torn from their families in Thebais, and shipped on the Nile, to be sent first to Alexandria, and then to their further destination. They were all very much cast down at leaving their homes against their will; they were also roughly treated by the soldiers who guarded them. When the ship touched one day at a large town on the shore, many of the inhabitants came down to the bank of the Nile, bringing the young recruits food and drink, and every kind of refreshment, consoling them and encouraging them to be hopeful and courageous, and showing so much kindness to these unknown and forsaken youths, that all were touched by it, and Pachomius especially. He inquired who these charitable and benevolent people were, and learned that they were Christians, people who believed in Jesus Christ, the only-begotten Son of God, and who endeavoured to do good to all men, and particularly to the sorrowful, the helpless, and the forsaken, and that they hoped to receive their reward in heaven, and not upon earth. Pachomius was deeply moved by this faith of the Christians; and, inflamed with divine love, he drew aside, and lifting up his eyes and hands to heaven, he prayed, saying, "Almighty God, who hast created the heavens and the earth, if Thou wilt deliver me from my present affliction, and wilt send me the true knowledge how to serve Thee most perfectly, I will dedicate all the days of my life to Thy service. Hear my prayer, and show me what I must do." The ship continued her voyage, and carried the young soldiers to their destination. Although many sednotions awaited him, Pachomius never forgot that he had promised himself to the service of God, and always avoided the worldly pleasures in which his heathen companions indulged.

Constantine's campaign against Maxentius was soon brought to a victorious conclusion, and the soldiers being dismissed in the year 313, Pachomius joyfully returned to his home, to place himself in another company, namely, that of the catechumens, who received instruction in the doctrines of the Christian faith. His ardent heart made him so zealous a disciple of this holy faith that he soon after received the sacrament of Baptism. The following night he dreamt that dew fell from heaven into his right hand, and was changed into honey, and that a voice said: "Pachomius! Christ the Lord gives thee great grace." His loving heart could not be satisfied save by sacrificing himself entirely to this gracious and loving Lord. Whilst he was considering how best to effect this, he heard of the aged anchorite Palemon, who, quite dead to the world, led a heavenly life in a desert of the Thebaid. All then became as clear to Pachomius as if the sun had risen inwardly upon him. He said to himself: "It is there that God will have thee," and he immediately set out on the road to Palemon's desert. He knocked humbly at the door of the poor hut, and begged for admittance. The aged anchorite only half opened the door, looked sadly and sternly at the youth, and asked him, "What dost thou wish? Whom seekest thou?" Pachomius, undiscouraged, answered: "The Lord God hath sent me hither. I seek thee, for I wish to learn from thee to be an anchorite." But with no less severity Palemon answered: "Many have said the same to me, but they all soon grew tired of their purpose. For the life of an anchorite is indeed pleasing to God, but it is a hard and a difficult undertaking, of which it is easy to become weary." "All men are not alike," said Pachomius modestly, " only try me, and by degrees thou wilt acknowledge my powers." " First go through the primary exercises of the spiritual life in a laura," said Palemon, still refusing; " there the company of others will afford thee more help, and their example will give thee encouragement, and thou canst more easily find solace when a penitential life seems hard to thee. Here, in this place, it is impossible to lead other than an extremely austere life, for all human help and support are absent. For my nourishment I only use bread or wild herbs with salt, and I watch during half the night and often the whole night long, in prayer and contemplation of the Holy Scriptures. In the daytime I am never idle for a single moment, and even when I sing psalms or pray, I am making hair-shirts, in order to be able to give their price to the poor and to strangers." The youth trembled at the thoughts of sacrificing a long life in this way; but grace overcame the resistance of nature, and he said resolutely: " I believe and trust in Christ the Lord, that He will give me strength and patience to persevere for His love in this course of life as long as I live, and I hope that thou wilt pray for me, my father." This faith in God's assistance, and this willingness to make sacrifices, was a sign to the aged Palemon that it was a supernatural vocation, and not pride or curiosity, which urged the youth to embrace the ascetic life. He bade him welcome, took him to live with him, and gave him the habit which all anchorites wore, so as outwardly to show the state of life to which they were dedicated—namely, the scapular of goat or sheepskin.

About this time Eusebius wrote in his " Proofs of the Gospel:"—

" In the Church of Christ there are two kinds of life which are both in conformity with grace, and one of them is supernatural, and excels the usual human way. For it allows neither marriage nor the begetting of children, neither possessions nor gains, and, entirely separated from the ordinary concerns of men, it dedicates itself, out of exceeding love, to the service of God alone. Those who lead this life are, as it were, already dead to this temporal life, and live only in the body upon this earth; their souls have by vehement desire already ascended to heaven. Like immortals, they look down upon the traffic of the inhabitants of earth, and sanctify themselves to the everlasting God for the whole human race, not by strangled bullocks, not by drink or smoke offerings, but by the simple precepts of true religion, by the dispositions of a pure soul, by the practice of virtue and good works, whereby they appease God, and offer Him a holy service for themselves and their brethren."

In such esteem did the ancient Church hold her ascetics; for they corresponded to her love for her Lord by their loving union with His propitiatory sacrifice, which won for them supernatural grace and strength to do penance for those who do none, and thus to acquire power of atonement for their brethren. Renunciation, out of immense unspeakable love, was the invention of the Incarnate God. He became Man in order to practise it in its highest perfection, and it has remained ever since the property of heavenly-minded men; for He not only showed to men the virtues pleasing to God, but at the same time gave them grace to practise them. Eusebius was by no means one of those enthusiastic souls, like Antony, Athanasius, or Augustine, who, inebriated as it were with divine love, made every breath they drew a hymn, and every pulsation of their hearts a sigh of love. He was in the Church of God devoted to learning rather than to love; but even his dry intellect acknowledged the supernatural depth and glowing love of asceticism, and basked in the holy flame of love of suffering which Christ enkindled upon earth.

Pachomius now lived with Palemon, practising the same spiritual exercises and labours as the old man himself. The nightly prayer was very trying to him, as he was not accustomed to night watchings, and was very often overcome by sleep. Then Palemon went outside the hut with him, and told him to fill a sack with sand, and to carry the heavy burden to and fro till he had become wakeful again. Palemon also admonished him to be always very attentive to prayer, and not to allow himself to be distracted by his work or by any other thought. He used to say, "Be watchful and fervent, my Pachomius! If thou art drowsy and lukewarm, the evil one will take advantage of it to inspire thee with disgust for thy holy purpose, and then all our labour and trouble will have been in vain." The pious youth received all the exhortations and teaching of the old man with perfect obedience, and thereby advanced from day to day in conduct pleasing to God, so that the aged Palemon rejoiced, and never ceased from praising Christ the Lord for such a disciple, whilst Pachomius, on his part, blessed God for giving him so holy a spiritual father.

On the holy festival of Easter, Palemon said, "To-day is a feast in the whole of Christendom; go out therefore, my Pachomius, and prepare a banquet for us for this glorious festival." The youth accomplished the order, and the feast which he prepared consisted in pouring a little oil upon the wild herbs which they usually seasoned only with salt. Then he came to Palemon, and said, "My father, I have done what thou didst tell me." But when, after offering up a prayer, Palemon's eyes fell upon the food, and he perceived that oil had been mixed with the pounded salt, he began to weep bitterly, and exclaimed, with tears, "My Lord and Saviour was given vinegar and gall, and shall I eat dainty food? No, I cannot indeed." Pachomius earnestly begged him to take a little of it, because it was the great day of joy, but in vain. The old man continued his lamentations. So Pachomius brought bread and salt as usual, and then Palemon was happy, and ate joyfully with his beloved disciple.

Once an anchorite came to them, and begged for shelter, which was willingly granted him. Pachomius had lighted a fire to bake some bread, and they all three sat near it in conversation. The stranger began to speak of faith, and suddenly said, "If either of you has real faith, let him place himself upon those glowing coals, and recite the 'Our Father' slowly." Palemon saw from this impertinent challenge that the good brother must be tormented with pride, and answered, "Do not let such words pass your lips again, my brother. An evil spirit has suggested them to you. It is the same spirit which summoned our Lord to throw Himself down from the pinnacle of the temple. If God commands thee to tread on burning coals, do so, but under obedience, and not out of the presumption of self-will." Instead of gratefully taking Palemon's advice, the anchorite stood up, and actually placed himself upon the coals. Either by the special permission of God, or by an illusion of the wicked one, he remained uninjured, and he then became so proud of his fancied holiness that he looked down upon Palemon and Pachomius with great contempt, and soon after left them. But he came to a sad end. Pride deprived him of true confidence in God, and of watchfulness against temptation, and he fell lower and lower, the blindness of his heart becoming so great that it gradually darkened his intellect, and, losing his mind, he died miserably. This occurrence was a salutary admonition to Pachomius to watch carefully over himself, that he might not only outwardly fulfil the precepts of God, but also that he might engrave them in his heart, and practise them with his whole soul. Day and night he read the Holy Scriptures, and, learning them by heart, and contemplating them, he endeavoured both to fix in his memory and to carry out in his actions their lessons of patience, humility, and love of God, and of our neighbour. Palemon secretly admired him, because he practised self-denial and mortification in so holy a manner that his soul became more and more cleansed and purified. Pachomius heartily loved his hard and difficult anchorite life, in which nothing was to be found save what was most repelling to sensual nature, because he thus lived over again a part of the Holy Passion of our Lord. In some spots the desert produced stunted thorn-bushes, the thorns of which are as long and as sharp as large pins, and which are, besides, so hard that they pierce each other like lances. At Jerusalem they are called the "Spina Sancta," because the holy Crown of thorns was made of them. One of these thickets of thorns was in the vicinity of Palemon's hut, and Pachomius collected there the twigs which he used for firing. When his hands and feet were painfully torn by the fearful thorns, he thought of the nails which pierced the tender Hands and Feet of our loving Saviour on the Cross, and no longer felt his own pain. Thus Pachomius went through a time of trial of many years' duration under Palemon.

One day's journey down the Nile from Thebes, on the left bank of the river, the beautiful temple of Aphrodite built by Queen Cleopatra, lies in the desert behind the village of Denderah, (the ancient Tentyris.) It was four hundred years old when Pachomius came into these parts, and as he then beheld it, it remains at the present time, even after the lapse of fifteen hundred years, except that its destination is altered, for it has now become a shelter for travellers in that country.[1]

This kind of building is called in the East a khan. It offers the traveller shelter for himself, his asses, horses, or camels, and nothing more. Under the twenty-four majestic and colossal columns, which, six in each row, form a magnificent hall, there is a layer of chaff a foot deep on the floor, as a sleeping-place for man and beast, and stones and black ashes lie about, the remnants of little fires, and lengthy water-troughs kneaded out of clay, for the cattle to drink from, reach from the interior to the entrance door. This employment for ordinary purposes forms a striking contrast to the severe and sublime architectural lines of the ancient Egyptian building, but not so striking as that between the deep seriousness of this very architecture and its childish and distorted decoration with chisel and brush. The purest creation of the spirit of the ancient Egyptians, and perchance of most other nations, was their architecture, probably because sensuality can be less impressed on that science than on any other. The village of Denderah lies under the palm groves, and in the midst of fields. But the cultivation soon changes into pasture land for sheep and goats, and gradually dies away into the yellow waves of sand out of which the temple of Hathor (the Venus of the Egyptian mythology) rises like a block of black stone. Beyond it the

[1] The well-known astronomical zodiac of Denderah in the Museum at Paris was carried off from the above ruined temple. But there is still a zodiac clearly visible, though somewhat blackened, on the roof of the external hall. It begins with the sign of the Crab, over which hangs a ball of light, which pours its rays over a wheat sheaf, thereby designating the summer solstice. Then follow the remaining signs which we know, intermingled with stars and symbolic forms, only in the place of the Virgin there is a snake.

boundless Lybian desert spreads its undulations into the very heart of Africa.

In this region there was situated a ruined and abandoned village called Tabenna. It is not known whether Christians had been expelled from it, or whether it had been earlier destroyed and laid desolate by the wars of the Romans, or even of still more ancient nations. Hither Pachomius once came when searching for a complete solitude. A voice from above said to him interiorly in prayer, " Pachomius, this is the place where thou shalt serve me, thou and many others. Behold." And an angel showed him a tablet, upon which were written the precepts which he afterwards gave to his monks as the rules of their order. Pachomius immediately hastened back to Palemon, and submitted all to his judgment. The old man gladly believed that a high destiny awaited Pachomius, and went with him to Tabenna, where he helped him to erect a cell, and then returned to his own little hut. There he was attacked by a long and painful illness, brought on by his severe fasts. Some of the brethren went to him, with the intention of nursing him carefully, and gave him better and more plentiful victuals. But his sufferings grew more violent, and he begged the brethren to leave him to his old ways. " Rest and joy are to be found only in God and in mortification," said he, " and therefore I will use even to the end the spiritual weapons which I took up for the love of Jesus." So he let himself be consumed by the disease, and died happily in the arms of his beloved Pachomius, who buried the venerable old man, reciting psalms.

Since Pachomius had become a Christian and an anchorite, he had never seen one of his relations. Great, therefore, was his joy, when his elder brother John came to him in the desert of Tabenna, with a view of sharing his hermit life. In those happy early times of the Gospel, the Christians distinguished themselves so much by their virtues, that the life they led after their conversion made a deep impression on such of the heathen as had preserved any virtuous dispositions. Pachomius had been gr atly struck by the neighbourly love of the Christians, and his brother John was similarly impressed when he heard of the ascetic life which his brother led in the desert for the love of God, seeing that it must be a divine faith which could inspire such a sacrifice. John learnt to know this faith, and, having been baptized, became an anchorite. Both brothers then advanced together to take the kingdom of heaven by storm, and each strove to excel the other in humility, patience, and self-denial. Pachomius mortified equally his body and his soul. For fifteen years, notwithstanding his strict fasts, vigils, and manual labour, he never lay down, but slept sitting in the middle of his cell, without leaning against the wall. At first he suffered exceedingly from this want of sleep, till nature was sufficiently overcome no longer to disturb the repose of his soul in God. He prayed for hours together with outstretched arms, as immovably as if his body had been fastened to the cross; and by constant elevation to God, and contemplation of the Eternal Beauty, he purified his soul to such a degree that it could not bear the smallest atom of imperfection on its spotless mirror without bitter repentance. What temptations the ancient enemy of human perfection prepared for him, and what snares he laid for him, may easily be inferred from these terrific austerities.

Inspirations from above informed him that the time was near in which he should collect around him many anchorites, and give them a rule of conduct for a community life. He and John were still entirely alone in Tabenna, but, like the boy Samuel in the temple, he was attentive to the voice of God, and therefore began by degrees to build cells. John, who was a great lover of poverty, blamed this supposed fault with some severity, and his reproaches deeply pained Pachomius; but he repressed all answer, and, behaving with the greatest gentleness, kept silence. In the night there came over him great remorse for this involuntary movement of sensitiveness. An ordinary man would have called being silent in such a case a virtue; but this holy man considered his interior emotion a sin. He went out and threw himself on the ground, weeping bitterly, and saying, "Woe is me! I still act always according to the flesh, and not according to the spirit! I burn with impatience because I fancy myself in the right. Thou didst not so, O Thou meek and humble Lord Jesus, and if Thou dost not find any of Thy grace in me, I am not Thy true servant. If, on the contrary, the wicked enemy finds any of his works in me, I am in his servitude; for it is written, 'By whom a man is overcome, of the same also he is the slave.'[1] How shall I dare to guide others in the spiritual life, if I cannot observe Thy holy law with an unspotted mind. O Lord! O Lord! cleanse my heart with the rays of Thy grace!" So tender a conscience could hardly be found where the natural man had not first been mortified and destroyed by holy asceticism.

John died soon after, and Pachomius was consoled by God with the frequent visits of an aged anchorite called Apollo, who strengthened him in his combats with the seductions of the devil. Once Pachomius complained to him of the sufferings of this combat daily renewed, and always under a fresh form. Apollo answered, smiling, "The wicked enemy has two reasons for fighting against thee with all his power—first, because he has never

[1] 2 Peter ii. 18.

yet overcome thee; and secondly, because he hopes to have an easy victory over us, if thou wert first conquered. Therefore resist bravely, O Pachomius! Thou dost outshine us all in divine grace; therefore thy fall would be an occasion of falling to many." In that holy simplicity which looks only to God, Pachomius continued his severe mortifications of body and mind, considering them as a means of facilitating his battle with sensuality and pride. When he for the third time felt the inspiration to found a community of anchorites, and to unite them in a common life by a fixed rule, he delayed no longer, but kept those with him who wished to learn from him the way of salvation, and to submit themselves to his rule. About the year 325, when Pachomius was nearly thirty-three years old, the monastery of Tabenna was founded, and he was its first Father, (in the Greek language Abbas, from which the English word Abbot is derived.) Pachomius founded afterwards eight other monasteries of Tabennasiots, as men belonging to this order were called; and also, by means of his sister, one of Tabennasiotines. She had also been converted to the faith, and soon after the foundation of the first monastery, she came to Tabenna to visit her brother. But Pachomius had made it a rule never to speak to a woman, and he would not make any exception even for his sister, denying himself this consolation. He caused her to be told through the brother porter, who received all the guests, that she had better dedicate herself entirely to the service of God, and assemble widows and virgins for the same end. If she was willing to do so, he would have a monastery built for her on the other side of the Nile from that on which the brethren lived, and he would draw up a rule of life for her community. The heart of the maiden became enkindled and inflamed with the fire of the

Holy Ghost, and she betrothed herself to the Divine Lover of souls; and in the year 328 she was living in the monastery called Men with some spiritual sisters, to whom she showed by precept and example the path of salvation. The venerable and aged monk, Peter of Tabenna, was commissioned by Pachomius to visit the nuns on certain days, in order to instruct them in the Holy Scriptures, and stimulate them to a life pleasing to God, according to the rule of their order, in poverty, chastity, obedience, and punctuality. The nuns could not see the male members of their families but with the permission of the superioress, and in the presence of other aged nuns, and could never receive the most trifling present from them. If buildings had to be looked after in the monastery, or other things done which women could not do, the most venerable, most silent, and industrious of the brethren were sent there from Tabenna, who executed the work, always returning at meal times to Tabenna, without accepting even a draught of water from the nuns. Except the priest, who with his deacon offered up the Holy Sacrifice of the Mass every Sunday, no man crossed the threshold of the monastery. The nuns had the same occupations as the monks. They prayed in community at fixed times during the day and night, reciting a certain number of psalms and hymns; and they each prayed alone and contemplated the mysteries of the faith, or the sentences and teachings of Holy Writ, during their work, whether it consisted of the household duties, cooking, baking, washing, and working in the garden, or of separate manual labours. They span the yarn out of which they wove their garments, and if they had more than was required for their community, they made clothes for the poor, and gave them away. When a nun died, the sisters laid the corpse in the coffin, in the habit of their order, and bore it to the bank of the Nile, solemnly reciting psalms, and holding palm-branches in their hands. Then monks came from Tabenna, across the Nile, also singing psalms, but with olive-branches in their hands, and, carrying away the body, buried it in their burial-ground with great rejoicing; for the battle of this life, so poor, and yet so rich in sacrifice, was won, and it rested from all earthly tribulation under the palms of victory and the olive-branches of peace.

Pachomius received with humble and holy love all who desired to offer themselves up in sacrifice to God by a life of penance and abnegation. He strengthened this purpose in them in every possible way, and constantly repeated this warning, "A monk must first renounce the world, then his relations and friends, and lastly himself, in order that, delivered from unnecessary burdens, he may be free to carry the cross of the imitation of Christ." At the commencement of the monastery, he was the sole servant of all the monks, prepared the tables for dinner, brought in the dishes, planted and watered the vegetables, filled the burdensome and laborious offices of porter and infirmarian, and yet persevered in all his fastings and watchings, and moreover gave all the spiritual instruction to the brethren, and set them the example of a fervent prayer inflamed with holy love. Before long the monks of Tabenna were reckoned by hundreds. Whosoever resolved to remain in the monastery, was kept for three whole years employed in manual labour, and in the minor household works, and then for the first time admitted to the spiritual exercises, and to his own place of combat. No one was received who was not free, who was under age, or who had contracted any indissoluble engagements in the world. No money or presents were taken from those who entered, as it might have been a source of vanity to the richer brethren, or of false shame to the poorer ones. Serving the strangers was the first humble occupation of the newcomer. If he could not read, he had to learn to do so, and whilst he was a novice, to learn by heart the whole of the New Testament and the Psalms. This was a good practice for impressing holy doctrines upon the memory, and for leading the mind to supernatural things. Besides, owing to the value of books at that time, and the great number of the brethren, it was impossible to provide each one with a copy of the Holy Scriptures, although some of the monks were always occupied in copying. A trumpet summoned them to the community prayers. At its sound the monks had immediately to leave their cells; and this they did with such punctuality that they never even finished the letter they had begun; this punctuality is, in reality, only conscientious obedience, without which no house or community can be kept in order. Every Saturday and Sunday the monks received the most Holy Sacrament. A priest from the nearest church offered the Holy Sacrifice, for there were no priests amongst Pachomius's first disciples, and he himself, like Antony, Hilarion, and Ammon, was a layman. No brother was permitted to receive holy orders, and if an ecclesiastic joined the community he had to submit himself to the same rule of life as all the others, because Pachomius wished to remove every occasion of dissimilarity or ambition. Prescribed prayers were offered up in community, at stated hours, and were each time commenced with singing psalms. If a brother was on a journey, or detained by business imposed upon him by obedience, he was bound to unite himself in spirit to the prayer of the brethren. The prayers were not very many, so that those fervent in devotion could add to them; whilst those less advanced in spirituality were not overladen. To practise obedience was the chief duty of a novice, and therefore he sometimes received commands whose object he could not discover, and which, indeed, had no other but that of subduing his will. This appearance of servitude was to give him true freedom, by delivering him from the yoke of his self-love. Whoever wishes to conform himself to the will of God must renounce his own will, and he cannot learn to do so otherwise than by obedience. A novice asked Pachomius for work. He stuck his staff into the ground, and said, "Water this stick." The youth obeyed that day and the next, for three hundred and sixty-five days. When one year was past, he did the same all through the second. And in the third year the staff began to put forth leaves and blossoms.

Amongst the numbers of men and youths who, eager for salvation, went to live with Pachomius, there was naturally a very great variety of capacities, of gifts, and of powers, both of body and soul. Some came to him who were already mortified, and soon reached the highest degrees of perfection, others progressed more slowly, and some not at all. But these last were always the exception. In order that all might be properly watched over and guided, they were divided into orders and choirs, and each order placed under the inspection of a superintendent, and these again were under the abbot of Tabenna. The remaining monasteries of the order had each a prior, who was subject to the abbot of Tabenna, although the monastery of Pabau was larger and more considerable than that of Tabenna. The hierarchical form was observed from the first beginning of the monastic life. In the various orders of monks all were distributed according to their various talents and capabilities, the weak in the easy occupations, and the strong in the difficult ones; but all, without exception, had to work. There was an order for each work that was required in the monastery—an order of cooks, of gardeners, of bakers, &c. The sick formed one order, and the porters another, which latter consisted of very circumspect and discreet men, because they had charge of the intercourse with the external world, and the preparatory instruction of those who wished to be received. Each order inhabited their own house, which was divided into cells, and three brethren dwelt together in each cell. But there was only one kitchen for all, and they ate in community, but in the deepest silence, and with their hoods drawn down so low over their heads, that no one could see whether his neighbour ate much or little. The holy abbot practised the same rule about food as about prayer; he was not too severe upon some, whilst he gave free scope to the zeal of others. Their usual meals consisted of bread and cheese, salt fish, olives, figs, and other fruits. Boiled vegetables were also served daily, but none ate of them save old men and children, or the infirm, and these also generally availed themselves of the permission of eating some supper, which was always brought to table, to give the brethren an occasion of self-denial. Pachomius and a few companions once visited a monastery where supper was laid before them. He remarked that the monks partook of everything. It was not against the rule, but this want of abstemiousness pained him so much, that quiet tears rolled down his cheeks. The monks were painfully surprised to see him so troubled, and still more so when, at their earnest request, he told them the cause. How much more must he have been pained when he saw the rules broken! At one time he had not visited the monastery of Pabau for two months. When he went there, many of the brethren came to meet him, and also some children, who had been sent by their parents to the monastery to be piously brought up. We see by this that even in their first beginning the monasteries were employed in this work, which became in later times so important and so noble. One of the boys said to him, " Only think, my father, whilst thou hast been away, we have not had either soup or vegetables to eat." The holy abbot kindly replied, " I will take care, my dear child, that it never happens again." He went into the monastery, and visited and examined all the classes, and then went into the kitchen. He found the superintendent of this class very busily occupied in plaiting reed-mats. " How long is it, my brother, since thou hast boiled any vegetables?" The brother immediately confessed that it must be full two months, but added, " As hardly any of the monks tasted them, I thought I might save the time and expense, and plait mats for the profit of the monastery." Pachomius asked, " How many mats hast thou plaited then?" " Five hundred," he answered. Pachomius said, "Bring them all here." And when they were all piled in a heap, Pachomius caused them to be burnt, and in the presence of the whole order reproved the twofold fault of the brother, saying, " Thou hast sinned against obedience, because the rule prescribes certain kinds of food, and also against charity, because the children and the aged have missed their necessary nourishment, and thou hast deprived the other brethren of the holy exercise of mortification." No economy, industry, or increase of gain, to the profit of the poor, excused in the eyes of the holy abbot the want of obedience and love. A chief steward superintended the domestic government of the monastery, and under him a procurator, whose care it was to supply the wants of the brethren out of the proceeds of their work, and to buy new materials, for example flax and cotton for weaving, parchment for the copyists, &c. What remained was sold for the benefit of the poor, and this amounted to so large a sum, that none of the poor, in that whole country, suffered from the famines which often visited Egypt. So great was the industry of the brethren, that two boats were constantly employed in these various affairs, going up and down the Nile, between Tabenna and Alexandria. They sanctified labour, which is also praiseworthy in itself, by contemplation of divine things; and by interior prayer, which is the breath of life to the holy, because it breathes out love, and draws in grace.

Brother Zaccheus was a very holy man, who had spent many years in extreme humility and mortification, and suffered very severe pains in his old age in consequence of his penances. He was given a separate cell, and obliged by obedience to occupy it; but he continued his austerities, and lived on bread and salt, slept little, rose at midnight, was unfailing at the community hours of prayer, and never complained, showing by his whole behaviour what consolation the love of God procures, and now light are temporal sufferings to those whose souls already inhabit eternity. As a matter of course, Brother Zaccheus worked with the greatest industry, although he could hardly hold himself upright from weakness and pain. He plaited mats[1] of reeds, and this is work which, being very rough, hurt his hands very much, and often wounded them severely. They represented to him that such work was too hard for one who was already martyred by sickness and suffering. Zaccheus answered that he knew no other work, and

[1] Reed mats, both fine and coarse, are universal requisites in an Eastern house. The clay or stone floors are covered with mats; mats are used to sleep upon, and to be stretched across whole streets where there is much commerce or traffic, as a shelter from the heat of the sun. For the same reason in Spain, where so much that is Oriental is found, fine mats are hung outside from the windows, and sprinkled now and then with water to give coolness and shade to the rooms. Mats are also hung over the inner court (patio) of the houses in Andalusia. Therefore to this day in Spain, the making of mats (espartos) is a great and important branch of trade.

that he knew still less how to be idle. They called his attention to the fearful wounds of his hands. Zaccheus answered, that the wounds in the Hands of the crucified Saviour were much deeper. At last a brother persuaded him to rub his hands with salve, so as to be better able to work. Zaccheus followed his advice; but instead of finding relief, the wounds and pain increased to such an extent that he could hardly move his hands. Pachomius visited the sick brother Zaccheus, and treated him as only one perfect man can treat another,—he reproved him because, from want of confidence in God, he had had recourse to human assistance. Zaccheus immediately accused himself of this failing, begging his holy abbot to implore God's mercy upon him, and wept for his fault to the end of his life.

On Wednesdays and Fridays each superintendent assembled his order, and gave them an instructive or an admonitory exhortation. On Saturdays the superior of each monastery preached once, on Sundays twice. Each order had also its little library, out of which the brethren were provided with books. Silence was faithfully observed, and speaking was only allowed at certain hours. Hospitality was nobly practised towards all comers. They were lodged and fed in apartments near the gate. They might share at will in the church services of the monks, but could not eat with them or dwell amongst them, not even if they were priests or anchorites. There was a separate building for female guests, in which they were hospitably lodged. And this beautiful virtue of hospitality is an inheritance which the monasteries of the East have faithfully preserved to this day, and which they exercise in an admirable manner towards all travellers. No monastery is without its adjoining building for pilgrims, and it is opened to all who knock, without distinction. In the Island of Cyprus, at Damascus, Jerusalem, Bethlehem, Nazareth, Rama, everywhere the good Franciscan Fathers receive with cheerful self-denial travellers of all nations, creeds, and conditions; and in the beautiful monastery on Mount Carmel, the most sublime and fascinating hermitage upon earth, the holy Carmelite Fathers make themselves poor to enrich their guests. Even the Greek monastery of Mar Saba, in the wild rocky desert of the Dead Sea, grants hospitable shelter. All who have ever travelled in the East know how to prize the hospitality of the monasteries at its just value.

The first monastic order which sprung from Christianity was so filled with the Holy Ghost that later centuries kept, unaltered in essentials, the rule which the great abbot Pachomius gave to his Tabennasiots, for it contained the incitement to every virtue, and gave scope for the attainment of the highest perfection.

But it sometimes happened that men entered the order who were deficient either in good will or in perseverance. They forgot the warning of our Blessed Lord, that he who has put his hand to the plough may not look back. They wished to be thought spiritual men, but to live as sensual ones. It was not yet the custom to take the three vows of the evangelical counsels on entering the order, after having finished the novitiate. In general, the faith was too ardent, and souls were too fervent to be wanting in zeal to persevere in the ascetic life. Besides, a recreant was as it were branded, because his return to the world was looked upon as evidence, to say the least, of extraordinary weakness. Pachomius felt great grief at one time on account of some monks who would not carry on to the end the interior combat. He spared himself no trouble in instructing them how to behave in prayer, in temptation, and in all kinds of delusions; he prayed for them with all the fervour of a tender father and a good shepherd, but in vain. His faithful vigilance over their behaviour became so hateful to them, and the evil desires of their passions grew so strong, that they persisted in returning to the world. But Tabenna, like a garden cleared of its weeds, only flourished and blossomed more brightly and more beautifully. Pachomius had such a gift of wisdom in the guidance of souls that the priors often brought him rebellious monks that he might pacify them. The prior of Pabau came once to Tabenna and brought bitter complaints of a young monk who would insist on becoming a priest, and whom he did not consider worthy to receive priest's orders. To his great surprise Pachomius said, " My advice is that thou shouldst comply with the brother's wishes. The desire to become a priest is good in itself, and may stimulate a slothful soul to greater perfection. Perhaps holy orders will sanctify him." The prior followed the advice of his holy abbot, and soon after the young monk came to Tabenna, threw himself at the feet of Pachomius and said, with flowing tears, " I thank thee, O thou blessed of the Lord, that thou wert so gentle and compliant with me. The denial of my wish only caused it to grow stronger and stronger. But when it was going to be fulfilled, I cast a glance into myself and shuddered before my imperfection, clearly recognising a satanic temptation to pride. I will remain what I am, a simple monk. But if thou hadst not treated me so wisely, I should have fallen away from the order and consequently from God Himself, who called me to it."

Pachomius was so extremely humble that although he worked miracles and signs, cast out evil spirits, and trod unharmed upon serpents and scorpions, he yet obeyed a child. He was visiting one of his monasteries, and after he had made an inspection of all the classes, and had offered up the community prayers, he sat down by the brethren who were making reed coverings, and began likewise to plait rushes. Then a little boy passed by, and, stopping near Pachomius, said, with the forwardness of his age, "My father, thou art not doing it rightly, our prior does it differently." Then Pachomius stood up as if one in authority were speaking to him, and said lovingly, "Then, my child, show me how the prior does it." The boy showed him, and Pachomius quietly continued his work in the way which he had just learnt. If he had acted according to earthly wisdom he would have given the child a reproof for his forwardness, but he acted according to heavenly wisdom, and gave the brethren an example of incomparable humility. Also when Athanasius the Great, the patriarch of Alexandria, visited the monastery of Tabenna, Pachomius hid himself amongst the monks and strictly forbade any of them to name him. But this was of no avail, for the saint recognised the saint. Pachomius feared that the great bishop would perhaps wish to ordain him priest, which he strove against with all his might, feeling himself unworthy in the sight of God. The saints became holy because they measured their virtue by what was above them, by the example of Jesus, and never by what was below them, the infirmity of their neighbour.

Pachomius had frequent extasies in which he clearly beheld future things and heavenly mysteries. Once, after long and fervent prayer, he was as it were raised above the earth, and saw in a vision the future of the monastic life, that much lukewarmness, worldliness, contention, and envy would creep in, especially because the superiors would not conscientiously maintain the rules, but would seek power and consideration in the world. Seeing this, he sighed and said, "O

Lord! if such things are to come, wherefore hast Thou caused me to begin the laborious undertaking in which I have served Thee night and day without giving myself any rest, and without ever satisfying myself even with dry bread?" Then a voice said, "Pachomius, do not glorify thyself, for what thou hast done for Me I have done in thee." Pachomius fell on his face and wept, and implored the pardon of God for his proud speech. And lo! a great light descended upon him, and angels surrounded him, saying, "Because thou hast implored the mercy of God to assist thee in thy struggle against sadness and pride, the King of Glory, who is Mercy itself, approaches thee, He who out of compassion has willed to become Man and to be crucified." And when the angels had raised him up Pachomius saw, standing before him in unspeakable beauty and glory, our Divine Saviour giving out rays of splendour as the sun, but with the marks of the Wounds and the Crown of thorns. "O Lord, have I thus crucified Thee?" asked Pachomius sorrowfully. "Not thou, but thy parents," answered the loving Lord. "Therefore be comforted and have courage and confidence. The work which I have begun by thee shall not be abandoned by my grace, but will subsist to the end of days. He who loves and seeks eternal life with his whole heart, and does not shun the battle, will find in this way the salvation of his soul, and hereafter eternal glory. But he who loves the death of the soul will remain in everlasting darkness." Pachomius heard these words with ineffable consolation, and when the heavenly vision disappeared he sought the brethren, offered up with them the evening sacrifice of praise and thanksgiving, and spoke to them so attractively of the joy of the glories to come, that they readily perceived the abundance of sweetness with which he was inundated. At the conclusion, he said, "Have, therefore, the hour of your death ever before your eyes, and think of the eternal punishments. Then every earthly pain, and every sacrifice will seem light to you. If you exercise yourselves in mortification in this way, you make room in yourselves for the operation of the Holy Ghost. He will enkindle fire and light in your purified hearts, which will make them capable of heavenly contemplation. And this continual contemplation will cleanse you more and more from earthly desires, and give you purity of mind and humility of heart. Then you will become truly temples of the Holy Ghost, and tabernacles of God as He Himself has promised: "If any one love me, my Father will love him, and we will come to him and will make our abode with him."[1] Then the holy fear of God will instruct you in the progress of the spirit better than the wisest teacher, making you clearsighted, and giving you knowledge above the conception of human understanding. Then you will know for what you are to pray to God, because "the Spirit himself asketh for us with unspeakable groanings. He asketh for the saints according to God."[2]

With this heavenly doctrine Pachomius enkindled holy love in the hearts of the brethren, and of a young monk in particular, called Sylvanus, who had hitherto given much scandal. He had been an actor, and feeling for a time disgusted with his mode of life, he had been led by grace to Tabenna, where Pachomius had admitted him in imitation of his Divine Master, Who did not break the bruised reed. But although Sylvanus never looked back wistfully to the follies of the world, his thoughts were still filled with their images, and he so often infringed the rule and discipline, out of levity and absence of mind, that he gave a very bad example to the younger novices,

[1] John xiv. 23. [2] Rom. viii. 26, 27.

and scandal to the elder monks. Pachomius alone had patience with him. At last it came to this, that some of the most experienced brethren represented to their holy abbot that Sylvanus caused too much harm by his light behaviour to be tolerated any longer in the monastery, to the prejudice of the weak. Pachomius, who was never tired of urging him with great sweetness to turn from the way of perdition, once more interceded for the frivolous and perverse youth, and he wept so long before God for the salvation of this soul that the spark of grace which slumbered within it increased till at length it became a bright flame. Sylvanus grew as penitent as he had formerly been frivolous, and he who had hitherto unceasingly talked and laughed now kept silence and wept constantly. He now again disturbed the brethren, but this time by his tears. Whether he walked or stood, at prayer, at work, at meals, he shed floods of tears. They begged him not to weep so bitterly, at least at table, as compassion prevented some of the brethren from eating anything. Sylvanus took very great pains to repress his tears; and as he did not succeed, he accepted with joyous humility all reproofs and punishments; but his sins were so continually before him that his whole soul was, as it were, dissolved in sorrow, and poured itself out in tears. He reached at last an unusual degree of holy compunction and hatred of self, and Pachomius said one day to the assembled monks, "My dear children, since this monastery was built I have only had one single brother who was perfect in humility. I protest this before God and His angels." The brethren tried to guess who this perfect monk was, and at length earnestly begged their abbot to tell them his name, for the edification of all. Pachomius answered, "My sons, if I did not know that he whom I shall name would humble himself all the more, I could not accede to your request. But he follows the grace of God so faithfully that the sting of earthly honour can no longer reach and wound him. He is no other than the youth whom you lately wished to expel from the monastery, Brother Sylvanus."

Once, during the fast of Lent, the monks of Tabenna had a wonderful example of mortification before their eyes. An aged workman asked Pachomius to receive him. The holy abbot was certainly endowed with the gifts of prophecy and of discernment of spirits; but nevertheless it pleased God at times to veil his supernatural sight, or to leave his prayers unheard. This, however, did not in the least disturb his holy indifference, for, in their fulfilment, as well as in their rejection, he loved the will of God alone. Pachomius told the aged labourer that he was much too old to begin a monastic life, for people began very early there to accustom themselves to the religious rule, and to submit themselves to discipline and obedience. His wish, therefore, could not be granted. But the old man prayed all one day, and the next, and for seven whole days, observing a continual fast all the time. On the eighth day he said to Pachomius, "I beg of thee to receive me. Whenever thou shalt see that I do not fulfil all the duties of a monk, in prayer and work, in fasting, watching, and silence, then, my father, I pray thee drive me away." Pachomius agreed to these conditions, and the old man was received just as the forty days' fast began. During that time the monks practised various mortifications; some ate a little towards evening, others only every second, third, or fifth day. Many watched the whole night through standing, and only resting a little in the daytime; many did all their work kneeling; in short, there was not one who did not take pains to retire with our Blessed Lord into the desert. But what did the old man do? He placed himself in a corner, and wove baskets out of palm leaves steeped in water. And there he always stood, without lying down, sitting, or kneeling, without leaning against anything, or speaking, without tasting a bit of bread or a drop of water. On Sundays only he ate a few leaves of salad, and he never left his place except at the community hours of prayer. He was ever diligently employed in his work, and was almost uninterruptedly in an extasy of holy contemplation and union with God. The whole class of basket-makers rose in insurrection, and said to their superior, "Where hast thou found this man, who has no longer anything human about him? Take him away. We can bear the sight no more, for it is impossible for us to keep pace with him. When we look at him we all fear to be lost." The superior of the class laid these complaints before Pachomius, who then himself carefully observed the doings of the old man. He was thereby filled with holy reverence for such a victory of the spirit over the flesh, and he betook himself to prayer to beg for light to see what he should do in this affair, in order that the brethren might be edified instead of discouraged by such extraordinary virtue. Then God opened the eyes of his soul. Pachomius went to the old man, led him by the hand before the altar, and said, "I greet thee, worthy friend of God, I greet thee, O thou blessed one![1] Thou art the great Macarius of whom I have heard for many years, and whom I have so ardently longed to see. I thank thee that thou hast humbled my spiritual children, and shown them that they have no cause to glory in their life. But I beg of thee now to leave us; thou art too far above us." Thus spake the great St. Pachomius, classing himself in the same rank as the most pusillanimous of the brethren, so that none should

[1] Macarius was called even in his lifetime by the title of Blessed.

despond, and humbling himself for them all, although he was in reality equal to Macarius.

That great man was born in Alexandria in a humble condition. At the age of thirty he suddenly abandoned his little trade of selling sugar in the streets, after the fashion of Orientals, and joined the anchorites whom Ammon had assembled in the country of Nitria. There he learned the practice of obedience, and then he followed the strong attraction that led him into solitude. He came into the desert of Scete, between Egypt and Lybia, which was so fearfully arid, that in its whole length and breadth there was no drinkable water. He who entered this dreadful desert was fain to be contented with the water of the marshy lakes, which was of a repulsive odour and bitter taste. And yet the anchorites were willing to spend their lives in it. As the desire of earthly goods stimulates worldly men to the conquest of blooming lands and the discovery of gold and silver mines, so the desire of heavenly treasures, of the bright gold of love, impelled ascetic men to search out places where seekers of pleasure would shudder, and where evil passions can find no food.

Macarius of Alexandria found a namesake and spiritual brother in the desert of Scete, the Egyptian Macarius, by birth a shepherd, but so early in life distinguished for his asceticism that the other anchorites called him "the young old man." His heart was overwhelmed with contrition for having stolen some figs as a child, and to confirm him more and more in humility God permitted some atrocious calumnies of him to be spread abroad and believed, whilst he was leading a hidden and penitential life in a small dark cavern in the hills. This trial passed over as all trials do, and when the time of honour began for him, when his miracles, the answers to his prayers, and the grace of God which worked in him, became known, he fled from the admiring crowds into the desert of Scete, where no one could follow him, unless it were a few disciples desirous of salvation. These were not wanting, although he exercised them severely in all the virtues of their state. But he did it with such gentle charity that his disciples clearly perceived his severity to be caused, not by harshness, but by the love he bore them. His favourite prayer was, " O Lord, have pity on me, as Thou best knowest and willest." He once sent a youth who wished to become an anchorite to the burial-ground of the brethren, and ordered him to praise the dead. When he returned, he said to him, " Go there once more and revile the dead." After the youth had obeyed, Macarius asked, " What did the dead answer thee, my son?" "Nothing, my father," answered the astonished youth. " Imitate, then, my son, their insensibility to the praise or the contempt of men; for eternal life depends not upon the judgments of the world, but upon the sentence of God." To another youth he said, " Receive poverty, want, sickness, and all miseries joyfully from the Hand of God, and with equal joy, consolation, refreshment, and all superabundance. By this uniform joy in the will of God thou wilt deaden the stimulus of thy passions." Some more aged anchorites accused him of too great condescension and too loving a demeanour towards his disciples, but he replied, " Oh, my brethren, I had to beg this grace from God for the space of twelve years before it was given to me. What does it profit us if we irritate or embitter those whom we have to correct? Punishment should be so constituted as to win the soul to virtue." When the sanctity of the Egyptian Macarius had gathered together many anchorites in the desert of Scete, who, like those in Cellia in Lower Egypt, lived in solitary huts, scattered over a distance of many miles, a church had to be built for them, in which they assembled according to the custom of those times, on Saturdays and Sundays for the celebration of the sacred mysteries, and the reception of the holy sacraments; and Macarius, by command of the bishop, was constrained to receive priest's orders, in order to supply the spiritual necessities of these children of the desert. By degrees three churches were built in the desert of Scete, and each was governed by a priest. But Macarius had a most terrible temptation to pride, and therefore besought God, day and night, to send him some wholesome humiliation. His prayer was heard. He received the command from heaven to visit two women living in a distant city, and to learn from them a degree of perfection to which he had not yet attained. They lived in the same house, and there was nothing extraordinary to be remarked in them, or in their circumstances. Macarius begged them to disclose to him their way of life. "Oh," said they, "that is not worth the trouble, my father. For fifteen years we have lived quietly and peaceably together; we have never exchanged an evil word, have been obedient to our husbands, have loved silence, and have kept ourselves in the presence of God in all our household affairs. That is all that we can do for love of Him, and it is, alas! very little." But Macarius returned to his desert edified and ashamed.

To him, the elder, came Macarius the younger of Alexandria, who was then beginning to lead an ascetic life. For seven years he lived upon raw vegetables; for three years upon from four to five ounces of bread daily. And at last he did in this way: he crumbled some bread into a jar of water with a narrow mouth, to soak it, and once each day he ate as many crumbs as he could take out in one handful. But that was very little, because if his hand was very full he could not withdraw it through the narrow mouth of the jar. In order completely to overcome every motion of sensual pleasure, he placed his dwelling for some months in a swamp over which swarms of flies hung like thick clouds. These bloodthirsty insects fell upon him, and tortured him to such a degree that he came back to the brethren, after six months, as wounded and disfigured as a leper. With immense labour he excavated an underground passage, which led to a distant and entirely unvisited cavern; then if strangers came and wished to speak to him about their affairs, he fled through humility into his place of concealment, and left the elder Macarins, or other pious solitaries, to despatch the business. The example of these two " blessed ones " excited all the brethren to emulation; and every one would have been ashamed of the sin of allowing himself any sensual enjoyment. A bunch of grapes was once given to the younger Macarius. He never even thought of eating it, but he took it to the anchorite who lived next to him. This one did just as Macarius had done, and the bunch of grapes travelled in this way over the whole desert of Scete, and after a long time returned to Macarius. When a disciple complained much of distractions in prayer, and was inclined to abandon it out of spiritual idleness, Macarius said, " Nay, rather lengthen thy prayer and say, Even if I cannot pray in peace, I will stay quietly in this spot for Christ's sake." The disciple followed his advice, and gradually overcame his distractions. The Patriarch of Alexandria hearing of the favourable influence which he exercised over souls, sent for him, and bestowed holy orders upon him. Macarius the elder accompanied him for a part of his journey. They travelled by the Nile, and had placed themselves humbly in a corner of the ship, and betaken themselves to contemplation. There were also on the ship two men of high rank, who were travelling with a large retinue. Their servants, horses, and litters, shone with gold and purple, and filled all the space. When they perceived the two poor monks in their mean garments, they deemed them happy in their plain and simple manner of life, and exclaimed, "Oh, how blessed are ye, who despise the world!" "We do indeed by God's grace despise the world," answered Macarius of Alexandria; "but how is it with you? Do you not also despise the world?" This speech made so obvious to one of the noblemen the emptiness and delusion of his state of life, that when he returned home he renounced all his vain grandeur and began an ascetic life.

Both the saints named Macarius, by their faith and holiness, their teaching and example, were true apostles and pillars of the Catholic Church, and were therefore bitterly hated by the Arians, and in particular by the Arian patriarch, Lucius, who gave no rest to the Emperor Valens, also an Arian, until he had driven both these holy men out of Egypt, and banished them to an island in the Grecian Archipelago, where idolatry was still in vogue. This took place in the year 373. But in banishment as in their home they won souls to the true faith, and it seemed as if God had wished to add to their other virtues that of the apostolate. This nowise coincided with the views of the Arians, so they were sent back to their own country. The elder Macarius sought once more his desert of Scete, and the younger went to Cellia, where he had the spiritual charge of the anchorites. Although he most conscientiously fulfilled this holy duty, and was indefatigable in all the offices of love which make the care of souls so arduous, he was nevertheless afflicted by the temptation of thinking that he ought to work still more for the honour of God, which he could only do in Rome. This thought followed him day and night. Neither work, nor prayer, nor occupation with the brethren, could drive away the torturing temptation. Then he filled a large basket with sand, took it upon his shoulders, and with this burden wandered all about the desert, in order to overcome his spiritual restlessness by bodily fatigue. In continual combats and labours, such as never lying down for the last sixty years of his life, he lived to nearly a hundred years of age, and died about the year 395. Palladius says of him that he was small and delicate in form, and that he worked so many miracles, that with him they were ordinary daily events. In the meantime the holy Abbot of Tabenna was leading his monks further and further into the regions of the spiritual life. Their mortification reached a very high degree even for that fervent ascetic age. It was the rule at the community prayers to keep as still as possible, never to cough or to clear the throat, or to move from one place. It happened once that Brother Titheus was violently stung in the foot by a scorpion during this time. The poison immediately caused the injured foot to swell, and Titheus felt it taking more hold upon him every moment. But in spite of the danger and the pain he stayed quietly in his place, and this heroic obedience moved Pachomius to beg of God his recovery and his life. He very rarely did so, for he generally said to the brethren who complained of their illnesses or pains, "Oh, my children, how can you wish to be freed from your sufferings? Do you not yet know that no mortification is so pleasing to God as the joyful, or at least patient, acceptance of the crosses He imposes? Fasting, watching and mortifying the flesh are good kinds of penance, but suffering in union with our suffering Lord and Saviour is incomparably better."

The salvation of all men lay very near to the heart of Pachomius. In the great deserts there are here and there fruitful spots around the water-springs, oases, which lie like green islands in the middle of the sea of sand. That which is called "the Great Oasis" in the Lybian Desert was also called by the Greeks "the Island of the Happy," because it was so beautiful. The Egyptian oases afforded pasture for herds of cattle, and were therefore inhabited by numerous shepherds, who became almost savages, and lost their faith from want of instruction. Pachomius went to the Bishop of Tentyris, and begged him to take pity on these poor forsaken Christians, and to send them a priest, and build a little chapel for them. Till that could be done, he and some of the brethren divided the pasture lands amongst themselves, and visited and instructed the shepherds in the faith. We seem to see a St. Alphonso Liguori, who in our own days, sought out the goat herds in the mountain valleys of Amalfi and Sorrento for the same end.

He who is completely reconciled to God has no longer a single enemy in the whole world. St. Jerome, who wrote the life of the great Abbot of Tabenna, relates that Pachomius could walk uninjured upon poisonous reptiles, and that crocodiles had offered themselves to him, and carried him over the Nile on their backs. Evil spirits came to attack him, but his heel crushed their head, and he obliged them to speak to him, and tell him by whose power they had been so fettered. "By the wonderful Incarnation of Jesus Christ," they said. Yea, truly, the Incarnation is the key-note of redemption; and the grandeur of the strong faith of Christian antiquity consisted in embracing this belief in its fullest meaning, and accepting all its consequences. But the tongue of the slanderer is harder to subdue than crocodiles or devils. Neither virtue nor solitude, neither sanctity nor miracles, protected Pachomius from calumny. Hatred and envy were busy in decrying him as an heretical